# Green Growth and Travelism

## Letters from Leaders

**Edited by**
Geoffrey Lipman, Terry DeLacy, Shaun Vorster, Rebecca Hawkins, Min Jiang

(G) Go⟨ hers Ltd

10 . 2012

**(G)** Published by Goodfellow Publishers Limited,
Woodeaton, Oxford, OX3 9TJ

http://www.goodfellowpublishers.com

*British Library Cataloguing in Publication Data:* a catalogue record for
this title is available from the British Library.

*Library of Congress Catalog Card Number:* on file.

ISBN: 978-1-908999-18-4

First published 2012

 Design and typesetting by P.K. McBride, www.macbride.org.uk

Cover design by Cylinder, www.cylindermedia.com

Printed by Marston Book Services, www.marston.co.uk

# Contents

## Letters from Leaders

# Preface

## Maurice F. Strong

**Founder Chairman, Cosmos International Group, Secretary General 1992 Rio Earth Summit**

## Travel and tourism – the green imperative

Maurice F. Strong, P.C., O.C., LL.D was born and educated in Canada. He has been working at senior levels in business, government and international organizations for over 30 years, and now spends most of his time in China. Current appointments include: Founder Chairman of Cosmos International Group; Senior Advisor to the Secretary-General of Nations Conference on Sustainable Development (Rio +20); Honorary Professor of Peking University (Beijing), Member of United States National Academy of Sciences. Some of Mr. Strong's past appointments include: Under Secretary-General and Special Advisor to the Secretary-General of the United Nations; Senior Advisor to the President, World Bank; Member, Foundation Board, World Economic Forum; Secretary-General of the United Nations Conference on the Human Environment (1972); First Executive Director of the United Nations Environment Programme; Secretary-General of the United Nations Conference on Environment and Development (Earth Summit).

Rio+20 comes at a time in which changes in the world economy are producing daunting challenges to the tourism industry. These challenges have also produced a new generation of opportunities, of which none is more important to the future of this industry than the 'green imperative'.

In its multiple dimensions, travelism – the travel & tourism socio-economic value chain – is one of the most pervasive industries, driving the processes of globalization and contributing to the economy of even the smallest communities, providing an ever expanding linkage between the local and the global. At the core of this challenge is the need for the industry to become a true leader in the greening of the economy. Indeed, the industry must see this as an imperative which will require the full commitment of its own leaders. Even at the most difficult economic times, travel increases and with it the environmental impacts of travel, particularly the increasing greenhouse gas emissions it produces.

Tourism involves travel and it requires that the destinations which attract visitors be protected and enhanced. The industry has strong incentives to do so as well as a great responsibility. For the environments which attract tourists are not only great assets for the industry but for the communities in which they are located.

Advances and innovation in technologies have led to a rapid expansion of travel by air, rail and road that has made our world smaller. This has led to the phenomenal internationalization of trade, communication, sport and recreation. And in turn, the systemic relationships being developed between them are inextricably linked to the expansion of travel and tourism. It is a relationship that is being strengthened by the internet and social media which are making travelism accessible to so many more people and destinations.

At the same time, a more accessible world also multiplies our risks and vulnerabilities – the rapid transmission of health threats, the impact of natural disasters, the costs of energy and food and volatility in the markets for so many key commodities. The resulting crisis conditions are now afflicting the economies of the United States and Europe, affecting most countries and impacting especially the poor and disadvantaged in both developing and more industrialized countries. Energy costs, which I believe will escalate to record levels, will place an especially heavy burden on the industry

The economic and financial crises also highlight the growing gap between the rich and the poor, the winners and losers, in all countries. This deepening rich-poor divide is producing growing tensions and citizen protests as evidenced in the rapid expansion of the movement which began with the occupation of Wall Street.

This is clearly a time of momentous change on a scale that will have a profound effect on the human future. Your industry has a responsibility to consider how green travelism contributes to this challenge and can best contribute to its solutions.

The environment as nature's capital is the greatest single resource for tourism and this provides a powerful incentive for the industry to protect it. It makes green tourism a necessity for the industry, not merely a fringe issue too often receiving more lip service than real commitment. Yet there is within the industry a disturbing tendency towards what we call 'green washing'. This clearly undermines global efforts to protect the environment on which tourism, indeed all life, depends.

The industry must integrate 'green' as an absolute necessity for its own future and the responsibilities it has for the entire human future. Simultaneously, this new travelism vision and its commitment to action must be integrated into the mainstream movement for radical global change. Rio+20 must give strong momentum to this movement. This is the reason that your industry needs to give high priority to its fundamental engagement.

Twenty years ago travel rose to the occasion – the sector's very participation in the Rio Earth Summit, the *Agenda 21 for Travel & Tourism* that you produced and the leadership you then showed provided a beacon for the sector that was truly worthy of your role as one of the world's largest industries.

Today the travel industry needs an enlightened but radically reinvigorated agenda for green growth transformation. You have made notable progress on which the industry can now build. But it needs real and continuing action, targets, measurement and a new mindset that links economic, climate, social and environmental response, as well as welcoming global and local inclusion. I am convinced you can make much more of your unique positioning if you fully integrate the interests of local communities into overall strategic policy in a meaningful way. In a sustainable green growth world, destinations will have the ultimate responsibility for their destiny.

Let me also call your attention to a fundamental issue in this change agenda – the importance of linking environmental and travelism education: particularly for the next leadership generation which will have to drive the most challenging changes.

I am involved in an initiative, with likeminded colleagues, to launch a World Environment University grounded in the Island province of Jeju in South Korea. Within that framework the establishment of a Green Growth and Travelism Institute is a priority element. As a torchbearer of the green growth 2050 vision, this is envisaged as the centre of a virtual global network of related organizations and institutions. This initiative is very well advanced with prospects of support from a core group of universities on every continent – this book with its leadership vision is an important underpinning to the focus for this sector on the green growth transformation journey.

That transformation must be started now and will be carried on by our children and grandchildren. Our task is to make the right choices now. No issue is more important in that context, than the growing risks of climate change, which provides the greatest threats ever to the sustainability and security of life everywhere. Travelism is a victim of as well as a contributor to climate change. It is now widely recognized that travelism accounts for some 5% of global carbon emissions and this is growing rapidly with aviation the leading and most rapidly growing contributor.

The initiative of WTTC in setting a goal of 50% reduction in $CO_2$ emissions by 2035 over 2005 levels and the International Air Transport Association's commitment to a mid-term goal of carbon-neutral growth from 2020 with reduction in emissions by 50% from 2005 levels by 2050 are commendable demonstrations of response to this challenge. I will expect that, based on this, your industry will move ahead in strongly supporting regulatory, voluntary and market-based mechanisms to ensure achievement of its objectives.

Travelism plays a key role in protecting the earth's natural capital – its biological diversity, the services that nature provides on which so much of our life and wellbeing depends. The eco systems – mountains, forests, islands, waters and coastal areas which provide some of the most attractive venues for tourism – are nature's gift to humankind which it is in our interest and responsibilities to protect.

Travelism also provides an immense range of opportunities for economic development and relief from poverty in some of the most disadvantaged areas. *Agenda 21 for Travel and Tourism* prepared in response to the 1992 Earth Summit, and more recently the very detailed report by the United Nations Environment Program on *The green economy, pathway to sustainable development and poverty eradication* define the many ways in which green tourism is essential to the development of the green economy.

Tourism creates jobs, opportunities for local entrepreneurship, small and medium sized business and economic development in virtually every community. There is no other industry that can have such a universal impact on economic development and the escape from poverty. The greening of tourism must be much more than applying a green veneer over underlining activities which are far from green. The greening must occur at every level of the travelism system. It has to be the heart and core of the industry which must take the lead in this. But it must be supported in and incentivized by much more enlightened and effective government policies and practices. This means that the green growth lobby must become much more active and influential than those who lobby for lesser measures.

Finally in this context, travelism thrives on peace and sustainability and it is an essential contributor to it. Tourism which is such an important factor in the economies of most countries provides them with a strong incentive to maintain internal security and protect the human rights of their people. The very conditions so necessary to the health of their tourist industry also helps to establish and maintain social stability and well being and provide expanding opportunities for their people.

No nation will have a greater positive impact on these developments than China where I spend much of my time these days and with which I have had a long relationship. After a century of internal turbulence and conflict, China has again emerged as one of the world's great nations with an immense and growing impact on its future. No nation has a greater variety and diversity of tourist destinations from the habitats of pandas to its vast heritage of historic, cultural and national wonders. Chinese travellers are great tourists within their own countries. Its domestic market is today twice as big as all of the international travel in the world. However Chinese international travel – where they are poised to become the leading global player – is less than 5% of its total travel.

There are few destinations in the world that do not receive Chinese visitors. Yet, tourism in China is still at its early stages and there are immense opportunities for tourism both in China and by the Chinese travelling internationally. In the early stages of China's remarkable economic growth, China, like the more traditional developed countries, gave little priority to the environment. It has paid a heavy price for this. China is fully committed to developing a green economy. The greening of its economy is a top priority and this will clearly contribute to its attractiveness for tourism. No country has greater potential for leadership in green tourism than China and this will continue to open up unprecedented opportunities for the greening of the industry.

Finally, my personal experience with travel and the environment have been integral to my own life. It is out of my own experiences that I have become so firmly committed to the systemic relationship between the environment and green travelism and indeed the imperative for this sector to fulfil its leadership destiny through the transition to green travelism.

# Dedication

We are dedicating this book to Maurice Strong, and to each and every individual that makes a modest bottom-up contribution to the sustainable development agenda, because they are the true champions of the green revolution underway.

For half a century Maurice Strong has been a global advocate for our planet and its people, becoming the architect and first head of the pivotal United Nations Environment Program. Twenty years ago, at the Rio Earth Summit, he led the charge to establish the framework for sustainable development and in shaping a planetary Agenda for the 21st Century. Today he is advocating the same message from his base in China, on which so much of our common future depends.

Maurice has also continuously encouraged our sector to reach forward to integrate the environment into its core business strategies. Many of us have been fortunate to become his friends and colleagues during this time, benefitting from his wise words and guidance. This guidance has helped steer the efforts to green the industry through *Agenda 21 for Travel and Tourism*, which was conceived during the Rio Earth Summit in 1992, the creation of the first ever green certification program a few years later and current efforts aimed at establishing a green growth focused global academic network.

Maurice recently urged the industry leadership in the World Travel and Tourism Council to fully integrate into mainstream Rio+20 initiatives, stating that 'My personal experience with travel and the environment have been integral to my own life. It is out of my own experiences that I have become so firmly committed to the systemic relationship between the environment and tourism. I firmly believe in the importance and indeed the imperative of making the transition to green travelism.'

We wholeheartedly share this view and it is for this commitment that we dedicate this book to his vision, in the hope that it can make a contribution to the process of transformation.

*G Lipman, T DeLacy, S Vorster, R Hawkins and M Jiang*

# About the editors

**Geoffrey Lipman** is Director of Greenearth.travel, a global think tank network, promoting green growth and travelism and specializing in strategy, innovation and funding. He is President of ICTP (International Council of Tourism Partners) & Associate of Cosmos China. Lipman is Adjunct Professor at Victoria University Australia, Visiting Professor at Oxford Brookes University, UK and Senior Tourism Research
Fellow at George Washington University, USA. He is a Member of the World Economic Forum's Global Agenda Council on Aviation, Travel and Tourism. Lipman joined the International Air Transport Association in the 1960s and rose to become its Executive Director before his appointment as the first President of the World Travel & Tourism Council from 1990 to 1999. Between 2006 and 2010, he served as Assistant Secretary General and spokesperson of UNWTO, the World Tourism Organisation, and prior to that acted as Advisor to the Secretary General.

**Terry DeLacy** is a Professor in sustainable tourism and environmental policy at Victoria University, Melbourne. He was previously Director of the Australian Government established, national Sustainable Tourism Co-operative Research Centre and dean of the agricultural and natural resources faculty at the University of Queensland. Terry's research area is in environmental policy specialising
in natural resources, sustainable tourism, climate change and most recently destinations in the emerging green economy. He is currently leading projects in Bali on developing a green growth 2050 roadmap and in the Pacific on developing vulnerability/resilience frameworks for the tourism sector to adapt to hazards and risks including to those from climate change.

**Shaun Vorster** is Special Adviser to the South African Minister of Tourism. He holds a DPhil in Political Science from Stellenbosch University. In his early career, he lectured part-time on international relations theory and European politics, and served as research and strategy manager for the official opposition in Parliament. He also served as Chief

Director in the Office of the Premier of the Western Cape, and, from 2004, as Special Adviser to the South African Minister of Environmental Affairs and Tourism. In the latter capacity, he was actively involved in international climate change negotiations. He is currently completing an MBA at Stellenbosch University, focusing on aviation, travel and tourism in the low-carbon economy. Views expressed in this book are in his personal capacity.

**Rebecca Hawkins** is a Director of the Responsible Hospitality Partnership (www.rhpltd.net), Research and Consultancy Fellow at Oxford Brookes University, and a Visiting Professor to the International Centre for Responsible Tourism at Leeds Metropolitan University. She has contributed to the responsible business agenda in this sector for the last 20 years and has worked extensively to deliver tools, training programmes and consultancy services to help hospi-
tality businesses operationalise responsible business programmes. Rebecca has also worked extensively in the area of sustainable tourism certification and destination management in an international context.

**Min Jiang** is a Research Fellow at Victoria University, Melbourne, Australia. She has been leading the climate change research group at the Centre for Tourism and Services Research of Victoria University and coordinating a number of research projects including a major one in the Pacific on developing vulnerability/resilience frameworks for tourism to adapt to climate change risks. Holding a Bachelor of Law (LLB), a Master of Law (LLM), and a PhD in environmental
law, Min has strong multi-disciplinary expertise in environmental law and policy, sustainable tourism, and the social and institutional dimensions of climate change adaptation. Min has built up a strong scholarly publication record of more than 40 publications of various kinds including international journal articles, book chapters, conference presentations and technical reports.

# Introduction and Overview

**Geoffrey Lipman, Terry DeLacy, Shaun Vorster, Rebecca Hawkins and Min Jiang**

We wholeheartedly believe that the Rio+20 Earth Summit confirms the international commitment to a long-term global green transformation to which the travel and tourism sector will make an increasingly powerful contribution. This is also the rationale for this book, which we hope can make a modest contribution.

**First,** we framed an outline concept of the goal of *'green growth'* (the new geopolitical paradigm to respond to the big economic, social, environmental and climate challenges of today, as well as to the population driven resource challenges of tomorrow) and the vehicle *'travelism'* (the entire travel and tourism value chain, including the destinations that it serves). We outline this in the initial section *Towards Transformation*, with a strong emphasis on recognizing the scale, scope and impacts of the sector; its real capacity for engaging in the forefront of global change and the importance of 'trans-cending the silos' (a phrase which we took from Minister Marthinus van Schalkwyk of South Africa).

**Second,** we asked a cross-section of thought leaders, mostly inside the travel and tourism system (public, private and civil society) for their views on the challenges and opportunities, as a contribution to the Rio+20 Earth Summit process. We asked them to keep it brief, strategically focused, practical and above all readable. We were delighted with the response from across the spectrum; from leaders heading international organizations and global initiatives; from government ministers steering the change; from business leaders including aircraft manufacturers, airlines, hotels, cruise liners, travel services and the like who are implementing the change; and the thought leaders in academia and the non-governmental sector who are contributing to shaping agendas. Of course there are gaps, but we know this is just the first step of a multi-decade transformational journey and the body of knowledge will grow as we move forward.

**Third,** we reviewed the papers critically and worked with some of the authors to update sections to ensure overall coherence or to minimise repetition. We did not seek to change or influence the ideas. Many of the contributions quote data and assert various positions not specifically supported by references, but by real life experience. We were comfortable with this as the book is not an academic reference work and the assertions contained in the letters stand and fall on the credibility of the leaders who have written them. In the final analysis, we decided to leave out all references and footnotes in the interest of readability. Instead we have produced a compendium which is available online in this book's page at the publisher's website: http://www.goodfellowpublishers.com.

The biggest challenge was to determine the order and the grouping of the viewpoints. In the end, in the main section, *Letters from Leaders*, we decided to simply list the contributions alphabetically by author. This is partly because so many of the views intersect and reinforce other contributions, but not in any logical grouping. It also testifies to the very idea of transcending traditional silos, rather than trying to force contributions into little boxes. And it's partly because we expect that people would not sit down to read this book from cover to cover, but rather to dip into particular parts over time, and hopefully draw on contributions for their own transformation processes. We made an executive choice on where to start because we thought that the letter from Thomas Enders, CEO of EADS (the parent of Airbus), captured so well the spirit and vision of the transformation need.

**Finally,** we have tried to identify some of the main strategic directions emerging from the letters. Key messages include:

- Travelism is a force for good, economic and social; but to fully capitalize on this, it must also be environmentally sustainable.
- The challenge is for the sector to leverage its core competencies of economic growth, job creation and as a conduit for cross cultural understanding, to deliver greater benefits for local communities and society, while 'future-proofing' the businesses through which these benefits are channelled.
- What is now required is to incorporate green innovation and carbon reduction into technologically, economically, and socially credible strategies for the next decades, with progressively enhanced implementation.

■ There is a need for greater policy coherence and coordination across the travelism value chain; most importantly, breaking out of the silos that still see tourism and aviation as separate economic activities. Travel and tourism should be positioned collectively as a strategic industry, with air transport as an interconnected core, not an isolated entity.

■ There is great value in cross-sectoral networks to help shape tomorrow's continuously evolving global socio-economic agenda, and there is a need for broad inclusion to encourage sound debate, avoid tunnel vision and embrace multi-stakeholder principles.

■ There is a need for better data and integrated measurement systems linking travelism (aviation and tourism data sets) and environmental accounting as well as factoring the emerging 'gross national happiness' concept into a more inclusive balance sheet of societal wellbeing.

■ Travelism's job creation capacity must be factored into main-stream strategies for green growth and social inclusion. Here the value of coherent and credible data across sectoral information presentation and messaging will be significant.

■ Given the volume of travel and tourism activity in developing and emerging market destinations, the sector can provide more equitable economic growth, which would promote social inclusion at a global level. Development agencies should focus on market driven solutions that use green growth approaches to meet consumer demand and contribute to the bottom line.

■ The importance of action at the local level in any transformation towards a green growth path should be recognized. This means taking globally evolving principles and treaties and translating them through regional and national regulatory frameworks into local community or city focused action plans for green travelism growth.

■ Aviation is a key driver in the development of sustainable travel and tourism, with connectivity a crucial element of a modern, resource efficient, global, green economy. Without aviation's connectivity, today's global economy simply could not function.

■ To secure a green growth economy while coping with growing challenges and shrinking resources, we need a coherent international approach to implement a new air transport R&D framework, and target concrete, resource efficient operational delivery, integrated with a priority educational revamp.

- Funding in particular needs an overhaul. Global revenues from aviation taxes could be used to fund the research, education and fleet renewal that would actually cut emissions and fuel a greener economy.

- It is vitally important to revamp education systems to fully integrate green growth and travelism into curricula and research disciplines, as well as more effectively communicating the importance of responsible travel to consumers. Social and environmental sustainability principles are integral to the expectations of young future leaders. They are more likely to feel attracted to and stay within companies that make a positive impact on the environment.

- Addressing the challenges of climate change should not be about sacrifice but about opportunity. There should be a healthy aviation industry, even when we have achieved the low carbon world of the future. But to make that a reality, we need new technologies, new fuels, partnerships and better policy.

- It is essential to agree a global market based mechanism for managing international aviation emissions, while avoiding double counting and double taxing of emissions. This must be designed to create price signals, provide offsetting opportunities, encourage long term R&D and promote behavioural change. Aviation's carbon burden should not be disproportionate. It must not become the 'cash cow' of the climate regime. This assumes that a significant portion of revenues from carbon pricing will be re-invested in green growth.

- There are real opportunities to reduce carbon emissions from air transport through operational, infrastructural and technological energy efficiency improvements, and by investing now in research and development for low carbon, sustainable, second generation bio-fuels to eventually replace kerosene jet fuel.

- Creating the essential global aviation bio-fuels industry will require a package of public policies, funding and partnerships at various stages of the technology life cycle and throughout a long value chain.

- There are 'low-hanging fruit' available to reduce emissions in the accommodation cluster, including through green building design, energy efficiency measures and renewable energy deployment; and in the land transport cluster through passenger modal shifts, more efficient vehicles and low carbon fuels as well as improved public transport in 'green cities'.

■ There is a need for strategies to assist local communities and SMEs to understand climate change vulnerabilities and increase their adaptive capacity. The large information gaps related to losses and damages of climate change has limited the place of tourism in major international climate change assessments.

■ There is significant potential for leveraging sustainability and development from technology innovation and this will require mechanisms for transfer, financing and capacity building in the world's poorest countries and small island states.

■ Ecotourism should be recognized as a specific green growth element and an important beacon for the sector: it is particularly important for developing countries and should be factored into both conservation strategies and development funding. This should not diminish from the imperative of applying stringent, enforceable standards for main-stream travelism transformation. Over time, success for a destination will not be judged by numbers of tourists, but by what beneficial effects tourism will have on the social, cultural, economic and environmental health of the destination.

■ There is a need to engage business fully, across the value chain, especially small and medium businesses, incorporating sustainability into strategies and routine operations, as well as company reporting systems.

■ It is also important to eliminate 'green-washing' and to encourage responsible sustainability benchmarks and certification programs.

■ Strategies are needed to connect the know-how and market access of multinational companies with businesses and entrepreneurs in less developed areas of the world. Successful bottom of the pyramid and inclusive business cases and practices need to be adapted and implemented in the travel and tourism sector.

■ Inadequate access to capital for SMME's is a major barrier for greening tourism. Creative public and private funding and risk sharing instruments are needed, as are prioritized government spending on public goods.

- Internet based technology can be a massive driver of travelism's green growth transformation, with innovations in mobile devices, consumer applications and broadband access opening up new markets – particularly in developing states.

- New forms of public private partnerships will reshape investment, development, environment and climate response across the travelism sector. Increasingly this will translate into infrastructure and human capacity building and will be focused on destinations where green growth strategies and CSR are mainstream priorities.

- Smart development of national parks is an important way to stimulate green growth, tackle the problem of biodiversity loss and engage communities: but it needs radical new communications strategies.

- Cities will also become major centres of green travelism growth and in this framework, sporting, entertainment or cultural events as well as green meetings can be important, globally projected and locally delivered.

- As consumer preferences evolve to demand greater sustainable performances by the companies from which they buy their travel, there is not only the opportunity to influence and educate the consumer but also to set the mould which others can follow. Business can influence local and international supply chains by demanding more sustainable products. This in turn creates a ripple effect and the potential global outreach is immense.

- The sector should be making sustainability commitments because we care about the environment. But we must also be making them because it makes good business sense. In spite of all the initiatives of the past decade, the main challenge is to fill the current gap between aspiration, policy design and implementation. Travelism can and should be part of the sustainability solution.

We trust that these issues and, more importantly, the *Letters from Leaders* will form a basis for informed public debate on green growth and travelism, will make a constructive contribution to the transformation of the sector, and will serve as one source of guidance for tomorrow's leaders. We are particularly mindful of the next generation of pathfinders who are currently studying for entry into the global workforce and those inside who are climbing their career ladders.

It is our conviction that future generations and their leaders will come to share the belief, expressed in all the letters, in the potential for travelism to make a seriously powerful contribution to green growth.

# Towards Transformation

**Geoffrey Lipman, Terry DeLacy, Shaun Vorster, Rebecca Hawkins and Min Jiang**

*Green growth is the global strategic response to the economic recession, persistent poverty, resource scarcity and above all climate change.*

*Travelism – encompassing the tourism & travel value chain– must be proactive in the transofmation; not only in its own interest, but more importantly because of the  overall contribution it can make to global sustainable development and cross-cultural cohesion.*

*Imaginative transformation strategies will be required for the travelism sector to play an increasingly relevant role in the evolving paradigm shift and to move from a fragmented, perceived secondary activity, to a recognized primary contributor to economic and societal well being.*

*Rio + 20 provides a vital stepping stone.*

## Green growth: a new paradigm

Green growth is gaining significant worldwide geopolitical momentum as a new economic paradigm. It is reflected in the strategies of such bodies as the G20, OECD, World Bank Group, regional government bodies on every continent, various agencies in the UN system, and an increasing number of industrialised and developing states. It is seen as a coherent strategy set to respond proactively to today's extreme economic, poverty and climate crunches; as well as preparing for tomorrow's anticipated food, water and energy crises; compounded by a population jump from seven to nine billion over the next four decades.

This strategic challenge is clouded by continuous pressures of dramatically volatile economics, markets and related politics; intensified by lightly regulated, superheated, globalization of capital and accentuated by recurring patterns of extreme natural or human caused disasters. But the long term direction remains unchanged. The generally identified transformation time frame of 2050 is linked to the mid century milestone the world community is targeting for stabilising global emissions to keep adverse impacts of climate change at manageable levels. There will be numerous opportunities for course adjustment en route, especially as scientific knowledge evolves, but identifying a long term pathway is an important starting point.

According to UNEP, the new green economy will be 'low carbon, resource efficient and socially inclusive'. Key components are reducing dependence on oil or coal and increasing reliance on clean energy, wind, solar, bio-fuel, geothermal, etc.; transferring technology and finance to developing and emerging countries; conserving eco systems for life sustaining biodiversity and linking information technology with energy technology to manage change. It will result in improved human well being and reduced inequalities over the long term, while not exposing future generations to significant environmental risks and ecological scarcities or reduction in quality of life. This is what France's Stiglitz Commission on gross national happiness refers to as 'natural, physical, human and social factors not traded in markets or captured by monetary measures but that make life worth living'. The complexity, scale and scope of this half century shift in every activity on this planet is almost incomprehensible, given different starting points, socio-politico-economic realities and the multi-trillion dollar cost.

Across the world, governments and industry stakeholders are now defining green growth principles, practices and enabling programs, progressively integrating them into national and local policy action. This includes a range of reforms to boost and sustain demand, foster job creation, contribute to rebalancing the allocation of capital, and increase growth potential. It also includes commitments to invest in clean energy and resource efficiency, low carbon technologies, greener cities and sustainable mobility. At the same time, industry generally is embracing the concept in corporate social responsibility (CSR) or transformational programs and consumer interest is gradually escalating.

The Rio +20 Earth Summit in June 2012, will see a new global effort to recommit to the green growth transformation. It is evident that the travel & tourism sector must seize the opportunity to reposition and respond pro-actively as contributor and beneficiary of this paradigm shift.

# Travelism

Travel & tourism, or for short, *travelism* (which is a term coined to encompass both the 'demand side' activity of non-commuting travel for business or leisure, international/domestic and the 'supply side' industry cluster of transport, tourism, hospitality, distribution and related delivery services), is increasingly identified as an important contributor to this evolving green economy.

- First, because of its size, scale and scope, as well as catalytic links to other sectors like agriculture, communications, financial services and transport.

- Second, because it has a critical role to play in advancing the development agenda and reducing poverty. In virtually all of the world's poorest countries it is an actual or potential services trade and employment leader, bringing investment and wealth creation as infrastructure is built and visitor spend is injected directly into local communities.

- Third, because human contact can spread cultural knowledge, understanding, tolerance, peace and happiness in ways that other traded goods and services cannot.

There is growing consumer demand to travel away from home for business and leisure, or for a combination of the two. This demand is increasingly seen as both a basic right and a valuable building block of modern society. It requires a complex mix of transport, food, accommodation and entertainment services, some of which are delivered by private entities, others by government. Some estimates suggest that a typical international trip can include up to 50 public-private interfaces, differing from country to country. In addition, while the 'thought leadership' has historically come from the major national and multinational players and institutions, the bulk of the sector, some 80%, are small and medium enterprises and most of the impacts are felt at the local level.

However, the overall impact of travel and tourism is generally misperceived, its contribution often undervalued, and its potential underdeveloped. The industry is very fragmented, between hospitality and transport; business and leisure; domestic and international; multinational and national. Not surprisingly, the systems and structures that measure, represent and regulate it have evolved in similar silos: from

the multilateral UN institutions, to fragmentation in national governments and industry associations.

As a result, the sector has not yet realised its real potential to
advance green growth and its engagement is less evident than that of
many other industries. Efforts to better quantify and manage this global
travel phenomenon have intensified in the recent past and will do so
increasingly as world economies rebalance, austerity budgets bite and
green growth becomes the norm. In addition, as global strategies trickle
down into local implementation there will be an increasing demand
for the true impacts of all travel related sectors, good or bad, to be
coherently identified and controlled in overall community economics,
environmental protection and lifestyles.

Travelism must be a part of the new paradigm and, significantly, it
can be a catalyst for transformation in otherparts of the economy. This
will require a new mindset about the nature of the sector, about its
real societal impact and about its role in sustainable mobility, lifestyles
and destinations. It will also require clear transformation strategies if the
sector is to move from a fragmented, perceived secondary activity to a
recognized primary contributor.

# The travel & tourism balance sheet is sound, but must be strengthened

## Assets

### 1 Economic

In conventional metrics, travelism's direct and indirect economic
contribution is massive by any standard. Today's international arrivals
are forecast by UNWTO to double over the next 20 years, led by BRICS
markets generally and Asia specifically, with the Gulf emerging as a key
global hub. Domestic travel is three to four times larger than international travel and evolving at similar rates.

At 9.1% of global GDP (or $6 trillion) in 2011, travel and tourism is
forecast to grow to 9.6% (or $9.2 trillion) by 2021 according to WTTC.
They also forecast total global investment in the sector of $652 billion in
2011 to more than double to US$1.5 trillion by 2021.

## 2 Employment

During this same period, direct and indirect travelism jobs will grow from 8.8% of the global workforce in 2011 (258 million) to 9.7% by 2021 (324 million). UNEP estimates that every job in the core workforce creates about one and a half related indirect jobs in the tourism related economy. There can be no indicator of more importance to global socio-economic development than job creation. Apart from the sheer numbers, the quality of jobs, gender equity and youth inclusion are all important factors. In addition, the capacity to create green jobs will be significant as the sector shifts to a low carbon, resource efficient model, particularly in linked sectors.

## 3 Development

These economic and employment deliverables are particularly important for developing, landlocked or small island states, where the contribution to improving livelihoods far exceeds the norm. Tourism services exports of developing countries are some 45% of their services exports, compared to a global 30%. It is a major source of foreign investment.

Significantly, most poor countries have the capacity to be producers of this offering simply because of their natural or cultural heritage. Moreover, tourism is a market based service where the product, with the right developmental support, is in the mainstream of evolving global demand. It can provide sustainable long term jobs, export income and competitive advantage. Direct impacts at community level are significant and catalytic indirect effects on other economic activities are substantial, particularly trade, communications, infra-structure and mobility.

The very qualities of underdevelopment mean that leapfrog strate-gies and technologies create their own green growth opportunities from a more receptive base. There is increasing evidence from UNCTAD studies that more sustainable tourism in rural areas can lead to more positive poverty reducing effects. And clearly this is now being deployed as part of national strategies in China and India, where the potential gains are dramatic.

## 4 Gross National Happiness

The balance sheet consists of more than economics. The wider intangible gains need to be properly accounted for, including positive impacts on global integration, trade and development, creating business or investment opportunities and facilitating connections. Travelism is also at the heart of leisure, rest, relaxation, sport and access to culture and nature. It is one of humanity's most fundamental vehicles for wellbeing and happiness. According to UNWTO's Global Code of Ethics it is 'an irreplaceable factor of self-education, mutual tolerance and for learning about legitimate differences between peoples, cultures and diversity'.

# Liabilities

## 1 Growing carbon and capacity impacts

On the negative side, travelism is an evident contributor to climate change. It also has a significant 'eco' footprint in terms of water, waste, marine biodiversity, and threats to local cultures and traditions. These elements will grow as a consequence of forecast sector expansion, unless radically modified by a range of government, industry and market initiatives.

As far as its carbon footprint is concerned, the total sector share of carbon emissions is some 5%, with aviation accounting for 40% of that total today. Despite technology, infrastructure or operating pattern improvements, aviation's share of total emissions will increase in the absence of alternative non-kerosene jet fuel.

Industry organizations have so far set targets with high aspirations and the challenge is to achieve them in the real world. WTTC members, for example, committed to an aspirational goal of a 50% reduction in $CO_2$ emissions by 2035 over 2005 levels. For airlines, IATA has committed to an aggregate annual 1.5% efficiency improvement up to 2020, with a mid-term goal of 'carbon-neutral growth from 2020' and a reduction in net emissions of 50% below 2005 levels by 2050. Some major carriers are committing to go further. ICAO has a goal of a 2% per annum improvement in fuel efficiency up to 2020 and an aspirational goal of extending this up to 2050.

This will require a range of public and private initiatives inside the sector, along with changes in externally related government action. A major challenge is that the window of opportunity to close the gap between aspiration and what is required by science is reducing fast. The later the peak, and the higher absolute emissions, the steeper future reductions would have to be to limit temperature increase to sustainable levels, and the more significant the role of uncertain breakthrough technologies will become.

## 2 Inadequate sector response

Within hospitality, initiatives have been ad hoc at a corporate level and nominally supported by the trade and professional associations, mostly through awards. Large corporations are increasingly engaging through CSR, green supply chain management and voluntary consumer offsets. There are numerous small scale measurement and certification approaches, with global agreements now being sought on mechanisms to unite these efforts.

For transport, the challenge runs deeper, because of the percentage of energy driven by fossil fuels. For aviation, specifically, the current absence of viable alternatives has even more significant implications. Aviation has generally been very active in sustainability and climate related policy development. This is due to a combination of reasons, including the historic recognition and organization of the sector in global trade and economic matters, the pro-active position of airlines, aircraft frame and engine manufacturers and airports, and the early experience of the sector in effectively managing noise pollution. Aviation, because of its trans-border nature and historic national controls over airspace and airlines, has frequently been dealt with as a special case in international treaties, regulation and operation. The Uruguay Trade Round is a good example; likewise the Kyoto Protocol where both aviation and maritime were left to specialised UN agencies to develop appropriate complementary policy frameworks.

Moreover, the special challenge of mitigating the impact of aircraft emissions on global warming has led to a policy impasse in international negotiations and intensifying government/industry rancour in some corners of the world. This has polarised around the EU's proposed inclusion of all airlines in its emissions trading scheme (ETS) in 2012 and non-EU states countervailing response, as well as government and industry efforts to finally deliver on a global ETS developed in ICAO.

Agreement on a global market based mechanism with an underlying carbon budget, national burden sharing, incentives and compliance mechanisms to ensure delivery against targets has so far been painfully slow.

Three major air transport issues will be important points of focus in the next decade.

1   The search for second generation biofuel alternatives to aviation kerosene. The financial viability, sustainability and scalability of drop-in biofuels are key challenges; but many opportunities beckon and major progress has been made to address barriers. There is increasing reason to believe that initiatives to create new and radically improved types of biofuel and a number of ongoing R&D and demonstration projects by aircraft/engine manufacturers with airlines could positively reduce aviation emissions.

2   The cat-and-mouse game on the introduction of a global emissions trading scheme has to have an end game. Irrespective of the merits, legalities or tactics in play, there can be no doubt that, as national or regional climate change mitigation policies and measures increasingly extend to other economic sectors, aviation cannot stay out of the game. In the absence of an ambitious regime for managing emissions, there are no real price signals in the market to stimulate behavioural change, the new investment required in R&D and the scaling-up and commercialising of game changing technologies.

3   Attacks which simply demonize aviation's climate impacts need to be put into an objective perspective and balanced with the airlines' real efforts to factor climate response into operational, infrastructural and technology driven efficiency improvements. But most importantly, they must be measured against the fact that aviation is the essential lifeline for travelism driven exports and jobs, most importantly in many least developed economies.

## 3 Inconsistent policy frameworks

Because of the fragmentation, misperception and historical development patterns, many public sector enabling frameworks are incomplete or even non-existent. Moreover, they are themselves in constant evolution to adapt to routine geopolitics and socio-economics, including green growth. The reality is that the institutional frameworks within multilateral institutions, the industry/government interface and the tourism/transport divide are not conducive to leveraging creative win-win solutions for the green growth paradigm.

Typical examples are the traditional policy splits between trade, tourism and transport (with aviation so often getting special treatment). Another is the historic failure of national accounts to reflect the total economic impact of the sector. Where UNWTO, WTTC and OECD have worked to create a satellite accounting framework, which is a major advance, efforts to integrate aviation or environmental economic measurement are still largely uncoordinated. At the industry level, airlines and airports have evolved in different silos, but have forged new alliances to respond to climate change. Security, immigration, trade and tourism are totally separate issues in government structures, but clearly have cross-cutting issues when it comes to border flows, airport efficiency and customer satisfaction. This is well articulated in the programmes in T.20, WTTC, UNWTO and WEF on e-visas and IATA's 'simplifying travel' initiative – positive steps towards more rational solutions which clearly link to green growth, increasing travel exports and creating jobs.

# Managing change

It is worth reflecting on the fact that the green growth transformation timeframe is almost 40 years. But we have to start now and move fast with the ambitious goals of stabilising global warming at acceptable levels; bridging the poverty divide; building a fairer inclusive society; conserving fundamental resources; and reshaping economies towards adequacy and away from greed. The landscape will shift quickly. On the one hand, 40 years ago internet, mobile phones, multimedia and PDAs didn't exist, there was an embryonic EU, no BRICS dynamics and international travel was a tenth of what it is today, so the potential for radical change is evident. On the other, the accelerating pace of change, around the clock multimedia exposure, geopolitical gyration and acute natural disasters will challenge the transformation targets. To stay on track, we will need some fundamental focal points.

## 1 Responding to extreme climate change

There can be no excuses for not joining the rest of society in its collective response to climate change. It is not necessarily to break the existing system, but rather to build on it by establishing best practice rules and procedures; creating implementation, incentive and compliance mechanisms; raising awareness and educating; building capacity and addressing the means of implementation; while providing checks and balances to ensure integrity.

At a more fundamental level, the challenge is to progressively decouple travelism growth and emissions growth: to decarbonise the sector. That means massive change, clean, low carbon transport; climate-proofed accommodation; efficient energy, waste and water practices; green growth support services; millions of redefined and trained green jobs; radically changed consumer habits; multimedia support and government led incentives and penalties. There is a huge unexplored scope for incentives in this area, as has happened for example with such issues as low carbon lighting, double-glazing and feed-in renewable electricity tariffs.

One of the major long term changes will be the role of China as it steps up its commitment by adjusting its socio-economic model and playing a leading role in the long term global green growth shift. There are clear signs that travelism will be an increasingly important element. Our sector has recently been identified in the 12th five year plan as a domestic consumption engine, in addition to its earlier designation as a strategic pillar of economic development. And the application of the 2008 stimulus package is daily translating into new airports, high speed trains and superhighways – this is the essential arterial network for travelism. Growing automobile production is another factor, as is the plan's goals to boost household income and wages. The opportunity to travel, for leisure and business, domestically and internationally, will simply become possible for more and more people in China.

Of course the thorny issue of sustainability is a major challenge accentuated in China by the speed and scale of development, as well as the historically low environmental starting point. It is clear that in its own way and at its own pace China is positioning to be a leader of sustainable development and particularly of renewable energy. These issues are also important elements of the current national plan. UN Secretary General Ban Ki Moon noted in 2011 that China's renewable energy investments are second only to Germany's and that its impressive roster of new cities can become global beacons of sustainable development. The sectoral perspective is to effectively integrate slowly strengthening travelism norms into the evolving national green growth agenda, particularly the highly focused low carbon dimension.

## 2 Better environmental stewardship

Here the challenges are different but equally pressing. Waste and water management issues, congestion and biodiversity destruction all escalate as more and more people want to visit prime tourism locations and fragile eco systems. Many of these impacts, and the travelism contribution, are not measured globally. Experience on the ground demonstrates that travelism can in some instances provide an incentive to reduce the occurrence of these impacts (especially biodiversity decline), whilst in others it exacerbates them (especially water consumption).

## 3 Boosting development support

The travelism potential is slowly being factored into development aid programs and World Bank thinking, but the amounts actually assigned for tourism are very small and the indirect linkage through infrastructure and other programs is somewhat tenuous.

Major new funding frameworks are needed for states generally, and Africa specifically, to use travelism as a development tool. This may come as states and institutions look to integrated approaches to job stimulus, Millennium Development Goal (MDG) fulfilment, and aid for developing trade and climate adaptation programmes. It will involve new approaches to public/private sector funding. The challenge will be to equitably meet international commitments in an age of austerity budgeting.

## 4 Creating green jobs

As the sector transforms as part of the ongoing green economy revolution, by definition many of its jobs will evolve into a green jobs classification, meeting sustainability criteria themselves or helping transformation. New jobs will be created in green skills and training programs for existing and new workers. As noted by UNEP/UNWTO: 'The greening of tourism, which involves efficiency improvements in energy, water and waste systems, is expected to reinforce the employment potential of the sector with increased local hiring and sourcing and significant opportunities in tourism, oriented toward local culture and the natural environment'. These jobs will be in such areas as energy management, retrofitting and maintenance of buildings, sustainable biofuel operations, ecotourism, conservation and national parks and in construction of high speed trains, superhighways, airports and new communication and information technology systems and tools.

## 5 Expanding financing frameworks

The financing world will also change for the green growth era with programmes and projects having to pass new green ethical and regulatory standards for investment from government, private equity, pension funds and the like. This will give new opportunities to place travelism in the mainstream, instead of on the edges where it has traditionally been.

New green funds can become accessible for travelism programmes related to transport infrastructure, renewable energy deployment, rural development or telecommunications, particularly where the goal is capacity building, knowledge/technology transfer or small/medium/ micro enterprise incubation. As UNEP has noted, government spending on public goods such as protected areas, cultural assets, water conservation, waste management, sanitation, public transport and renewable energy infrastructure can reduce the cost of green investments by the private sector in green tourism. Governments can also use tax concessions and subsidies to encourage private investment in green tourism. Time-bound subsidies can be given, for example, on systems, equipment and technology that prevent waste, cleanse water or process biomass; that encourages energy and water efficiency, that conserve biodiversity and that strengthen linkages with local businesses and community organisations.

## 6 Revamping education and training

Education is another fundamental issue in long term transformation. Transport, hospitality and travel services have so far evolved in their own educational silos with differentiated quality and little connectivity. Most emphasis in this sector to date has been on vocational training in secondary and tertiary education systems. Geography and economics have been important surrogates for the former, with engineering, marketing, finance and general management for the latter. Classic university disciplines are limited, despite the multiplication of hospitality colleges and faculties around the world in recent years.

Even the key industry and international organizations have only played on the edges of a meaningful education and training strategy. There is no coherence in fundamental school, vocational, entrepreneurship, graduate and postgraduate components, nor between the public and private sectors; nor a leadership mind-set attuned to the potential global positioning of the sector.

The green growth paradigm offers a step change opportunity, because it will mean a strategic re-orientation in all education systems. In this context two new initiatives are worthy of note.

1 The creation of a global green growth knowledge platform by UNEP, the OECD, World Bank and Korea's Global Green Growth Institute to 'identify and address major knowledge gaps in green growth theory and practice'. This platform will improve local, national and global economic policy-making around the world by providing rigorous and relevant analysis of the various synergies and trade-offs between the economy and the environment. It will complement other efforts by emphasizing policy instruments that yield local environmental co-benefits while stimulating growth, providing a compelling set of incentives for governments.

2 The concept of a World Environment University, advanced by Maurice Strong to mainstream sustainable development in academic structures, can be an important element because a Green Growth and Travelism Institute will be an important founding component. This Institute has been designed to become an education reference point for academic, industry and government thought leaders committed to the mainstreaming of the sector in green growth. It will operate as an education network committed to best practice learning techniques based on new media and mobile delivery.

## 7 Intensified community focus

The main directions and principle strategies for transformation will be multilaterally charted, in global and regional processes gradually embracing unique national characteristics. But the real impacts, challenges and opportunities will occur at the local, destination level. While government strategies will form the base, the sector itself, with corporate social responsibility as a mainstream determinant, will increase its commitment and strengthen its role in decision making. Large multilateral bodies will continue to provide leadership vision, but action will be demanded by regulators and the marketplace. Moreover, small and medium sized businesses, as well as civil society, will become fully engaged in those processes.

Communities start from different geographical, political, economic and capacity vantage points, but with a common desire to have a major impact on their own destiny and a shared need to frame their 2050 roadmaps. While mitigation of GHG emissions must form the baseline of most strategies, it is only part of the narrative.

Strategies have to consider the enhancement of environments and eco systems as well as factor in economic and cultural trends on a global, regional and local scale. Other vital considerations include changing and greening market demand (i.e. green consumerism), supply chain dynamics, destination competitiveness, brand positioning and funding options. Key factors underscored in UNEP's tourism report are the need to engage a wide variety of agencies and programs to effectively understand and eventually manage tourism's dynamic impacts for community benefit and again, the importance of public/private transformation financing.

The complexity and integrative nature of these factors complicate effective and targeted policymaking and consequently, while tourism master plans may have provided a framework in the past, the concept needs revamping for the green growth era. What is now required are dynamic cross-sectoral approaches that build green growth plans from the destination perspective.

# New Directions

**Geoffrey Lipman, Terry DeLacy, Shaun Vorster, Rebecca Hawkins and Min Jiang**

## 1 A changed mind-set

There is emerging consensus that all sectors must contribute to the evolving green growth paradigm and clear evidence that travelism can make an important contribution as change agent, a wealth generator, jobs creator and cultural integrator. According to UNEP, a green economy investment of a mere 0.2% of annual global GDP (US $135 billion at current levels of GDP) between now and 2050 would allow the tourism sector to continue to grow steadily over the coming decades, contributing to much needed economic growth, employment and development while ensuring significant environmental benefits such as reductions in water consumption (18%), energy use (44%), and $CO_2$ emissions (52%) compared to today. Because of the transformation time frame, the fragmented cluster of industries that compose travelism can reposition and coalesce, but the sooner it starts the better.

What is missing is the mind set and the mechanisms for delivering green growth at policy, business and destination levels. The thinking process has started: for example, the UNWTO's Davos climate change process and roadmap for recovery, UNEP's green economy studies, WTTC's climate roadmap, IATA 2050 Vision and WEF's work on low-carbon tourism and aviation. But much of the content is aspirational and significant work remains to develop coherent links.

We must recognize the transformation potential and get squarely behind the green new deal. It is still early days in the global acceptance of this kind of economic approach, but we must understand it, and the pros and the cons, to maximize our contribution and our benefits. We must start from the need for energy efficiency for long term survival and advocate 'smart tourism' that is clean, green, ethical and quality driven. We must intensify public private sector collaboration. Governments have to create the enabling framework with incentives for public private partnerships. And we must work to position the sector during the window of opportunity where governments are putting together the massive transformational funds for poverty alleviation, climate adaptation, decarbonisation and aid for trade.

## 2 Cross-sectoral vision

We need a common vision across all clusters, change management vehicles that deliver locally, and a strategic game plan that starts now and can adapt with policy and market shifts. To date, knowledge has been accrued within individual silos, whether government departments, business sectors or specific destinations, and often deliberately kept there for self-interest or simply due to a lack of a shared win-win vision.

New technologies and policy concepts that can help to spread consideration and collaboration more readily are already emerging across the sector. Forty years ago typical game changers like the internet, mobile phones, Skype and Twitter did not exist. Looking 40 years into the future, most technical collaboration barriers will likely be long gone. The human and political ones will be more challenging.

Collaboration mechanisms should enable all players in the travelism system to think about the green growth agenda in new and different ways, and to use this thinking to define the role the sector as a whole can play in a new growth paradigm.

We will need to consolidate within the sector itself, bridging the fragmentation between tourism, aviation, travel, hospitality and related services – recognizing that the broader synergies of collaboration far outweigh the fragmented sectoral ways of doing business. Despite nice 'sounds', too little has so far been done to bring public and private sector, or tourism and transport, into any sort of cooperative framework. But things are moving fast, and the informal travelism coalition built around the UNWTO and WTTC nucleus are surely a very positive step in the right direction.

Defragmentation cannot just take place in the rarefied closed door fora at the top of the industry; the real impact and action should be felt at the bottom of the pyramid, in destinations and among the small players that make up 80% of the sector. Multi-stakeholder mechanisms are needed within the travelism sector, linked to broader socio-economic decision making processes.

# 3 Mainstreaming

Government and industry initiatives to convince the G20 heads of state and government to recognize the importance of the sector are an important start. The awareness raising must be broadened, to regional and national institutions and decision makers, as well as into non-travelism media and events. In this respect, the T.20 Ministerial Platform is an important one. There is great merit in its initial focus on the rational improvement to travelism trade flows by the use of e-visas or other travel facilitation programmes, including electronic visa processing and issuance and regional visa schemes. These simplify and speed up border crossings while increasing essential security measures. It boosts export trade, creates jobs and 'greens' the process.

Global initiatives must cascade into local policy development structures. It must be linked to trade facilitation and it must be communicated widely to the travelling, hosting and servicing publics, who in the end should be the ultimate determinants of policy in the market and at the ballot box.

Mainstreaming must be increasingly supported by standard data sets, with tourism satellite accounts embracing aviation and integrated with environment and climate accounting.

Travelism must also be reflected coherently in green growth fiscal strategies, with historical special treatment progressively phased out, full costs accounted for, discriminatory taxes eradicated and incentives made fully available, particularly where developing states, small islands or small and medium enterprises are involved.

# 4 'Glocal' delivery

This is the key starting point for wide-scale progressive transformation, taking globally evolving principles and treaties and translating them through regional and national regulatory frameworks into local community or city focussed actions. Over time these locally based experiences will form a continuous feedback loop that will enrich and reshape the broader framework.

Local governments, communities and businesses need to establish mechanisms for coordinating with ministries responsible for environment, energy, labour, agriculture, transport, health, finance, security and related areas. Clear requirements are needed in areas such as zoning, protected areas, environmental rules and regulations, labour rules, agricultural standards and health requirements.

## 5 Implementation now

We have passed the analysis, aspirational targets and declaration stages. What is needed now is committed implementation, engaging a fragmented sector and uniting it with shared goals, while maintaining separate but coordinated momentum. Travelism has only scratched the surface of its clean, green potential – now it is time to deliver change.

We will routinely have to adjust course but the journey has to begin with an end point in mind and move progressively towards it. There is no upside in delay; the window of opportunity to deal with the transformation is narrowing fast and volatility is increasingly a given. We need to better understand the potential of travelism in a global green growth future and seek to contribute effectively with coherent global and local actions.

# Letters from Leaders

## Thomas Enders

**CEO of EADS**

## One born every minute

Thomas Enders (1958) is currently the CEO of EADS, having been a member of the Executive Committee since 2000, first as CEO of EADS' Defence and Security Systems Division and later as Co-CEO of EADS. Tom served as President and CEO of its subsidiary Airbus from 2007-2012. In an aerospace and defence career spanning more than 20 years, Tom has been President of the German Aerospace Industry Association (BDLI) since 2005. Prior to joining industry, he worked in the German Parliament and the Ministry of Defence as well as in various foreign policy think tanks. Tom studied economics, political science and history at the University of California and completed his doctorate at the University of Bonn.

Not so long ago, the aviation industry pushed the boundaries of technology. Microprocessor capacity grew to meet our needs. We didn't just drive aeronautics; we drove a whole raft of new innovation. Today, the average games console has more capability than some single-aisle aircraft, but the airlines can't even use that fully because key infrastructure dates from the 1950s. Kids playing with pocket games have a direct data link at their disposal, but we're still using VHF radio for pilot to ground communications!

What's more, it currently takes 20 years to implement safely a significant step change in aviation technology on an aircraft programme, which has a typical life span of 30 years. The last one off the production line will fly for another 30 years. That gives us an 80 year cycle, which would be a bit like people still driving around in Ford Model B's or having to spend six weeks on a boat to get to Australia.

Throughout this book you'll read about how air traffic has grown by over 50% in the last decade, while demand for aviation fuel has only risen by 3%. How we've cut fuel burn and emissions by 70% and noise by 75%, while growing to support almost 60 million jobs and $2 trillion in GDP. Certainly those are great achievements. But achievements that were only possible because of technology from an intellectual infrastructure that is gradually crumbling around us.

It's simple. To secure a green growth economy we need to put the focus back on technology and the education required to deliver it.

That doesn't just mean the much awaited step change in aircraft performance. It means a step change in our traditional industry model. Neither airline profitability nor emissions targets can wait while we launch a series of new aircraft one after the other as the technology matures. We need to treat research and development programmes like aircraft programmes, with a single minded focus on value and maturity. If necessity really is the mother of invention, perhaps it is even time to think about reinventing commercial aircraft. Perhaps we need a more flexible approach, like a robust upgradable platform that could quickly evolve in line with economic and environmental demands; the kind of thing we see already in some military products?

Delivering the right basket of technologies takes time, investment and risk. That's why we need both a long term vision and the tangible steps to get us there. In Europe, initiatives like ACARE and FlightPath 2050 are central to that, with targets for 75% reduction in $CO_2$ emissions and a 65% reduction in noise by 2050. There's a similar approach in the US with NASA's Environmentally Responsible Aviation project. It aims to move from good ideas to flying hardware by demonstrating a 50% cut in $CO_2$ emissions by about 2025 using innovative scaled test beds.

However, the problems tackled by ACARE and FlightPath 2050 are not only European. The problems being tackled by NASA are not only American. The problems being tackled by strategic partnerships like INSPIRE and ASPIRE are not only in the Indian Ocean and Asian

Pacific. Yes, the IATA and ICAO targets provide a more global vision. But faced with growing challenges and shrinking resources, we still lack a cohesive international approach to fund and implement the concrete steps to deliver them.

Funding in particular needs an overhaul. A global industry tackling a global problem needs global research. Some national taxes are invested in local research, but that restricts opportunities for wider co-operation, which creates duplication and slows the delivery of solutions. Perhaps instead, global revenues from aviation taxes could be used to fund the research, education and fleet renewal that would actually cut emissions and fuel a greener economy? After all, taxes don't cut emissions or create jobs. Technology and talent do both!

There is already precedent for treating our taxes differently. After all, ICAO was formed because the world's governments agreed that an industry with such a unique role needed special treatment. The Chinese government announced it will redirect passenger tax revenues to a development fund for airports, energy saving and emission reductions, including research and development. The EU FlightPath 2050 targets also indicate an intention to go down that road. However, we have yet to see how that will translate into action.

The European Emissions Trading Scheme situation may change radically by the time this book goes to press. If not, there are some serious questions to be asked about plans to spend the $20 billion the world's airlines will pay to comply between now and 2020. As food for thought, that would be enough to implement an upgraded European air traffic management system, which would cut emissions by 10%; to build enough biofuel refineries to meet the EU's target of producing two million tonnes by 2020; to develop an entirely new aircraft model that would provide a significant step towards our target of halving aircraft emissions by 2050; and still have enough left over to educate about 20,000 engineers.

And believe me, those engineers would go a long way to solving the current shortage of talent coming into this industry. Technology holds the key, but there is no innovation without education and while the baby-boomers are heading for the golf course, we're not filling the gap behind them. That's where our efforts for a green economy have to start.

Look at some of the formidable products developed by Russia in the past. Most of those engineers are now in their seventies and that capability is being lost. A similar trend is appearing elsewhere, with around a third of US aerospace workers already hitting retirement age.

That problem is echoed in the fact that America now spends $4 on people over 65 and $1 on the under 18s, with some areas investing twice as much in prisons as in higher education and less than 5% of undergraduates studying engineering. It's a similar tale in Australia. Only half the required number of engineers graduated during the last decade, with failure and dropout rates running at around 40%. Likewise, Europe needs 12,000 aeronautics engineers a year, but only 9,000 graduate and up to 40% of them switch to other careers. Even in Germany, there are half as many engineering students as there were a decade ago, with the Chancellor encouraging young Spanish engineers struggling to find jobs to develop their careers in Germany. Gone are the days when it was low paid or unskilled workers that had to migrate to find work. And ironically, while overseas students still flock to the traditional bastions of engineering and technology, visa restrictions often mean they leave again straight after graduation.

Worst of all, we are still not realising the potential of almost half of the population. Despite twice as many boys having literacy problems in high school, only around a third of the maths, science and technology graduates from Europe and the US are female. The number who go on to pursue careers in engineering has dropped steadily over the last decade to around 10%, with many then leaving the industry.

The problems start much further down the chain though. Only one in five twelfth graders in the US achieve proficiency in the core science subjects and the same scores in Europe are below the OECD average, with 20% also struggling in literacy. Even at home, four out of five American aerospace workers would not recommend their children follow a career in the industry.

The impact of all of this is starting to show. Recent Information Technology and Innovation Foundation rankings of 40 countries indicate that Europe and the US are strong performers today. They also reveal that in terms of what has been done to improve innovation capacity in the last decade, Europe ranks 15th and the United States at the bottom.

E

Now it's true that so many numbers probably invite some retorts about how every good statistic automatically generates another. But even if people debate the figures themselves, the important thing is that they paint a picture worth understanding. That applies, not only to education, but to matching skills with industrial requirements and developing long term career satisfaction that will attract the best engineers to aviation. Aircraft have become so complex that it is increasingly difficult for individuals to understand how it all comes together and skills sets are changing accordingly, with mechanical engineers now expected to master software development.

Don't get me wrong, there are some good initiatives underway to turn this around. President Obama's Council on Jobs and Competitiveness includes a special task force to generate 10,000 more engineering students per year. Australian academics are teaming up with UNESCO to push the issue up the agenda. The Europe 2020 strategy is starting to show results. Special incentives are in place to recruit more STEM teachers and education is now a key element of ACARE, which is pushing for 'centres of excellence' that would allow industry, research centres and education to join forces in attracting and retain talent.

Emerging economies put huge priority and investment into educating a workforce that will drive growth and competitiveness. The traditional economies need to up their game quickly if we are to create a truly global talent pool. School children should be encouraged to understand why science and engineering can be such a great world to explore; to understand how the world around them actually works. Teachers should be properly trained, equipped and supported. Qualified engineers should be enticed back into the fold. Who knows, perhaps we could even rehabilitate a few who strayed into the financial sector and turn them into more useful members of society that actually help the economy?

What worries me most is that, like many people in this book, I've been saying these things for over a decade now. Technology, partnership and education feed economic and environmental performance. There's nothing new in any of it. Shifting engineering demographics takes time. Educating a kid through school and university or an apprenticeship takes time. Developing and implementing new technology, air traffic management or aircraft takes time. Evaluating environmental pressures and implementing solutions takes time. Yet we've wasted an entire decade debating these issues instead of resolving them.

There are 250 kids born every minute. Among them are the engineers, scientists, teachers and policy makers who must take global transport beyond the age of fossil fuels and build a truly sustainable economy.

Today kids use iPads before they can walk. They think nothing of getting their bedtime stories via videophone. But if we don't sort ourselves out quickly they will cut their transport teeth on technology that has been around since before most of the people reading this book were even born.

# Patricia R. Francis

**Executive Director, International Trade Centre**

F

## Greening the tourism sector – building the competitiveness of developing countries

Patricia R. Francis, is the Executive Director of the International Trade Centre (ITC). Prior to joining ITC in 2006, Ms. Francis was President of Jamaica Trade and Invest since 1995, and a member of Jamaica's Cabinet Committee for Development. She served twice as President of the World Association of Investment Promotion Agencies, has chaired the Organization for Economic Cooperation and Development's Caribbean Rim Investment Initiative, as well as the China-Caribbean Business Council, and is on the advisory board of the IESE graduate business school. During her tenure at ITC, the annual project implementation has almost doubled with larger, multi-year, multi-stakeholder programmes now representing more than 50% of the portfolio. Ms. Francis has overseen ITC's change management process which has instilled a strategic planning and reporting cycle, mainstreamed MDG programmes for gender, environment and poverty and introduced results-based management principles.

## Tourism and developing countries

Travel and tourism is an important sector for reducing poverty, employing 7% of the world's population. Developing countries have a competitive advantage in tourism over developed countries in two areas: the relatively low price of the services they offer and their unique natural and cultural resources.

For the environment, tourism is a double edged sword: it can promote local environmental protection, but can also damage local environmental assets. The sector is not only a contributor to climate change but also a victim, particularly in island states, which are at the highest risk of flooding from rising ocean levels and associated storm surges.

This letter outlines the scope for developing countries to strengthen their competitiveness in the tourism sector, particularly in the green niche, and the important role international agencies like the International Trade Centre (ITC) can play to support this process.

Tourism is a particularly important growth driver for developing countries. It is also the main source of foreign exchange for a third of developing countries and half of the Least Developed Countries (LDCs). Cambodia, for example, derives 18% of its GDP from travel and tourism, with the sector employing 14% of the country's labour force. Tourism has been identified as a priority sector for development in 90% of LDCs in the Diagnostic Trade Integration Studies (DTIS) conducted by the Enhanced Integrated Fund (EIF). These studies assess the competitiveness of countries' economies and the sectors that are engaged, or have the potential to engage, in international trade. The studies found that tourism already creates jobs and is becoming a significant industry for many LDCs, with a direct link to poverty reduction.

## Developing country advantages

The World Economic Forum's (WEF) Travel and Tourism Competitiveness Report compares destinations according to a comprehensive set of indicators in 14 areas. These range widely from price competitiveness, safety, hygiene, and infrastructure to natural resources. The index allows countries to compare their strengths and weaknesses with others. In all but one area, advanced economies rank significantly higher than developing countries. The only area where developing countries as a group outperform developed ones is 'price competitiveness'. According to WEF, 11 LDCs are in the top half of the ranking for price competitiveness, with Gambia and Nepal in the top ten. These are also countries that prioritize the development of the tourist sector.

Many countries also rank highly in several other areas including their richness of natural resources. A clear testimony to their tourism potential is that the majority of LDCs rank in the top half of the WEF's ranking for natural resources, with Tanzania ranked 2nd out of 139 economies, Zambia 15th and Uganda 29th. This suggests that there is a strong case for allocating resources to build competitiveness in tourism, based on their natural resource assets, for example, in ecotourism.

## Natural resource-based competitiveness

Ecotourism is defined as responsible travel to natural areas that conserves the environment and improves the well being of local people. Costa Rica is often looked upon as an example of how a developing country took the strategic decision to develop its ecotourism offering and so deliver green growth in the tourism sector – and is reaping the benefits with higher earnings for tourism per visitor than countries such as France.

According to the International Ecotourism Society (TIES), ecotourism has grown at three times the rate of mass market tourism since 2004, and this has been good news for local populations. TIES reports that 80% of revenue for package tours goes to airlines and hotels. By comparison, eco-lodges tend to hire and purchase locally, resulting in a high proportion of earning returning to the local economy.

## What governments can do

Ensuring continued green growth of the tourism sector requires the right enabling environment. Stable political conditions and good governance are needed for the private sector to grow in an environmentally sustainable way. ITC proposes a number of specific actions that are necessary for supporting green growth in the tourism sector.

### 1 Understand the costs of destroying natural assets

Nature provides society with a vast diversity of benefits such as food, fibres, clean water, carbon sequestration and more. Unfortunately, economic incentives are often stronger for the destruction of nature than for its preservation. Legislation and enforcement in developing countries often provide weak protection for natural assets, leading ranchers and farmers to cut down forests for financial gain. Tourism can build economic value in nature, removing its 'economic invisibility' as described by *The Economics of Ecosystems and Biodiversity* report by TEEB.

The value of nature is revealed through eco-tourism. For example, whale watching was estimated to generate US$2.1 billion per year in 2008, with over 13 million people undertaking the activity in 119 countries.

## 2 Focus resources on niche markets

Price-based markets are still hugely important for developing countries. However, as the world's middle class grows in affluence, demand will increase for holidays based on natural resources, including eco-tourism.

The potential for further growth is still significant:

- For example, in Costa Rica tourism (mostly ecotourism) generates US$ 1,000 per visitor while in France the average tourist spends only US$ 400.
- In Dominica, overnight tourists using small, nature-based lodges spend 18 times more than cruise passengers visiting the island.

## 3 Take actions to reduce environmental impacts

The International Union for the Conservation of Nature (IUCN) has described tourism as a 'double edged sword'. The tourism sector makes positive contributions to conservation by providing economic incentives to protect the natural environment that attracts tourists. However, tourism development also typically has major negative impacts on the environment. These result from:

- Loss of habitat (e.g. hotel construction)
- Disturbance and damage to wildlife (e.g. scuba diving)
- High levels of energy and water use
- Disposal of waste
- High sectoral emissions of greenhouse gases

Governments can encourage the growth of ecotourism through implementing policies to protect nature and so maintain the assets that attract tourists.

Certification also has a role to play in promoting environmental performance. The ISO 9000 (Quality Management) and ISO 14000 (Environmental Management) series of standards have been used in tourism services to improve the overall quality of service. Private voluntary standards have also emerged: Green Globe draws from the ISO standards and is used to assess the sustainability performance of travel and tourism businesses and their supply chain partners. Other private voluntary schemes include the Blue Flag label, which is awarded on the basis of environmental performance of beaches, marinas and boats. Securing the appropriate certification could also help tourism providers attract a higher number of visitors and move up market.

F

## 4 Draft strategies for climate change adaptation and mitigation

Climate change will undoubtedly change the competitiveness of tourism in developing countries. Some will benefit, many will lose. Small island states are particularly exposed to rising water levels, ocean acidification and extreme weather events. This will have both specific impacts that threaten the viability of ecotourism as it may destroy the natural resources it depends upon, but will also threaten the wider industry.

The Quantification and Magnitude of Losses and Damages Resulting from the Impacts of Climate Change report by UNDP modelled the impact of a one metre sea level rise in the Caribbean by the end of the century. Results predict that nearly 1,300 km² of land area will be lost, over 110,000 people displaced and at least 149 multi-million dollar tourism resorts will be damaged or lost.

By 2050, the mid-range estimate for the annual economic costs (e.g., lost amenity values) of climate change in the region will be almost US\$ 4 billion and the cost of rebuilding is predicted to reach US\$ 26 billion (6% of GDP).

The challenge for Caribbean states is to reduce their vulnerability, through investment, insurance, planning, and policy decisions, and inform UNFCCC negotiations regarding adaptation assistance from international funds. These challenges are not restricted to island states, but are common to many coastal developing countries, particularly LDCs.

The tourism industry also has a role to play in reducing emissions, particularly from air travel. Business-as-usual scenarios see tourism's emissions growing by 152% by 2035. Setting the right economic incentives for reducing aviation emissions is key to making the tourism industry less carbon intensive.

## 5  Support SMEs in greening the tourism sector

SMEs dominate the tourism sector, accounting for 80% of all hotels worldwide. Providers of goods and services to the industry also tend to be small, local businesses. SMEs, however, can also cause significant environmental impact and are often ill-prepared to deal with economic and environmental shocks.

As the UNEP *Green Economy* report highlights, green tourism awareness exists mainly among larger companies, rather than SMEs. Capacity building support is therefore needed to help businesses understand the practical aspects and advantages of sustainability.

Governments can increase the share of spending on protecting natural assets, improving waste management and public transport. Investment in green technologies and tourism reduces the cost of energy and waste, and enhances the value of biodiversity, ecosystems and cultural heritage.

### ITC's role

ITC's World Economic Development Forum (WEDF) held in Turkey in 2011, within the framework of the Fourth United Nations Conference on the Least Development Countries (LDC IV), focused on solutions for developing sustainable tourism with a key message to support private sector led development in a supportive policy environment.

ITC supports the green economy through its Trade, Climate Change and Environment Programme (TCCEP). In Zambia for example, the programme is providing technical and marketing support to a natural products company supplied by 500 women collectors living and working in remote rural areas. These products are sold at a premium price to high-end eco-lodges. This link to the ecotourism trade provides the women with a vital cash income to supplement their earnings from subsistence agriculture.

At the policy level, ITC has provided support to the Government of Rwanda to integrate the green economy into its most recent DTIS update in 2010. This highlighted the importance of protecting the country's gorilla population to ensure the continuation of income generation from ecotourism for communities living around the country's national parks.

As this example demonstrates, the green economy increasingly forms part of the Aid for Trade dialogue and allocation of donor resources.

## Conclusion

F

The green economy is a market opportunity for developing countries, including LDCs. In response, ITC is providing environment-related Aid for Trade programming at both the policy level and directly to producers and exporters. Tourism is a key sector in this respect.

However, one must remain realistic about what the green economy can achieve on its own. Developing countries will not always achieve wealth creation and green objectives simultaneously. For this reason, they will build on their current competitive advantage of price-based tourism, which has some negative environmental impacts. Ecotourism also presents an opportunity for developing economies to build on their competitive advantage and deliver environmental protection and greater social inclusiveness.

In the near to medium term, the sector faces a huge challenge from climate change. Governments and the private sector will need to support the development of adaptation strategies to safeguard the industry particularly in more tourism dependent economies, whilst taking actions to reduce emissions from the sector.

# Edwin D. Fuller

### President of Laguna Strategic Advisors, Former President International Marriott

## Helping to manage change by sitting at the table

Edwin D. 'Ed' Fuller, distinguished corporate leader, best-selling author and noted educator and speaker, is Chairman and Co-Founder of Irvine, California-based Laguna Strategic Advisors, a global consulting firm focused on destination management, management leadership, transformational organizational engagement, risk management and delivering grounded business solutions. His performance-driven corporate career with Marriott International spanned four decades culminating with the company naming him President & Managing Director for International Lodging. His career included extensive multi-faceted global experience in developing long-term strategies that applied corporate philosophies, delivered on brand promise and enabled ethical decision-making and sound direction. His colorful and real-world experiences are recounted in his top 20 best-selling book, *You Can't Lead with Your Feet on the Desk*, published by John Wiley & Co., in 2011. . He has spent a lifetime of service to philanthropy and education, sits on the boards of several charitable bodies and has received numerous awards for this service.

It's an old axiom that when change is inevitable, it's best to be part of the solution so that contemplated changes can be effectively managed. The alternative is to stand aside and let the tidal wave of change swamp your best-laid plans. It's also axiomatic that a collaborative response to an anticipated change is often more effective than attempting to stand against the tide alone.

Today, I believe our industry is at a crossroads – one path can result in our being recognized as a major player in helping to bring about transformational change on a global scale as a wealth generator, jobs creator and cultural integrator; the other will leave us at the mercy of the decisions and policies that others promote. We can continue to do what we admirably do in our respective arenas and reap the benefits of what we sow; or we can take a new path – one open with limitless possibilities that will raise all boats.

It's true that none of us can lose sight of the fact that we're in business to serve our respective stakeholders, including our shareholders. The bottom-line IS the bottom-line. But, we also have the opportunity to significantly help others and enhance the stage on which we operate while continuing to help ourselves.

**F**

Today, we have the power to be an extraordinary force for positive change, as global leaders address the economic and societal challenges of our time – challenges that include extreme poverty and congestion, food and water shortages, and energy depletion. With more than 1 billion tourism arrivals anticipated this year alone and an average of 4% growth each year for the next 10 years, we are in a unique position to impact a lot of people and, thereby, foster understanding of these challenges, broaden cultural appreciation and, more importantly, contribute to the global solution.

Over the past two decades I've had the privilege of working with scores of our industry's most thoughtful and committed leaders who are genuinely concerned about the sustainability of our most treasured antiquities and of our most pristine beaches and majestic mountains, given the positive growth projections of tourism. Most of us take enormous pride in the fact that our industry – through our individual efforts and through collaborative programs like Youth Career Initiative – is providing first-time employment and the promise of economic security for many who have long lived in despair. For nine of its 17 years I served as a Chairman of the Prince of Wales's International Tourism Partnership, an organization in which all of the members recognize that conserving energy resources, recycling, conducting periodic clean-up campaigns and the like make good business sense, and we are reaping the community and consumer good will that comes with these practices.

At Marriott International, we have long recognized our responsibility to mitigate our business impact on the natural environment. Both in our hotels and beyond, we have worked to understand and act on the direct and indirect environmental impacts of our business operations. Our goals are focused in five areas: to further reduce energy and water consumption by 25% per available room; to create green construction standards for hotel developers; green our multi-billion dollar supply chains; to educate our associates and guests to support the environment;

and to invest in innovative conservation initiatives including rainforest protection and water conservation.

Why preserve the rainforest and be concerned with water conservation? What does this have to do with successfully operating hotels? Because climate change – caused by carbon dioxide and other greenhouse gas emissions – threatens species, biodiversity and life on Earth as we know it.

According to Conservation International and other environmental experts, the destruction of tropical forests contributes 20% of the world's greenhouse gas emissions and fuel climate change. To help mitigate this challenge, Marriott has committed $2 million to help protect the 1.4 million acre Juma rainforest reserve in the State of Amazonas, Brazil.

In China, the need for fresh water is expected to exceed its supply by 25% over the next 15 years. As a result, Marriott joined forces with Conservation International on a program to protect the source of fresh water in Asia for more than 2 billion people. Located in Sichuan Province, the program helps improve water quality in the rural communities of Pingwu County, promotes sustainable businesses in the rural communities, reduces erosion and sedimentation and educates the local populace on the importance of water and forest conservation.

Setting both these initiatives apart is the fact that they are the result of public/private partnerships we formed – in Brazil with the Amazonas Sustainable Foundation and in China, with Conservation International (CI). In addition, we worked with CI to become the first global hotel company to calculate its carbon footprint.

None of the challenges facing the world, and our industry, today will be resolved easily or in quick order. And whatever solutions are proposed will result from evolving information and conditions. No one entity or person has all the answers. What is known, however, is that it will take the best and most creative thinking and resolve of all of us.

Our industry is rich with promise and unlimited potential. The world's rising middle class is eager to taste and experience all that we have to offer. Our people take pleasure in providing great service. We've made great strides in conservation, sustainability and providing opportunity, but much more needs to be done. We owe it to future generations of guests and employees and the communities we call home to do our best and to be at the table when society's challenges are addressed.

# Angela Gittens

## Director General of Airports Council International

**G**

## Aviation and green growth – an airport perspective

Angela Gittens, a 25-year airport veteran, began her tenure as Director General of Airports Council International (ACI World) in 2008. She was formerly CEO for two of the largest US airport systems, Miami and Atlanta, and deputy at another, San Francisco International Airport. Ms Gittens previously served as Vice-President, Airport Business Services for HNTB Corporation, where she led the firm's practice in airport business and strategic planning. As Vice President at TBI Airport Management, she oversaw the transition to private ownership of London Luton Airport and managed operations contracts at several airports in the US and Canada. Ms Gittens has served on numerous aviation industry boards and committees including FAA and NASA advisory committees, the Executive Committee of the National Academy of Science's Transportation Research Board and the Board of Directors of JetBlue Airways.

## Aviation sustainability

Environmental stewardship at airports is becoming as important as safety and security. The dialogue on environmental management has shifted from basic consideration of limiting or reducing the environmental impacts to addressing sustainability, allowing for a broader, more balanced consideration of issues.

The Brundtland Commission of the United Nations provided a widely used definition: 'Sustainable development is development that meets the needs of the present without compromising the ability of future generations to meet their own needs.' This clearly refers to environmental stewardship – the preservation of air, water and land quality, the careful use of finite resources and the increasing use of renewable resources. Furthermore, in the case of aviation, meeting the needs of future generations implies the growth of the capacity of airports and the global aviation system to meet the ever increasing demand.

Sustainability involves the consideration of environmental, social and economic demands – these are considered to be the 'three pillars' of sustainability. As virtually all of man's activities (starting with breathing and eating) can adversely impact the earth's environment, sustainability is about minimizing the adverse effects to the environment and society, while maximizing the benefits to society and its economy.

## Permission to grow

If mankind chooses to continue to develop our societies and pursue the alleviation of poverty, hunger and mortality, the best known avenues for this remain modernization, technology, education and prosperity. Increasing economic activity and individual wealth leads to increasing demand for transportation. Goods need to be transported to markets, business development often requires travel, and individuals expect to travel for holidays or social occasions. Economic growth and demand for aviation are closely coupled.

To achieve this growth, the aviation industry needs approval from society. Granting such 'permission to grow' should allow society to reap the economic and social benefits while stakeholders acknowledge the environmental consequences and mitigate these impacts.

## Growth and environmental pressure

Growth is not without consequences. For airport operators, economic development often generates a growing demand for housing and pressure to develop residential areas. Many airports built outside urban areas find that residential encroachment, even in noise affected areas, is a tide difficult to turn back.

Additionally, wealth generation and increasing standards of living mean that people have an increased expectation of the quality of life. For airports this can mean an increasing sensitivity to issues such as noise and complaints coming from people living further from the airport, well outside traditional airport noise contours that indicate areas of high noise.

Growth in airport traffic can lead to increasing impacts of noise and emissions of aircraft and road vehicles, resource use and waste generation. Where a local regulator imposes limits, perhaps on noise levels or

local air pollutant concentrations, continued growth in airport operations can lead to exceeding these regulated environmental limits.

Increased aircraft noise events can also lead to increased levels of
community adverse reaction. Individuals or community groups can
exert pressure for new environmental limits or more stringent existing
ones. This environmental pressure encourages government to expand
regulations such as operational restrictions and partial or total night
time curfews. Such artificial limitations impede the efficient use of cost-
intensive airport infrastructure resources.

Airport operators are increasingly recognizing that often it is not
the physical effect alone (e.g., the noise level) causing community
annoyance, and that perception issues and attitudes toward an airport
or aviation can be at the root of the adverse reaction. Such perceived
impacts are no less valid than physical impacts, however the resulting
environmental pressures can be much more difficult to address.

As airports get busier, throughput may approach the operational
capacity limitations of either the runways, the terminals or other
infrastructure bottlenecks. This can lead to congestion and delays to
operations rendering the system inefficient and unreliable.

## Planning permission

An airport operator needs to plan the development of infrastructure
to meet projected traffic levels. In most jurisdictions, airports need
planning permission from local government for large projects, such as
terminal buildings and runways. Usually, a public consultation process
is required and some form of public approval must be obtained. The
lack of public approval could lead to legal action and projects can be
delayed in review panels or courts for many years.

Winning this 'permission to grow' requires that the airport authority
addresses environmental pressure by establishing a track record on
environmental stewardship and demonstrating plans to continue
compensating for the environmental impacts of growth. By presenting
a case for sustainability and the need to cater for future generations,
the permission process can include consideration of the social and
economic needs and benefits of airport growth.

## Aviation and climate change

The International Civil Aviation Organization (ICAO) has established a framework for addressing aviation's contribution to climate change that includes the following features:

- A basket of measures for States to implement to reduce aviation emissions.
- A global goal of an average annual efficiency improvement of 2% through to 2050, including fleet and operational improvements.
- A global aspirational goal of achieving carbon neutral growth from 2020 onwards.
- A set of principles for the design and implementation of market-based measures for international aviation emissions.
- A target to implement a new $CO_2$ emissions standard for aircraft by 2013.
- A process for ICAO to collect data from states on their Action Plans for achieving these goals.

The agreement of these goals and principles by ICAO Member States represents an important achievement, unparalleled by any other international industry and is a significant step towards incorporating international aviation into any post-Kyoto climate agreement.

The aviation industry stakeholders include industry associations of airports (ACI), airlines, air navigation service providers and the aircraft airframe and engine manufacturers. The joint aviation industry position on addressing aviation $CO_2$ emissions is closely aligned with ICAO's goals. The industry goal for average annual efficiency improvement is 1.5% (less than ICAO's 2%, but not including the portion that falls under the responsibility of governments such as releasing military airspace) and industry has the same goal for carbon neutral growth from 2020.

Industry has a further goal of achieving absolute $CO_2$ emissions reductions of 50% (relative to 2005 levels) by 2050. This will be achieved by a combination of aircraft technology advances, fleet renewal, operational improvements and, crucially, aviation fuels produced from biomass sources.

Biofuels for aviation have moved from concept to reality in five years and are a potential game changer for the sustainability of aviation. In mid-2011, fuel with 50% bio-derived synthetic content blended with conventional fuel was officially certified for aviation. These fuels are 'drop in' substitutes and will not require changes to aircraft or airport fuel delivery infrastructure. By early 2012, there had been over a thousand commercial flights of passenger aircraft with some of the fuel made from biomass sources.

The biomass sources include crops such the jatropha nut, the camelina grain and algae, and others such as municipal and forestry waste material and spent cooking oil. Great care is being taken by the aviation industry to identify and develop biomass sources that will not adversely affect food, water and land supply. Many challenges lie ahead, especially the massive scaling of biomass production and refining capabilities.

## Airports and climate change

As airports are the interface between aviation (aircraft) and ground transportation, the management and responsibility for emissions are less clear-cut for airport operators. Activities and emissions sources need to be categorised according to ownership and influence. ACI provides recommendations to its airport members in the publication *Guidance Manual on Airport Greenhouse Gas Emissions Management*, which categorises emissions into 3 scopes:

- Scope 1 emissions are from sources that are owned or controlled by the airport operator, such as an airport power or heating plant, airport fleet vehicles, construction, and fire fighting.
- Scope 2 emissions are those from the off-site generation of electricity purchased by the airport operator.
- Scope 3 emissions are those from airport-related activities from sources not owned or controlled by the airport operator, including aircraft, most ground support equipment and most ground access vehicles, such as private cars and public transport.

Some examples of measures for an airport operator's Scope 1 and 2 emissions reductions include the modernisation of the power, heating and cooling plants; the generation or purchase of electricity and heating from renewable sources; and the modernisation of fleet vehicles especially using alternative fuels, such as compressed natural gas (CNG), hydrogen, electricity, compressed air and hybrid vehicles.

In addition, airports can reduce aircraft emissions (Scope 3) by actions such as improving taxiway layouts and reducing aircraft queuing with options such as slot management, virtual queuing and delayed push-back. Ground-based electrical power and pre-conditioned air also reduce aircraft emissions.

Non-aircraft Scope 3 emissions are dominated by transport activities on the ground, essentially public and private vehicles travelling to and from the airport and airport ground handling vehicles themselves.

Working with different stakeholders, airports can help reduce these emissions by efforts that range from the provision of new public transport links such as new train services through to encouraging the use of alternative fuel or hybrid taxis, rental and other cars using incentives such as priority queuing, parking cost reduction and priority parking areas.

## Carbon neutrality and accreditation

ACI encourages its members to set goals on both GHG emissions sources within their control and those in the control of stakeholders, which they can influence. For an airport's Scope 1 and 2 emissions, the ultimate target is for the airport to become carbon neutral.

Carbon neutral status can be achieved by reducing emissions as much as practicable, then purchasing carbon offset credits for the remaining emissions. Offset credits must comply with international standards and be fully verified.

Airports can attain recognition for their achievements in carbon management with *Airport Carbon Accreditation*, which recognise four levels of progress – Inventory, Emissions Reduction, Stakeholder Optimisation and Carbon Neutrality.

The project started in Europe in 2009 and, during the first and second year of operations, contributed to reducing $CO_2$ emissions from airports by 411,000 tonnes, and 730,000 tonnes, respectively. Participating airports represent more than 50% of European passenger movements and Abu Dhabi is the first in the Asia-Pacific region which was included in late 2011.

## Major airport environmental issues

### Airport noise

Despite massive reductions in individual aircraft noise emissions in recent decades, aircraft noise remains the most pressing issue for local communities and the issue most likely to trigger environmental pressure or mobilise local residents against airport infrastructure or capacity expansion. There are two distinct, but linked, battlegrounds. The aviation industry is seeking approval of its $CO_2$ roadmap from global society and the UNFCCC. Airports require permission to grow from regional governments and local communities whose main concern is noise. The $CO_2$ roadmap, however, is dependent on mitigating airport and airspace congestion.

Airport operators have three fundamental avenues for managing aircraft noise, although none is fully within their control.

1 Reducing the level of aircraft noise emissions requires the use of the latest aircraft with the best noise technology and flight procedures to reduce incident noise levels. Airports can introduce measures such as noise related landing fees to incentivise airlines to switch to quieter aircraft.

2 To reduce the number of people exposed to high noise levels, airports must work with local governments to discourage residential encroachment and can partially improve sound exposure with sound insulation programmes.

3 Airports can work to improve community acceptance of the airport and its activities. They need to proactively foster community relations based on open and clear communications and social programme initiatives. Specific actions can include monitoring noise levels in the community and publishing the results in accessible, non-technical formats; fielding and responding to individual noise complaints; and establishing and maintaining community liaison groups for consulting and dealing with issues that arise.

### Local air quality (LAQ)

An airport with a history of non-compliance with LAQ regulations can be subject to pressure from regulators and communities when planning permission for infrastructure expansion is required.

Starting with the relevant national and regional LAQ regulations, an airport operator should assess compliance for each pollutant species and determine which emissions sources are contributing to any non-compliance. This assessment can include monitoring LAQ pollutant concentrations and conducting emissions inventories and dispersion modelling. This should indicate the relative importance of various emissions sources and activities at airports such as aircraft, ground support equipment, fleet vehicles, power and heating plants and local road traffic.

Addressing LAQ problems is fundamentally achieved by reducing emissions and virtually all of the GHG mitigation measures described above will also mitigate LAQ emissions.

Given the strict Swiss LAQ regulations, Zurich Airport has one of the most comprehensive airport LAQ management programmes including monitoring, modelling, inventory, aircraft APU restrictions and landing fees with a NOx emissions component.

### Water use

Potable water use can be reduced by modern plumbing practices including low flow taps and showers, detector controlled toilet flushing, maintenance and leak detection. Much potable water use can be replaced with water from other sources including rain water from roofs and tarmac, treated waste water and recycled cooling water.

Landscape planting should use native or arid zone plants needing little water. Brisbane Airport achieved a potable water use reduction of 72% in a four-year period, a reduction equivalent to 24,000 households.

Storm water can be collected from roofs, tarmac and landscaped areas. Depending on the collection, storage and possible contamination, the water may require treatment ranging from settling ponds to a proper water treatment plant. Use will depend on water quality and could range from landscaping to vehicle and building washing, and toilet flushing. A crucial task of storm water management includes keeping water with tarmac residues from contaminating surface water courses.

### Soil and land management

Soil and surface and ground water can be contaminated by storm water run-off, fuel spills, de-icing fluids and other spill incidents. Spill prevention and reaction to incidents are operational and environmental responsibilities. Poorly planned land management can provide habitat that creates a bird and wildlife hazard.

### Solid waste

There are many streams of solid waste at an airport including, municipal waste from concessions and passenger areas; waste from airfield operations and maintenance such as derelict equipment, pallets and hazardous material like paint thinners; de-planed waste that might require incineration, and debris from construction and demolition. Some streams are regulated, some materials can be recycled, and some can generate income.

### Community relations

The perception of the environmental impact by neighbouring residents can be as important as the physical effects. Fostering positive community relations can make a vital contribution to the mitigation of adverse environmental pressure resulting from airport operations.

The goals of an airport's community engagement programme should include establishing and maintain the trust of the community, because if the public does not believe the information provided, there is no foundation to achieve community engagement. This trust is built upon a long-term culture of honesty and transparency.

If communities can grant the airport permission to operate and grow, and airports can undertake sufficient voluntary measures, then overly restrictive regulation and court actions can be avoided.

## Conclusion

The aviation industry recognises the significant effects brought to the environment and community. However, as a vital component in society and the economy, the aviation industry sets out to address the concerns and mitigates environmental issues while maintaining continual growth. In order to expand and operate sustainably for generations ahead, the airport operator must constantly communicate and engage its local community while addressing pressing environmental issues. Together with permission of both the government and community, airports will be able to play an active role in dealing with sustainability and emissions-related concerns.

# Harold Goodwin

**Professor of Responsible Tourism
Management at Leeds Metropolitan
University**

## Mainstream tourism and
sustainability

Dr Harold Goodwin, Professor of Responsible Tourism Management at Leeds
Metropolitan University, (www.haroldgoodwin.info) has published extensively on Responsible Tourism, and tourism and poverty reduction. He is an
advisor to the World Travel Market on World Responsible Tourism Day; chair
of the Advisory Panel of the International Tourism Partnership (part of the
International Business Leaders Forum) and Chair of the Judges for the annual
Virgin Holidays Responsible Tourism Awards. He is an Expert Advisor to ABTA,
the UK's Travel Association, on Sustainable Tourism and to UNEP's Global Partnership for Sustainable Tourism; a member of the IUCN's World Commission
on Protected Areas and an advisor to *RT Reporting*. Harold provides advisory
support to VisitEngland on Wise Growth on a voluntary basis. He is also a
director of the International Centre for Responsible Tourism which he founded
in 2002 and which promotes the principles of the Cape Town Declaration.

Rising prosperity in the developing economies of Brazil, China,
India, and Russia, combined with continuing growth in established and emerging markets, means that we can expect to see
continuing growth in domestic and international tourism. It is clear
from the patterns of growth over the last 40 years that once people have
the leisure, and resources, to travel, their propensity for conspicuous
consumption as tourists is high. Whilst it seems likely that the cost of
flying will increase as fuel costs rise and that this will dampen demand,
mass tourism will continue to grow.

To the question 'can mainstream tourism be more sustainable?'
the brief answer is 'yes', but it depends on the choices we make and
how we manage the continued growth in domestic and international
tourism. The industry and local governments need to exercise more
responsibility for minimising the negative impacts and maximising the

positive economic and social impacts of tourism. We know a great deal about how to make all forms of tourism more sustainable, but we are not making anywhere near enough progress in establishing sustainable ways of living for the world's growing population, whether on holiday or at work. We need to do much more if the challenge is to be met; over the 20 years since Rio not enough has been done. There has been too much talk of sustainability and too little taking of responsibility.

**G**

Travel and tourism are conspicuous forms of consumption. As tourists we take our holidays in other peoples' homes, we are at leisure when they are at work and we generally consume more when we are on holiday than when we are at home. Tourism attracts attention in part because it is associated with conspicuous consumption, and rightly so. Tourism remains a privilege of the relatively wealthy, made more apparent by the juxtaposition of the tourist consuming leisure and the waiter or cleaner at work. Levels of daily water consumption by tourists, which may be higher than at home, are often well above those of the waiter or cleaner, and in water stressed areas may result in tourists and tourism businesses consuming water luxuriously whilst others struggle to secure enough for their minimal daily needs. Tourists in hotels may well have electricity at the expense of the local population who suffer cuts in supply – tourists and tourism businesses get priority of supply because of their relative wealth. Tourism reveals inequality and should challenge us to think about our sustainability. It is fundamentally true that on known technology our earth cannot sustain all of us at the levels of consumption enjoyed by those with the wealth to travel – whether they are consuming as tourists or at home.

Twenty years on since Rio the travel and tourism industry has been slow to face up to the challenge. There have been too many cul-de-sacs. The early focus on ecotourism, a tiny niche, was convenient for the mainstream industry; sustainability was addressed in the niche rather than in the mainstream. Little attention was paid to the fact that the ecotourists used the same transport infrastructure as everyone else and worse, ecotourism created the persistent myth that the consumer would pay a premium for sustainable tourism. They won't.

There has been considerable emphasis placed on the green agenda, forgetting that the twin objectives of Rio were environment and development. Community-based tourism was a favourite with donors and NGOs, appearing to offer a way of using tourism for community economic development. Whilst there have been a few successes, this niche has been characterised by economic failure; communities have not secured the economic benefits promised by those who promoted the idea.

Efforts to achieve sustainable tourism have been bedevilled by endless list making. The Global Sustainable Tourism Criteria provide a long list of 'issues'; consensus has been built by including everyone's priorities; time has been wasted on definition, when focused action on local priorities would have begun the process of making tourism more sustainable in destinations where local economic, social and environmental issues need to be addressed and managed. The sustainability of destinations cannot be reduced to the certifying of businesses.

The elephant in the room is of course the carbon pollution caused by travel to the destination – particularly by flying. The airline industry has successfully argued that its emissions are international and cannot be subject to national accounting or regulation. There is much talk of new fuels and of carbon offsetting, the purchasing of a mediaeval pardon, one which removes any incentive for the airline to improve its carbon efficiency. Both approaches are designed to allow the airlines to continue business as usual and to put off making the radical changes which with known technology can radically reduce, at a price, the carbon pollution caused by flying. Change will come with rising fuel prices but has been too slow; governments have failed to regulate and force improvements in the carbon efficiency of flying.

Ten years on from Rio in 2002 in Cape Town, at a side event of the World Summit on Sustainable Development in Johannesburg, the Cape Town Declaration on Responsible Tourism in Destinations was agreed. Drawing on the ideas of Jost Krippendorf, the 1996 South African White Paper on *Development and Promotion of Tourism in South Africa* and the *National Guidelines* published in 2001, and on work with tour operators in the UK, the Cape Town Declaration asserted that all forms of tourism could be more responsible and that it was important to address mainstream tourism. Tourism is what we make it; we have to take responsibility to make it more sustainable. Accommodation providers, outbound and inbound tour operators, national and local governments, attractions, local communities, holidaymakers and travellers all need to take responsibility and do everything they can to make travel and tourism more sustainable. Responsible Tourism is about making 'better places for people to live in and better places for people to visit.' In that order, it is about using tourism rather than being used by it. It is about identifying the locally significant issues and acting to deal with them.

**G**

For example the city council in Cape Town has identified seven local priorities: reductions in water and energy consumption and waste; increased local procurement and enterprise development; social development and skills development. The city council and tourism businesses in Cape Town are taking responsibility, managing tourism to achieve these sustainability objectives and progress is being measured against clear agreed criteria. In this way progress towards sustainability can be driven across the whole tourism sector in Cape Town and delivery measured and reported.

In the UK, ABTA, the Travel Association, has committed its members to take responsibility for sustainability in a finite word, and to create rewarding jobs and thriving destinations. Companies like Thomas Cook and TUI are now addressing the sustainability of their businesses and their impacts in the destination and in providing transport to them. They have established priorities and they are reporting progress against their targets to their clients and to investors in sustainability reports which can be accessed on-line.

More carbon efficient transport and accommodation, reductions in water use, hardened sites and stronger visitor management all contribute to making the activity of tourism more sustainable where people take responsibility and act. Policy makers, consultants, journalists, travel writers and academics need to focus rather more sharply on the positive and negative impacts of tourism and how they are managed rather than rehearsing their aesthetic prejudices. Not all forms of ecotourism are sustainable; not all all-inclusives are unsustainable. We need to manage all forms of tourism so that they are more sustainable. All forms of tourism should be scrutinised against local priorities for sustainability – environmental, economic and social – if tourism is to be used to make better places for people to live in and better places for people to visit.

# Gloria Guevara

## Secretary of Tourism, Mexico

## Tourism, green growth and sustainable development

Gloria Guevara Manzo is Tourism Secretary of Mexico, and a Member of President Calderon's cabinet. She is the CEO of the Mexico Tourism Board. Under her leadership the National Agreement for Tourism was signed in February 28, 2011 and Mexico achieved a new record in domestic and international tourists. She chaired the T20 Ministerial which delivered a ground-breaking communique to the G20 on the socio-economic and job creation importance of Travel & Tourism  For three consecutive years, Gloria was named one of the 50 most influential women in Mexico by *CNN Expansión* She holds a BS in Computer Science from Anahuac University and an MBA from Kellogg School of Business, Northwestern University, as well as marketing and project management qualifications Gloria began her professional career at NCR Corporation in 1989, and during the last fifteen years, she worked for Sabre Travel Network and Sabre Holdings, in the United States; Latin America and Caribbean, ultimately as global Vice President in the Information Office.

## Role of governments in the development of new responses

Today the world faces many challenges. More and more countries are experiencing limitations to keep growing and to provide better living conditions for their inhabitants. The effects of environmental degradation worldwide as well as climate change represent a real threat to humankind.

In order to solve both crises, economic and environmental, simultaneous solutions have to be provided. The crucial point is to break the dilemma of economic growth versus the environment. Above all, because of the life threatening consequences of climate change, we have to move towards a low carbon economy and integrate that into the broader evolution towards green growth.

The Mexican Government has promoted, in different international forums and through different diplomatic levels, the need to establish a clear path to sustainable development.

Mexico strongly believes it is necessary to define and establish a set of public policies regarding the green roadmap, starting with measures that involve individuals, companies, communities, as well as local and federal authorities.

The role of the government is to coordinate the efforts of the different stakeholders towards a common goal with clear actions and concrete solutions. This has to be done with a local and a global perspective and by creating conditions that incentivize good corporate or individual responses, while discouraging bad.

To this end, Mexico promoted a series of important agreements within the framework of the Conference of the Parties 16 in 2010. Two of the main results were the acceptance of the creation of the Green Fund and, for the first time, a 2 degree Celsius limit to the rise in world temperatures. We also established the Cancun adaptation framework and the technology transfer mechanism, and also formally recognized the importance of the REED+ mechanism.

Despite these important efforts, we have to progressively increase our efforts and identify new, innovative answers to achieve a more sustained and sustainable growth. One of these responses, with great promise and with great significance for Mexico and globally, is in the tourism industry.

## Tourism as an alternative to achieve sustainable development

The tourism industry is a key sector for ensuring long-term economic, social and environmental development. Building on the premise that economic growth does not come at the expense of environmental decline, tourism is a sector able to generate jobs and growth, and which, if carefully managed, can have a positive impact on sustainable development.

Mexico is a great example of how nature can coexist with tourism. This economic activity represents 9% of Mexico's GDP and over five million direct and indirect jobs, but also it has a great potential to empower local economies, protect wildlife, guard culture, and celebrate heritage, with a soft environmental footprint. This has been possible thanks to the joint participation of both the public and the private sectors – which will be increasingly necessary as global economic conditions put strains on all stakeholders.

There are many examples of these efforts to mitigate greenhouse gas emissions, promote adaption in tourism businesses and destinations and invest in new technologies.

The Government of Mexico is undertaking efforts towards developing Nationally Appropriate Mitigation Actions (NAMAs) in several sectors, including small hotels. With the support of the German Agency for International Cooperation, we are collaborating with some small hotels in the design of a NAMA for energy efficiency in boilers and refrigerators.

Mexico is one of the first developing countries with a cross-cutting climate change program: the Special Climate Change Programme (PECC, for its acronym in Spanish) with different actions regarding renewable energies; energy efficiency; housing efficiency; sustainable management of forest areas and solid urban waste. For tourism the following goals were established: six goals for mitigation, five for adaptation and 19 cross-policy. These goals represent a clear guide for the entire industry.

The Ministry of Tourism has implemented the Sustainable Tourism Programme, in order to generate sustainable development in touristic destinations. This Programme represents the leading policy about sustainable development of tourism industry and involves three main strategies:

a) diagnostic of tourist destination's status;

b) transversal action plan; and

c) best practices promotion.

We also established a Sectoral Fund for Research, Development and Innovation in Tourism studies, for mitigation and adaptation before climate change and signed an agreement with the Federal Environmental Protection Agency, which led to the recognition and certification programs for better environmental practices of tourism service providers, called 'Calidad Ambiental Turística' (Tourism environmental quality) and 'Destino Turístico Limpio' (Clean tourism destination).

The Mexican Tourism Ministry is working on sustainability certification of services. In this regard, the EarthCheck Programme was selected, as result of an analysis of the different international certification programmes, because it is aligned with the The Global Sustainable Tourism Criteria, and goes beyond the current version if ISO 14001, by specifying expected areas of performance improvement. It also takes in consideration the Greenhouse Gas Emissions Protocol developed by the Intergovernmental Panel on Climate Change. Thank to the active participation of the private sector, the Mexican tourism destination Huatulco received the Gold Certificate EarthCheck as a sustainable community, becoming the first worldwide tourist destination to obtain this certification level. We will intensify these kind of initiatives in the years ahead.

In developing countries we are looking at the vulnerability of certain tourism destinations to the devastating impacts of climate change, ranging from rising sea levels and the destruction of coral reefs, to the loss of basic tourism services such as water supply and food security.

We need to take a global approach towards tourism and climate change; and not overlook the ability of tourism to fight poverty and to promote the development of host communities. We must also recognize the imperative of protecting biological diversity, for its own sake, but also to maintain its socio-economic contribution to tourism.

We will face the future with optimism – innovation in the use of technologies, alternative energy sources, changing consumption patterns and generating new technical and administrative capacities in all levels of government, social and private, will create new opportunities to meet the challenges of global climate change, economic volatility and poverty alleviation.

We have to be clear that for any country, the measures implemented in order to promote green growth, are cheaper than the consequences of climate change.

And we have to recognize that Tourism can make a massive contribution to green growth and sustainable development. This is the case for Mexico and I am firmly convinced that it is also a big part of our shared global solution.

# Peter Harbison

## Chairman, CAPA-Centre for Aviation

## Sustainable aviation and green growth - blood, sweat and tears

Peter Harbison is Executive Chairman of Sydney based CAPA-Centre for Aviation (formerly the Centre for Asia Pacific Aviation), today the world's largest publisher of B2B commercial aviation information and analysis. An aviation lawyer, consultant and commentator on industry issues, Peter established CAPA in 1990. CAPA additionally presents major conferences on key aviation topics and provides education and training courses for the aviation and tourism industries. Peter is also Chairman of CAPA AeroPark, an affiliate of CAPA, and of CAPA India, the company's consulting arm for the sub-continent. Over the past 25 years, he has conducted more than 200 consultancy projects in aviation and authored and/or edited numerous reports. His career in aviation spans more than 40 years, including two years with the Australian mission to the International Civil Aviation Organisation in Montreal and 10 years in the International Air Transport Association, IATA, in Geneva.

Happily for aviation there is a near-perfect synchrony between commercial necessities and reducing fuel-related emissions. Reducing emissions is, to a large extent, synonymous with lowering costs. Thus, consuming less fuel per passenger has been an industry priority for many years, a feature that became more pressing as low cost airlines forced the recognition that the search for lower costs must be a continuing one.

This is a healthy starting point from which to build. But inevitably once the focus moves to specific cases, the general proposition becomes more complex.

There's probably no better example of the need for reconciliation of positions – meaning actions, not words – than the role that the aviation and tourism industries must play in providing for a green future.

And nowhere is this more applicable than for some of the supposed outriders of the climate change movement, many of whom are in the rapid growth countries of Asia.

Reconciliation is necessary because tourism is much more than merely wealthy nations' playthings; it has become the staple for many emerging countries, and central to much of that activity is the airline industry. As the world's axis of economic power shifts towards Asia, that vast and poorly understood financial equation becomes even more uncertain. To restrain aviation growth is to curtail economic development for many countries; yet clearly there cannot be a straight line expansion in the industry's climatic impact. Hence the massive dilemma now confronting the aviation industry and its regulators.

Only five decades ago, years before the first commercial jet airliner flew, the fastest way for humans to travel above the ground involved large amounts of hot air. On that evolutionary basis I think it is pretty fair to assume that the next 50 years will bring developments in travel and propulsion we equally cannot even imagine today.

It's impossible therefore to envision that annual projected global passenger traffic growth of around 4% will actually mean that annual aircraft movements in five decades' time will consume 700% more fossil fuel and emit the equivalent in additional annual emissions. Assuming a straight line growth in all of these components implies mindless expansion. That is patently not something the airline industry can ever be accused of. Yet that is what some suggest will be the case.

But on current trends, there will inescapably be vastly larger amounts of hot air, political and actual. Only a tiny proportion of it will be down to the always-innovative airline industry. Yet clearly we are neither in a position to say with confidence that sufficient alternative fuels can be developed, nor that propulsion efficiencies can be improved on a scale which caps and even reduces the current levels of emission – per passenger and overall.

Even though the first 50 years' technological development hasn't been as obviously matched by the past half century, there have still been enormous strides in the efficiency rate, most notably in fuel usage per passenger. Even aside from much greater engine and aerodynamic efficiencies, the combination of larger aircraft, more direct services, much higher seating density and load factors and en route flying improvements, along with a heightened consciousness about fuel usage, have all combined to ensure that straight line was severely skewed.

The great dilemma of the moment – and one which is guaranteed to escalate through 2012 – relates to the dynamics of accelerating the reduction in airline emissions. For reasons mostly to do with the extreme visibility and high profile of the aviation industry (whose emissions are greatly less than, say, the shipping industry), political pressures are much more intense.

Following the failure of Copenhagen, few governments have moved to take serious action to combat climate change, but the European Union has very conspicuously, and equally controversially, imposed measures nominally designed to force airlines to reduce carbon emissions. That is, all airlines flying to Europe, not merely locally based companies. Whether or not the European Commission's Emissions Trading System (ETS) is merely a tax and whether the money raised could be more effectively used in seeking solutions to the global problem is one thing.

But more pertinently the question is whether it is better to have a 'unilaterally' EU-imposed ETS, or to await a global approach. The former risks dividing those who actively support some form of action to reduce emissions. And indeed, when we talk of outliers, a fast growing country like China has in practice already undertaken proportionately much greater emission reduction measures at home than many of those who would lecture it.

The result is thus to force other national governments into a choice between accepting what is *de facto* (even if not *de iure*) exercise of extra-territorial jurisdiction on the one hand – and adopting serious measures to combat climate change on the other. This dilemma is both unproductive and divisive. It will inevitably lead to some airlines being forced to pay the ETS 'taxes' and others, whose governments have the political clout to say no, being immunised.

In many ways this aviation case study is a microcosm of the worldwide issues. Full consensus on airline issues in the UN's aviation body ICAO, is about as likely as achieving consensus at the wider UN level. In those circumstances, is it wiser to leave resolution to a regional body like the EU, promoting reciprocity (based on mutual exemptions) and thereby developing a quasi-multilateral system, or to continue to strive for a wider multilateral approach?

The answer may soon become obvious, as the EU's payment demands on foreign airlines will be generally unenforceable in practical terms. The EU Commission itself cannot demand payment from a foreign registered airline; that can only be done at national level and the system proposed is for the government of the country to which a particular airline operates most services to be responsible for collecting the tax – on threat of suspension of service in the case of non-payment. Thus for example, when push comes to shove, it is hardly likely that the German government will rush to suspend service into German airspace by Air China. Quite apart from the high level political fallout from such an action, Germany's airlines would immediately see their reciprocal rights to fly to China withdrawn. And Lufthansa's two decades of investment in China would be at risk.

Even if the EU did try to stand behind an individual government, it is barely conceivable that national governments would accept an even broader EU-wide cancellation of service – with reciprocal suspensions for *all* EU airlines.

As this complex scenario unfolds, other sectors and government bodies will be watching closely. The EU has set itself up – largely unwittingly – as a test bed not only for aviation but also for the wider climate change response regime.

There is a footnote: the more subtle undertone to this fractious debate highlights the dangers when political forces are allowed to overwhelm more targeted and effective measures. Some scientific experts maintain that the broad-brush obsession with carbon emissions is disguising other, more serious aviation issues – indeed that some of the more harmful flight by-products, such as nitrous oxide, may actually be increased as the airlines rush to conform with regulated carbon standards.

Rapid action is undoubtedly necessary to combat climate change, but even more importantly, that action should be effective, not merely cosmetic.

# Donald E. Hawkins

### Eisenhower Professor of Tourism Policy, The George Washington University

## Green growth development strategies for the travel and tourism sector

Dr. Donald E. Hawkins is Eisenhower Professor of Tourism Policy, School of Business, The George Washington University, Washington, DC. In 2003, Dr. Hawkins received the first United Nations World Tourism Organization Ulysses Prize for individual accomplishments in the creation and dissemination of knowledge in the area of tourism policy and strategic management. He serves as Board Chairman for Solimar International, Sustainable Travel International and the SAVE Travel Alliance, is Chairman of the Tourism Cares Global Outreach Initiative,  and is on the Board of Directors for VEGA and Tourism Cares. He has contributed 122 publications over the past 42 years. He has recently been engaged in tourism consulting in the Republic of Georgia, Dominican Republic, Jordan, Sri Lanka, Bulgaria, Portugal, Spain, Tanzania, Ethiopia, Mozambique, Canada and the United States.

As one of the largest global industries and employers, tourism has a significant role to play in both developed and developing economies. Acknowledging this reality, economic development agencies and development assistance programmes are increasingly using tourism as a means of fostering sustainable development, since it can contribute directly to the three pillars of sustainability: economic growth, environmental conservation, and social equity. This letter will focus mainly on challenges in developing countries that need to be addressed thorough international cooperation facilitated by developed economies and multinational companies.

Development assistance for tourism has a relatively short history of about 40 years. In most developing countries, tourism continues to be an ongoing social, economic, and environmental challenge. With nearly 50 bilateral and multilateral donor agencies involved in development assistance for tourism, international cooperation faces many challenges. In 2004, The George Washington University and the UN World Tourism Organization (UNWTO) sponsored the Tourism Policy Forum, in Washington, D.C., which convened development assistance donors and recipients for the purpose of improving tourism's contribution to sustainable development. The Forum produced the *Washington Declaration on Tourism as a Sustainable Development Strategy*. The Declaration called upon the development assistance community to build partnerships to foster buy-in for the concept of sustainability in all sectors of the tourism industry and to promote the preservation and conservation of cultural and natural resources.

## Development Assistance Network for Tourism Enhancement and Investment (DANTEI)

One of the specific outcomes of the Forum process was the establishment of the DANTEI (http://www.dantei.org/). DANTEI is a web-based platform developed to share information and knowledge about best practices, tools and guidelines for tourism directed toward sustainable development outcomes. The site was created to help potential development assistance recipients (particularly government and civil society) access funding resources. It is envisioned that DANTEI could serve as a portal in which development agencies could share information and access resources and tools

## Global Sustainable Tourism Alliance (GSTA)

In response to the challenges set forth at the Forum, the GSTA was formed in 2006. The GSTA was comprised of 15 non-profit and for-profit organizations in the sustainable tourism field working together with USAID Missions to apply a holistic and market-driven approach to sustainable tourism development. This alliance enabled its members (including leading tourism development institutions, conservation organizations, the private sector, and USAID) to combine resources, expertise and outreach in exciting and innovative ways in the following countries: Ecuador, Dominican Republic, Montenegro, Mali, Ethiopia and Uganda

In each GSTA country leading tourism development institutions, conservation organizations, tourism practitioners, private sector tourism industry leaders, and USAID jointly designed, co-financed, and implemented tourism activities that adhered to the GSTA's core principles:

- Make optimal use of environmental resources, conserve biodiversity, and protect natural heritage;
- Respect the socio-cultural authenticity of host communities – including their traditional values and heritage;
- Provide fairly distributed socio-economic benefits to all stakeholders; and
- Encourage investment in sustainable tourism products, services and related infrastructure.

## USAID online courses on Sustainable Tourism

USAID and the GSTA partners produced an online tool kit and resource series last year which can be accessed free by going to: http://lms.rmportal.net/course/category.php?id=51. The tool kit includes:

- Global Tourism: Achieving Sustainable Goals
- Project Development for Sustainable Tourism: A Step by Step Approach
- Tourism Destination Management: Achieving Sustainable and Competitive Results
- Tourism Investment and Finance: Accessing Sustainable Funding and Social Impact Capital
- Sustainable Tourism Enterprise Development: A Business Planning Approach
- Tourism Workforce Development: A Guide to Assessing and Designing Programs
- Tourism and Conservation: Sustainable Models and Strategies
- Scientific, Academic, Volunteer, and Educational Travel: Connecting Responsible Travelers with Sustainable Destinations
- Powering Tourism: Electrification and Efficiency Options for Rural Tourism Facilities

The resources listed above can be used to facilitate the transformation of the travel and tourism sector by using a green growth approach to lower carbon emissions, promote biodiversity conservation and to stimulate local economies through enterprise development and job creation.

## Illustrative green growth initiatives

There are encouraging signs that the travel and tourism sector can contribute positively to green growth initiatives that can benefit both developed and developing countries:

## Global Sustainable Tourism Council: Travel Forever

The Global Sustainable Tourism Council is a global, multi-stakeholder membership organization dedicated to increasing the reach, awareness and recognition of sustainable tourism practices through large and small enterprise operations and to endorsing the principles of the GSTC Criteria. For detailed information, go to http://new.gstcouncil.org/.

In 2008, the Partnership for Global Sustainable Tourism Criteria (GSTC Partnership), a coalition of more than 50 organizations working together to foster increased understanding of sustainable tourism practices and the adoption of universal sustainable tourism principles, developed a set of baseline criteria organized around the four pillars of sustainable tourism: effective sustainability planning; maximizing social and economic benefits to the local community; reduction of negative impacts to cultural heritage; and reduction of negative impacts on the environment.

The Rainforest Alliance, United Nations Environment Programme (UNEP), United Nations Foundation and the United Nations World Tourism Organization (UNWTO) initiated the Partnership in an effort to come to a common understanding of sustainable tourism. The Global Sustainable Tourism Criteria are the minimum requirements that any tourism business should aspire to reach in order to protect and sustain the world's natural and cultural resources while ensuring tourism meets its potential as a tool for poverty alleviation.

To develop these criteria, the GSTC Partnership consulted with sustainability experts and the tourism industry and reviewed more than 60 existing certification and voluntary sets already being implemented around the globe. In all, more than 4,500 criteria were analyzed and the resulting draft criteria received comments from over 2000 stakeholders. Since the launch in October 2008, the GSTC has focused on engaging all tourism stakeholders, from purchasers to suppliers to consumers, to adopt the criteria. Currently, efforts are underway to develop and validate criteria for tourism destinations.

## Green Globe

Green Globe was established by the World Travel and Tourism Council almost 20 years ago as the first sustainable tourism certification scheme. Its objectives were to be a global scheme suitable for all types of tourism businesses and destinations to certify their sustainability practices against specific accreditation standards established for each sector.

Green Globe evolved to include mandatory earthcheck benchmarking of performance in areas such as GHG emissions, energy use, water use, waste production and local employment. Annual benchmarking updates encourage continuous improvement. The system also incorporates independent third party auditing against the sector standard.

Over the years Green Globe has morphed into several ownership models from industry organizations, not for profits and private companies.

## Sustainable Travel International

STI was founded ten years ago on the idea of providing market-driven solutions to support sustainable tourism development. Throughout its early years, STI focused on establishing sustainable tourism criteria and indicators, educating the travel trade about sustainable tourism, providing membership services, and delivering climate solutions to travelers and businesses of all sizes. STI's carbon management model was a pioneering approach that drew the attention of larger corporate clientele and major international NGOs.

Since 2009, carbon management has evolved beyond a B2B carbon model to include carbon tourism solutions for island economies. Simultaneously, the demand for STI to work on destination advisory projects and B2B projects has grown in scale and diversity. Recent highlights include an EU-wide sustainable tourism indicator project, and projects under development such as (a) a carbon neutral tourism strategy for Northern Tobago, (b) a 'Trash to Treasures' recycling project in Haiti, and (c) a certification program for sustainable tourism professionals.

STI also established the Sustainable Travel Leadership Network (STLN) in 2010, an executive-level forum for industry leaders who are committed to achieving the highest levels of sustainability in travel and tourism. STLN members are focused on identifying and assessing key issues in global sustainability, while creating an unparalleled forum for knowledge-sharing and innovative solutions.

## Challenges for the future

Green jobs need to be created by the travel and tourism industry including sustainability operations, energy efficiency and renewable technologies, environmental management, natural resource conserva- tion, smart growth/building strategies and on-line technologies. Career development programmes need to be established by education and training providers in close collaboration with employers to meet green growth workforce needs and opportunities.

An international green growth strategy is needed to connect the know- how and market access of multinational companies with businesses and entrepreneurs in less developed areas of the world. Successful bottom of the pyramid and inclusive business cases and practices need to be adapted and implemented in the travel and tourism sector. Economic development agencies and development assistance donors need to focus on market driven solutions that use green growth approaches that meet consumer demand and contribute to the bottom line.

# James Hogan

**President and CEO, Etihad Airways**

## Green growth and travelism

James Hogan has served as President and Chief Executive Officer of Etihad Airways since September 2006, and brings more than 30 years of aviation and travel industry expertise to the Abu Dhabi-based airline. He has overseen rapid growth of the UAE's national airline since his appointment, and under his leadership, Etihad has become the fastest growing airline in aviation history. The airline currently operates to 84 passenger and cargo destinations with a fleet of 67 modern, environmentally friendly aircraft. James has previously held senior positions with Hertz and Forte Hotels in Asia and Europe. James is a fellow of the Royal Aeronautical Society and a former non-executive director, and member of the Board's Audit Committee, of Gallaher Plc. He serves on the Executive Committee of the World Travel and Tourism Council and the International Air Transport Association (IATA) Board of Governors, and is vice chairman of Air Berlin plc.

A viation's biggest challenge, among the many diverse external pressures on its sustainability, is undoubtedly to address its impact on climate change while ensuring continued sustainable growth of the industry.

There is a no doubt that aviation is essential for business and leisure. Aviation is pivotal to global trade, and makes a major contribution to global economic prosperity, currently estimated at US$2.2 trillion. It provides significant social benefits, facilitates tourism and supports over 56 million jobs worldwide.

However, its true value has been demonstrated most clearly by its absence, when events such as 9/11 and the Icelandic volcano paralyzed aviation with massive global consequences across all sectors. Over 10 million passengers were affected over the week-long volcanic eruption and the cost to the global economy was estimated at US$5 billion.

Despite the setbacks arising from the 2008 global financial crisis and the prolonged economic crisis in the Eurozone, the industry continues to grow in response to increased demand, especially from emerging economies and their newly affluent communities.

This means that the carbon emissions associated with aviation will continue to grow.

IATA's 'four pillar strategy' combines a range of measures to decouple growth and the impact of aviation on the environment. These pillars are technology development, operational efficiency, improvements to infrastructure, and market-based measures. These have been deployed across the industry with reasonable success – the growth of the industry averages about five per cent per annum while carbon emissions have increased by nearly three per cent.

Today, airlines have access to the most advanced aircraft available, and airframe and engine manufacturers use fuel efficiency and lower emissions as key selling points – as carbon emissions have replaced the challenge of noise in recent years – and we have invested heavily to support a sustainable business strategy. Tweaking engines, modification to the airframe, reduction of weight, adopting fuel efficient flight techniques and accurate fuel uplift are all standard practice for the most successful airlines.

However, the industry is still constrained by the absence of any substantial investment in infrastructure development and modernisation. We see serious inefficiencies in the use of airspace, which often override the benefits of our own advanced route planning systems, preventing us from taking advantage of jet streams and available airspace to calculate the most efficient routes, adding time, wasting fuel and leading to unnecessary emissions.

Inroads have been made here, driven by the industry's jointly agreed commitment to annual emissions reduction targets and sustained engagement with the broad stakeholder community. Partnership is essential in driving this change and green flight programmes require serious collaboration with air navigation service providers, airports and governments in identifying and introducing flexible tracking systems, airspace redesign, addressing congestion around airports and other fuel and flighttime saving measures to make essential improvements to the carbon footprint of our industry.

In 2011 Etihad Airways engaged with over 20 stakeholders in the INSPIRE partnership. INSPIRE – the Indian Ocean Strategy Partnership to Reduce Emissions – identified many opportunities for fuel and emissions savings, which were implemented on a number of commercial flights between the UAE and Australia. On one Etihad Airways flight alone, over 15 tonnes of carbon dioxide were saved using initiatives such as preferential taxi and runway use, and unconstrained take off and descent, and by using preferred routings.

However, even with extensive efforts on all these fronts – design and innovation, investment and collaboration – it is only through the commercial adoption of an alternative to oil-based fuel that we will achieve the necessary step change in the decarbonisation of our industry.

Despite the significant advances in the use of alternative fuels in other industries, and the fact that aviation cannot realistically rely on any other form of alternative energy, their adoption in the aviation industry has not gained meaningful momentum until very recently. The current spike in activity is quite inevitably attributable to historic oil price highs and in response to the imposition of carbon taxes.

The development of an alternative fuel for aviation is not without its challenges, not least the requirement that any alternative should be fully mixable with regular fossil-based fuel. The scope and size of the industry and the fact that alternative fuels could only be a partial replacement in the short- to medium-term, means that an alternative needs to be used in parallel.

The biggest challenge to a sustainable alternative fuel is cost. Fuel is our single greatest operating cost. It was 35 per cent of our operating costs at Etihad Airways in 2011 and this would have been even higher were it not for an aggressive fuel hedging policy.

Other challenges include the development of appropriate feedstock as the source of aviation biofuel. Many of the more proactive airlines, including Etihad Airways, have committed to a stringent set of principles on the production and use of alternative fuels as part of membership prerequisites for the Sustainable Aviation Fuel Users Group. Membership of this group, whose airlines account for more than 25 per cent of commercial fuel demand world-wide, requires that in the production of biofuel, the sustainability and ethical issues around competition with local food and water resources, and the social impacts of biofuels, must be taken into account.

Locally Etihad Airways is a founding member of the Sustainable Bioenergy Research Consortium, together with Boeing and Honeywell's UOP. The Consortium is hosted by the Abu Dhabi-based Masdar Institute and is presently engaged in evaluating the viability of locally grown bio-fuels – specifically, a venture looking at saltwater tolerant, high oil-yielding plants alongside fish and shrimp farming along the coastal areas.

It is innovative research for a harsh desert environment, with the potential to be deployed in many similar habitats, which are otherwise of little economic or ecological value. Etihad Airways will continue to work with Masdar and others over the coming years to address all the issues we face, to find solutions, and to pass our findings on to policy makers and the broader community of local and international stakeholders.

Despite the enormous efforts by the industry and its commitment to mitigate its impact on climate change, airlines continue to face a range of measures that have the potential to damage their long-term sustainability, in particular their capacity to invest and improve.

Market-based measures are intended only as a final resort, in the event of the other initiatives not being enough to meet the emissions reduction targets. Despite reports to the contrary, the industry accepts that these measures may be necessary, as long as they are implemented fairly and equitably, and recognize the very significant collaborative efforts already in place.

They include levies and charges that are disguised under an environmental protection banner. The UK Airport Passenger Duty is a perfect example, as it was originally introduced as an environmental measure. In 2012 this will provide over US$4 billion to the British Government, a substantial sum which could be used many times over to offset the emissions associated with flights into and out of the UK.

Given the pressure being placed on airlines, more so than on other areas of the travel and tourism industry, we have to engage tirelessly, proactively and decisively with our associations and airline partners to lobby governments not to impose arbitrary taxes and levies under the guise of addressing climate change. All these actually do is create an additional tax stream and rob the industry of the finances it needs to improve and invest. The threat of a proliferation of schemes around the world is very real.

What we want is a global response that takes into account the efforts we have made and continue to make. We welcome the global goals agreed at the last ICAO Assembly for a two per cent efficiency improvement across the aviation industry and the aspirational goal for carbon neutrality after 2020. We now need to work on how this can realistically be achieved.

The industry doesn't have many options left. We need to be able to do this sustainably and be able to keep up with demand. We see great value in partnering, but also need the support of governments in recognizing the demands placed on us, and indeed the whole of the travelism value chain. The world needs mobility and we need to ensure it is achieved in a way that allows us the flexibility to meet these demands.

# Brian King

## Centre for Tourism and Services Research, Victoria University

### and

# Chris Buckingham

K

## Chief Executive, Destination Melbourne

## A liveable and sustainable city that loves visitors

Brian King is Professor of Tourism Management in the School of International Business at Victoria University where he has also served as Pro Vice-Chancellor. Brian is a specialist in tourism marketing with an emphasis on cultural dimensions and emerging markets. He is Editor-in-Chief of the journal *Tourism Culture and Communication* and has extensive tourism industry experience in tour operations, airlines, cruising and destination management. He is Fellow of the International Academy for the Study of Tourism and has been a visiting professor in the USA, Hong Kong and Italy. He is a Board Member of Destination Melbourne.

Chris Buckingham leads Destination Melbourne, the regional tourism organisation for Melbourne. Chris works with a team of dedicated professionals who are passionate about the visitor industry and optimistic about the future of Melbourne and Victoria as an outstanding global visitor experience. His priorities include: building a culture of co-operation and collaboration between business, community and government; supporting the development of leaders who are proud to be part of the visitor industry; communicating the value of visitors; and connecting the visitor industry with the broader Melbourne agenda. Chris is an active member of the Victoria Tourism Industry Council; a Fellow of the Australian Institute of Management and a Graduate member of the Australian Institute of Company Directors.

With a population of over four million, Melbourne is Australia's second city. The city's global reputation peaked in 1956 when it hosted the Olympic Games, though this also marked the beginning of a gradual decline as she yielded dominance in the financial services sector to its noisy neighbour to the north – the very beautiful and glamorous Sydney. Despite the global fascination with Sydney, it is Melbourne which has taken the mantle of the country's leading events city, a function of the passion of Melbournians for sport of all kinds and the long (by New World standards) history of the city's cultural events and institutions. This status fits comfortably with the green growth agenda. Melbourne is cultivating its credentials as an international leader and a sustainable destination that hosts sustainable global and community events. Its government and corporate institutions are pursuing a range of sustainability initiatives that seek to address the interests of both residents and visitors.

Having hosted the widely praised 2006 Commonwealth Games, Melbourne continues to deliver a series of annual hallmark events including the Formula 1 Grand Prix, the Australian Tennis Open (one of the world's four 'Grand Slam' events) and the largest of them all, the Spring Racing Carnival which includes the Melbourne Cup (128,243 interstate and international visitors). In this letter we explore some ingredients of being a successful 'events' city, both currently and into the future and why Melbourne's strategy to offer high quality liveability for residents and visitability for non-residents is an important driver of the green growth agenda. The strengthening nexus between business, community and government will support Melbourne's primacy over coming decades.

Melbourne's success as a destination in recent times has been well documented. Having recovered from a period of economic gloom and restructuring during the late 1980s and early 1990s, it subsequently weathered the global financial crisis relatively unscathed. Melbourne has progressively attracted a growing share of Australian domestic visitors and increased its share of international visitation to Australia, with China recently becoming the top source market in terms of both volume and value. Melbourne's success is generally attributed to its consistent marketing and branding, to a busy calendar combining hallmark and community based events and to a consistent strategy of attracting business events and conferences. Tourism 'Melbourne-style' is self-consciously a team game, with most aspects enjoying bi-partisan support from both major parties which have occupied government for extended periods. The city is now Australia's most desirable domestic holiday destination, having overtaken the nation's iconic beach destination the Gold Coast (source: Roy Morgan Research). The city's residents are adjusting to the idea that Melbourne is a place which is sought after for holidays, study, investment, migration and visiting friends and relatives.

In its 2011 global liveability survey, the Economist newspaper rated Melbourne as the world's most 'liveable' city. There was gentle celebration in the world's southernmost metropolis and serious consternation within erstwhile and recently dislodged leader Vancouver. Tourism Vancouver's Chief Executive Rick Antonson visited Melbourne in October, 2011 to speak about why 'liveability' contributes greatly to Vancouver's reputation as a great place to visit. He identified five primary considerations for both residents and visitors:

- safety
- access and transport
- a sense of community – no matter where you are from
- confidence
- good infrastructure that serves the people

This list emphasises the interconnectedness of residents and visitors. It prompted consideration about how Melbourne would be rated if there was a global 'visitability index'. Hong Kong is an example of good practice within the Asia-Pacific region, having conducted annual monitoring of visitor satisfaction from various source markets with experiences provided by different sectors of the visitor industry. However the connection between liveability and visitability is less evident in Hong Kong. The Antonson perspective was significant because it drew attention to parallels with Vancouver and reaffirmed Destination Melbourne's commitment to advocate for the visitor experience. In responding to this new line of thought, the recently endorsed Destination Melbourne strategic plan captures this sentiment by aspiring to establish and sustain Melbourne as a: 'compelling global destination of outstanding visitor experiences.'

In contemplating Melbourne's appeal to non-residents, most residents appear reconciled to the absence of city icons – there is no obvious equivalent of the Rock, Reef, Opera House, theme park or giant pineapple (giant objects representing local industry or identities are commonplace across Australia!). Almost unconsciously, Melburnians have replaced the urgency to create or invent an icon with an acknowledgment that the appeal for actual and potential visitors is the subtle elements of the city's fabric. Rather than an iconic attraction, Melbourne offers visitability – the sum of parts leading to outstanding and memorable visitor experiences. This involves a longer term and holistic commitment to sustainability.

To capitalise on the comparative advantage associated with liveability and visitability, how can business and government be encouraged to support the visitor experience in a collaborative and strategic manner? Over an extended period, Melbourne's visitor industry has worked collectively to elevate the destination brand and to provide compelling reasons to visit. However, it is timely to begin broader community conversations about the visitor experience that generate greater ownership amongst residents. With interstate and inbound migration at historically high levels, residents are being asked to cope with unprecedented population growth which is placing pressure on infrastructural and service provision, including health, education, transport and aged care (the city population is expected to grow from 4.1 million to 5.4 million over the next two decades). When confronted by such challenges, most residents may be expected to prioritise more immediate concerns over capacity building for hosting visitors. In acknowledging this potential conflict, the visitor industry is advocating for investment in infrastructure, services and culture to support visitors as well as community life – the essence of visitability. The guiding principle is that by offering an unqualified commitment to looking after those who find Melbourne sufficiently compelling to visit the lives of resident will be enriched.

Destination Melbourne has articulated the Melbourne Visitor Experience as a central component of our new strategic plan. Over the next 3 -5 years we will:

■ Influence and measure the provision of visitor experiences.

- Be a catalyst for new ways of working and thinking about the way the visitor experience enriches Melbourne.
- Have greater engagement and representation of the visitor industry in the broader Melbourne agenda.
- Encourage Melburnians to understand the value of visitors and the benefits they bring to the community.
- Position Melbourne to be renowned globally for providing outstanding visitor experiences.

Providing residents with greater cause to reflect on the quality of the visitor experience will create opportunities to inform them about what makes the city liveable. The plan nominates industry leadership as a basis for delivering outstanding visitor experiences. It is based on the premise that Melbournians can be inspired to support the city's development as a welcoming and safe place to be enjoyed equally by residents and visitors. It is time for more community conversations about how residents in both the inner urban and outer suburban areas can take responsibility for being good hosts – doing so will almost certainly make our city a better place to live. Though Melbourne rates very highly on liveability indices and the authorities are determined to retain this positioning, its performance on sustainability leaves room for improvement. According to a ranking system devised by one of Australia's premier environmental groups Melbourne is rated as more sustainable than Sydney, but it is middle ranked and lags behind Darwin and Brisbane.

Melbourne was the second city in the British Empire during Victorian times and continues to enjoy the benefits of the transport investments that accompanied its wealth – an extensive rail and tram system. However in the post war era Melbourne spread out in a low density fashion, leading to a high level of car dependence. Meanwhile 85% of the state's electricity is produced through the combustion of locally mined brown coal (lignite). While lignite does not have the same sulphurous qualities as black coal, it has high water content, leading to lesser efficiency in the power generation process and emissions of larger quantities of carbon. At the time of writing Australia is on the threshold of implementing a new carbon tax to drive GHG reduction and Australia's visitor industry is actively assessing how this will impact upon operations.

At a time when the Australian Government is embracing major tax and regulatory reform, thought is needed about how the pursuit of a more sustainable approach to tourism will support liveability and visitability. The cornerstones of Melbourne's visitor infrastructure – public transport, parks and open spaces and green buildings – have been conceived and implemented by visionary leaders who have an understanding of the relationship between nature and built form. According to the sustainability index mentioned previously, Melbourne scored highly for its number of green buildings and for achieving a relatively high level of health and education among residents. However the city trails the nation in public participation – the percentage of volunteers – and is below par for its use of public transport and its support of biodiversity

One area of Melbourne with a high concentration of 5 and 6 star green rated buildings is Docklands. The extensive Docklands area is adjacent to the central business district and consists of about 200 hectares of land and water and seven kilometres of waterfront. The precinct incorporates a combination of corporate offices, retail and residential development. It also has one of the world's biggest public art programs. Docklands draws residents to the waterfront for a variety of festivities including various water-borne events and regattas. It is also home to Etihad Stadium, a multi-purposes stadium with retractable roof which hosts diverse sporting events including Australian rules football, soccer, rugby, cricket and various entertainments. From a sustainability perspective, Etihad Stadium has strong public transport links with Melbourne's residential areas, thereby emphasising sustainable means of the transport when major events are staged accommodating a large concentration of spectators. As part of the government's determination to stimulate activity in the inner urban area which is better connected through the transport network, the facility replaced a stadium (subsequently decommissioned) which was located in the heavily car dependent outer suburbs. Etihad Stadium is adjacent to the main regional railways station and to a recently completed extension of the city's original tram system.

Also located on the waterfront, though in this case on the Yarra River, the Melbourne Convention and Exhibition Centre (MCEC) is emblematic of the state's pursuit of sustainable buildings. It is the largest in

Australia and was the world's first convention centre to receive a 6 star green rating (in 2008). All aspects of the centre are consciously green, from the heating and cooling to the water systems. The latter is of particular importance in light of Australia's status as the world's driest continent. The implementation of solar hot water and renewable power leads to a reduction in emissions, a message which features prominently in the key proposition for event organisers.

International research has shown that green buildings that are able to demonstrate environmental stewardship, increase energy efficiency and reduce greenhouse gas emissions attract a higher proportion of grants, awards, subsidies and other incentives. MCEC has received many environment related awards, including the 2010 Victorian Architecture Medal, the 2009 Banksia Foundation Built Environment Award, the 2010 Australian Construction Achievement Award and recognition by the Design Institute of Australia for its contribution to Victoria's public amenity. A 2009 survey by Meetings and Conventions magazine found that 56 per cent of conference organisers enquire about green initiatives when selecting a meeting venue, while another 15 per cent plan to start doing so. Moreover, 51 per cent said that they had recently increased their focus on green meetings. Such considerations are particularly important for conference settings such as Melbourne, located far from the traditional North American and European markets. Whilst closer proximity to Asia is an advantage, attracting conference delegates and event participants from Europe is increasingly challenging as the environmental costs associated with long haul travel are increasingly passed on to travellers by European governments.

The events focus is not confined to the natural environment. MCEC management has connected the visitor experience that occurs within the facility with the activities of local food producers. The Centre 'thinks local' and supports sustainable and responsible Victorian producers and suppliers. This involves reducing transport related emissions while supporting producers who share a vision of making the world greener. The MCEC philosophy of 'Farm to Fork' gains particular prominence during the annual Melbourne Food & Wine Festival (MFWF) where it is incorporated within the Festival's Cellar Door & Farm Gate initiative. This is indicative of Melbourne as a 'meetings place' where built forms are playing a major role along with outdoor festivities.

The provision of protected areas is another connection between the city and the countryside. During its Victorian development, Melbourne's founding planners and surveyors incorporated a network of parks and gardens which were described as the 'lungs of the city'. More recently the government entity that has stewardship over the parks – Parks Victoria – received an extended brief to handle both city (metropolitan) parks and rural (regional) parks. Significantly the remarkable 17% of Victoria's landmass which is designated as parks and reserves gives Parks Victoria a major role in the visitor experience both inside and beyond the city. The Parks Victoria initiative, 'Healthy Parks, Healthy People' is a symbol for Melbourne's desire to connect residents, visitors and the natural environment.

The City of Melbourne has implemented an extensive range of sustainability-related initiatives and these have a major impact on the visitor experience. Prominent amongst these are water related activities since Australia is the world's driest continent and Victoria only recently emerged from a prolonged period (over a decade) or drought. Victoria has an established reputation, previously featured on car registration plates, as Australia's Garden State. Trees are one of the city's defining features and the council owns 60,000 of them! Though parks, gardens, green spaces and tree-lined streets contribute to Melbourne's livable city status, trees are under increasing threat after a decade of drought. As a consequence of these hostile conditions as well as pressures for development, it is anticipated that Melbourne will lose 27 per cent of its tree population over the next decade and 44 per cent over the next 20 years. Progress is being made – since 2006, the City of Melbourne has cut water use in parks by 62 per cent. In acknowledging the critical relationship between trees and water, the city has drafted its *Urban Forest Strategy 2012–2032*. The title of the strategy is indicative of bringing features more commonly associated with rural areas into the city.

As is the case in other progressive cities, Melbourne's leaders are encouraging residents and visitors to make greater use of low carbon emitting transport modes. The Council spends more than $3 million annually on cycling, including implementation of the city's Bicycle Plan (covering the period 2007–2011). The plan has improved the provision of on- and off-road bike paths and bike facilities. The plan includes upgrades to bike routes to improve safety, connections and way-finding. The city operates a bicycle account, based on the Copenhagen equivalent. The Melbourne Bike Share scheme offers visitors and residents an opportunity to cycle around the city and is a joint initiative between the Victorian Government, the motoring organisation, the City of Melbourne and Bicycle Victoria.

A City of Melbourne environmental intervention with direct impacts on the tourism industry is the Green Hotels Savings in the City initiative, which focuses on water management and energy use and waste disposal by providing support, recognition and advice and the distribution of tool-kits. 30 hotels and serviced apartments have been participating in the pilot program which is a partnership involving the tourism and water authorities

Melbourne is also playing its part in global networks and institutions. Such collaborations strengthen the prospects of delivering on sustainability initiatives by raising awareness of international benchmarks and combatting complacency. In 2002 Melbourne became headquarters of the United Nations' Global Compact Cities Programme. This initiative is dedicated to the promotion and adoption of the Global Compact's ten principles by cities, and provides a framework for translating the principles into day-to-day urban governance and management. It focuses on collaboration between all levels of government, business and civil society in order to enhance sustainability, resilience, diversity and adaptation within cities and in the face of complex urban challenges. This is consistent with the types of activities being undertaken in Melbourne and mentioned in this letter.

There is a famous sporting slogan – if you want to stay number one you have to train and play like you are number two. Melbourne embodies the spirit of being a second city that enjoys leadership across many dimensions of achievement. The pursuit of the green growth agenda exemplifies Melbourne's commitment to best practice and global aspirations (what leading Australian futurologist Peter Ellyard has described as 'Globalism'). Combining an holistic and sustainable philosophy and reconciling the interests of residents and visitors, Melbourne is well placed to play its part in implementing the Rio+20 agenda.

# Karen Kotowski

## CEO, Convention Industry Council

## Meeting as a green growth strategy

Karen Kotowski is the Chief Executive Officer of the Convention Industry Council (CIC). The CIC is a federation of 32 organizations in the meetings, exhibition, events and travel industry. Karen is responsible for the day to day management and strategy of the CIC, delivering several signature programs, including the Certified Meeting Professional (CMP) Designation, Accepted Practices Exchange (APEX), and the CIC Hall of Leaders. Karen has more than 20 years of meeting planning, education and program management experience for non-profit associations and private sector companies. Karen graduated from the Pennsylvania State University with a degree in Public Service and she holds both the industry's illustrious designations, the Certified Meeting Professional (CMP) and the Certified Association Executive (CAE).

In 2009, with enhanced scrutiny on the meetings sector within the United States, the Convention Industry Council (CIC) initiated a plan to demonstrate the economic value of face-to-face meetings by commissioning a study on the economic significance of meetings to the US economy. We were in a fight for the future of our industry as a result of both the economic downturn and a political and media-made crisis which painted the meetings sector as a colossal waste of money, without regard to the beneficial outcomes derived from meetings, nor the economic benefits which build communities.

The results of the study proved that the meetings sector produced 1.8 million meetings, $263 billion in direct spending, 1.7 million American jobs and almost $26 billion in federal, state and local taxes. The meeting sector's $106 billion contribution to the Gross Domestic Product far exceeded that of the automobile industry ($78 billion), an industry which was also receiving its own attention as a government bailout recipient. These significant figures only consider direct impacts. When indirect and induced figures are added, the impacts are even more astounding.

So what does this have to do with sustainable meetings you might ask? Well, everything. Just as the meetings industry has significant impacts on the economies of countries, cities and communities, it also has a significant impact on the community, country and global environment.

According to the US Environmental Protection Agency, the average conference delegate produces 20 pounds of waste per person, per day. Those same attendees would produce an average of five pounds of waste a day at home. Each delegate uses approximately *846* gallons of water. An event with 10,000 attendees, therefore, would use approximately *8.5 million* gallons of water. Multiply both resource usage figures by the 1.8 million meetings held every year, and the amount of waste produced and water resources used is staggering. As an industry, we know we must do better. If every meeting sponsor made an effort to reduce the waste produced during their meetings or events, it could make a huge impact.

For this reason, the Convention Industry Council, in a partnership between the US Environmental Protection Agency (EPA) and the Green Meeting Industry Council (GMIC), sought to answer the need in the meeting and event industry for a uniform measurement of environmental performance. The result was the recently published APEX/ASTM Environmentally Sustainable Meetings Standards. These standards lay out specific sustainable practices in nine areas ranging from accommodations to transportation.

These standards are an attempt to create a level playing field of what constitutes 'green' for the meetings and events industry. While the standards are voluntary, demand and use by planners and competition will drive adoption. The standards are specific, measurable, performance-based criteria and are intended to be adopted internationally and to work hand in hand with other management system-based standards such as British Standard 8901 Sustainable Events Standard and the currently under development ISO 20121 standard, which are written to inform the process of organizing an event.

According to a Meetings Professionals International Future Watch study, 76% of European and 63% of US meeting planners reported that Corporate Social Responsibility (CSR) is a focus for their organizations, and sustainability as part of CSR activities continues to be a top trend on their bi-monthly *Business Barometer Report*. Further, a 2010 Meetings & Convention Magazine Research study showed that 51% of meeting planners reported that green meetings have become more important and 56% inquired about green initiatives on RFPs for meeting venues. 66% said that a venue's green initiatives are somewhat or very important to the process of selecting a meeting venue.

'Leading companies are already building comprehensive climate-change strategies tied to their business strategies that are designed to help them mitigate the financial and reputational risks, as well as pursue the emerging opportunities and reap the rewards,' according to a PriceWaterhouseCoopers report on global warming. Successful hotel companies, food and beverage providers, transportation companies and the myriad of businesses supplying products and services to meetings, events and exhibitions must engage more comprehensively in the green meetings growth movement, with the right strategies to capture the attention and business of those consumers. The meetings industry can be an important player in the green growth paradigm.

As sustainable meetings practices become more ingrained in how meeting planners and suppliers produce events, recognized standards such as the APEX/ASTM Environmentally Sustainable Meeting Standards, Global Reporting Initiative and ISO 20121 will provide transparent reporting mechanisms by which companies can align and communicate corporate strategy and results on the environmental, social and economic performance of their meeting and event activities. As a result, meeting suppliers can become a reliable and credible partner in this process.

While we have made progress as an industry in developing tools to implement and record change, we have by no means reached the tipping point which Malcolm Gladwell would define as 'the "mysterious" sociological changes that mark everyday life.' The same MPI Business Barometer Report mentioned earlier, does predict that CSR and green initiatives will increase. However, it also acknowledged that survey respondents said that 'green initiatives suffered during the recent economic turmoil,' and these practices will 'increase in popularity as a responsible and cost-saving strategy,' and that standardized processes and government regulation will also play a role. It is my hope that education about sustainable practices, cost reductions and the ability to track results, irrespective of the state of the economic condition will drive change to that tipping point, rather than government mandate.

Market forces are always a much more efficient and effective game-changer for consumer and business behavior than government inter-vention. And in the world of sustainability, demonstrating progress towards those goals with specific measurable outcomes will help drive those efforts forward as well as provide business opportunities for those that can assist companies meet and/or report on achievement of sustain-ability goals.

In the 2012 Green Biz State of the Industry Report, one of the trends highlighted in the report was the fact that CFO's are becoming more involved in sustainability efforts because the 'growing calls for trans-parency and disclosure of sustainability impacts (require)... more, and more reliable, information about increasingly deeper levels of company operations and supply chains.' Further, the big four accounting firms have become acutely aware of the business opportunity and growth strategy related to assisting their customers with this critical sustain-ability reporting just as they do with providing financial reporting services. Meeting professionals within organizations will be key to developing and implementing sustainability reporting for an organi-zation's meeting activities as a part of its overall communication of sustainability impacts.

Another trend, according to the Green Biz study, likely to drive behavior change in the green growth movement is green gamification. 'As consumer product companies jump on the gamification bandwagon, some are likely to use it to promote green behaviors – and sell green products.'

The meetings industry can also use this strategy to promote and encourage green behavior in both practices and purchasing decisions. The Green Meetings Industry Council (GMIC), a CIC member, intro-duced *Game On!* at its 2011 Sustainable Meetings Conference. The *Game On!* format was an attempt to increase both engagement and learning about sustainable meeting practices, by involving attendees in a prac-tical experiment to test and influence behavioural patterns in ways that could be replicable across the system. It also demonstrated that market forces could drive behavior as the 'marketplace' delivered constant reward and feedback, through virtual currency, tokens, and additional 'lives' that gamers received in the competition. *Game On!* was designed to drive engagement, competition, and learning, and succeeded in all three.

Another case study in gamification of meetings was Event Camp Vancouver 2011, a meeting which integrated a mobile application-based game called *Get Your Green On*. The game engaged event attendees in 'Acts of Green' which resulted in points for performing sustainability actions. For instance, participants received points for transit use in travelling to the conference. This resulted in 168 individual vehicle trips not taken by walking, taking public transit or car-pooling and avoided an estimated 17 kg of emissions per trip, or 2.85 metric tons of $CO_2$. Even simple acts were awarded such as buying fair trade, organic coffee roasted locally, unplugging appliances in sleeping rooms, abiding by 4-minute showers, and participating in the hotel's linen reuse program. Timers were distributed to encourage water conservation and 73 water wise showers were recorded, and 21 attendees practiced linen reuse. Both practices helped to conserve 2,385 L of water, and each individual act of green resulted in a $1 contribution to charity as an incentive to improve event sustainability.

These are but small examples of how market and individual competition as well as incentive forces can be a driving force of change. With those changes, come market opportunities for businesses within or new to the green growth economy. When we again consider the overall economic output of the U.S. meetings industry, it can be a transformative player in the ever-growing green marketplace.

The green meetings movement is no longer a fringe element but is evolving into the way we can and must do business. Green products and services offered by industry suppliers offer a competitive advantage and over time those companies whose businesses embrace sustainable practices stand to gain the most from opportunities to grow along with the vast and robust global meetings industry.

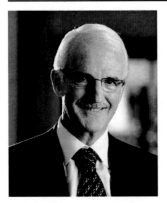

# Gerald Lawless

## Executive Chairman, Jumeirah Group

## Green growth in Dubai – delivering sustainable community benefits

Gerald Lawless is the Executive Chairman, Jumeirah Group. He has helped establish Jumeirah as one of the premier luxury hotel brands in the world. He joined the company in 1997 after a 23-year career with Forte Hotels. A graduate of Shannon College of Hotel Management in Ireland, Gerald holds an Honorary Degree of Doctor of Business Administration in Hospitality Management awarded by the Johnson & Wales University, State of Rhode Island in the U.S.A., and an Honorary Degree of Laws by the NUI Galway, Ireland. Gerald is a member of the Executive Committee and Vice Chairman of Corporate Governance for WTTC; a fellow of the Institute of Hospitality; Vice Chairman of the Aviation, Travel and Tourism council (WEF); member of the Dubai Holding Executive Committee; Non-Executive Director, Travelodge; and Chairman of the Board of Governors of the Emirates Academy of Hospitality Management.

I t is hard to overemphasize the importance of travel and tourism globally for both developing and developed economies. According to the latest figures released by the World Travel & Tourism Council, there were 981 million international arrivals in 2011. The global GDP share of travel and tourism was equal to 9.1% and the industry supported 255 million jobs, which equates to 8.7% of the employment around the world.

At a time of rising unemployment in many markets, travel and tourism has a crucial role to play in generating and sustaining the economic recovery. Moreover, travel and tourism is a direct export and therefore influences a country's balance of payments. So investments made in a well thought through tourism strategy can deliver the kind of returns that make both economic and social sense.

Dubai is a great example of what can be achieved through the coordinated development of travel, tourism and hospitality. Having lived in Dubai from 1978 to 1982 and again since 1991, I have seen first-hand how, with careful planning and visionary leadership, a country can develop its tourism industry from nothing. Dubai now welcomes over eight million visitors a year, yet the population of the city itself is only two million. Dubai airport has already exceeded 50 million passengers in 2011 making Dubai, a 'universal aviation hub'.

The Government of Dubai understood at an early stage the potential benefits of tourism to its economic development. Hotels, such as Jumeirah Beach Hotel and Burj Al Arab, helped to position Dubai as a tourist destination, but the key to success lay in ensuring a coordinated approach between the private sector and the government to promote the destination and, most significantly, the development of Emirates Airlines since 1985. No destination can realistically expect to succeed in the development of tourism without having adequate airlift.

So now that Dubai has achieved its goals in relation to tourism, what are the benefits to the country?

Economically the figures speak for themselves: in 2011 the travel and tourism industry contributed around 18% to Dubai's economy. There have also been immense social benefits, not least of which the ability to generate a greater degree of understanding between different cultures. Most prejudice, I believe, is based on ignorance and if people can dispel that ignorance through travel by exposing themselves to other cultures and customs, we can go some way to undermining prejudice.

A fine example of this in Dubai is the Sheikh Mohammed Centre for Cultural Understanding. Jumeirah has tapped into the amazing resources that are available within this foundation – guests can sign up to visit a local mosque, share breakfast with local Emiratis, listen to an imam discuss the background and the values of Islam, the similarities between Islam and other Abrahamic religions such as Judaism and Christianity and ask about local customs. All the guests leave the mosque feeling totally enriched by their experience and we see this ability to deliver an enriching experience as a very important part of our role.

Many of our guests are looking for an experience that goes beyond sun, sea and sand. Of course they love to do this, but at the same time we offer them the opportunity to deepen their understanding of the destination – its history, its traditions and its people. One example of this is pearl diving, which along with trade and date farming was the mainstay of Dubai's economic activity in the past. Pearl diving died out when the technique of developing cultured pearls was perfected in Japan – but it is now being re-introduced as a way of connecting people with Emirati heritage. Our guests can now go out on a traditional dhow, dressed in authentic cotton diving tunics, sing the pearl-divers songs and dive for oysters off in the Arabian Gulf. All the oysters they collect are opened on the deck of the dhow and the excitement they feel if they are lucky enough to find a pearl, however small, is unforgettable. Beyond the excitement is the fact that in taking part in the activity they are experiencing a direct connection with the lives of the grandfathers of today's Emiratis and a deeper understanding of the culture they are visiting.

Jumeirah is also very concerned about environmental and conservation issues. In the Arabian Gulf, the hawksbill turtle is an endangered species. With the support of the Dubai Centre for Turtle Rehabilitation we rescue turtles that are washed up on the beaches of the Arabian Gulf as a result of accumulating an encrustation of barnacles, injury or illness. These turtles are taken to our marine biology centre in Burj Al Arab where they are nursed back to health. When they have sufficiently recovered, the turtles are then transferred from Burj Al Arab to the canals of Madinat Jumeirah where they complete their recuperation. Once they are fully back to health the turtles are ready to be released back into the wild. These releases have become big public events, with local schools and our guests being invited to take part. And the benefits in terms of raising awareness of the plight of these endangered species and educating the public on what to do if they find them are critical in helping preserve the species. In addition, some of the larger turtles have satellite trackers glued to their backs to allow the marine biologists to learn more about turtle behaviour – as well as allowing turtle fans to follow their progress on Facebook.

Within Madinat Jumeirah we have 110 acres of landscaped grounds, and the resort has become the first in the United Arab Emirates to implement a Bokashi compost programme to recycle food waste as compost to be used on its gardens. In 2011 the resort recycled over 56 tonnes of food waste into compost which is used in the gardens instead of traditional or chemical fertilisers.

We see these activities as a means of engaging not only with guests, but also with the community and with bodies that are concerned with environmental and related issues. As a company we talk about 'conservation as conversation', as it allows us to demonstrate our commitment to being good corporate citizens and to participate in the development of a greater understanding of issues that are relevant to the region.

Jumeirah is currently in the process of setting up a charitable foundation which will be known as The Jumeirah Foundation. It is our intention to ensure that as we develop hotels and resorts in other parts of the world, we provide means by which the local communities can benefit from development of these hotels. This would take the form of consulting with the local population to ensure they benefit from the economic activity we bring to the region, especially their young people. At one level this may take the form of providing educational and healthcare support; at another, the opportunity to integrate local crafts in the hotel, and to provide potential employment for those who have taken advantage of our educational support in the time between us signing a management agreement and the hotel being ready for operation. An added benefit is that this kind of initiative encourages young people to stay and work in the own villages and not migrate to the cities or overseas.

Many of our colleagues based in Dubai have already volunteered to help with such projects and will themselves be enriched by the experience of rolling out this plan.

These are just a few examples of how the travel and tourism industry can help to engage in a way that is economically, environmentally and socially relevant with the local community. It is relevant to the reputation of the industry and most importantly it is relevant to our guests, for whom it is increasingly important that the values of the hotel company they are staying with are aligned with their own values. It allows them to experience what we call 'luxury without guilt': a more meaningful and enriching experience that will stay with them for a lifetime – and not just until their suntan has faded.

A key area of growth for the travel and tourism industry this decade is China and India. It is expected that China will provide over 100 million outbound travellers per annum before 2020, and India over 50 million. This brings a new dimension to the challenge of environmental sustainability in the travel and tourism sector. Apart from hotels taking initiatives to reduce their impact on the environment, it is essential that the aviation industry continues in their efforts to develop cleaner technologies for aircraft – this naturally extends into the role of other industries to play their part. For example the development of biofuels as a step towards addressing the carbon emissions restrictions that are now being implemented throughout the world and have already started in Europe.

Travel, tourism and hospitality are definitely a force for good. But we have to strike the right balance. Sustainability is not just about environmental issues, it is also very much about social, cultural and developmental issues. As people travel more and as more people travel, the hope is that their minds are opened to new experiences and to different cultures. This new-found inter-cultural engagement has the potential to influence the prospects for peace – or at least to mitigate the potential for prejudice in the world.

# Manfredi Lefebvre

## Director and Chairman, Silversea Cruises

## The green economy – travel and tourism and the cruise sector

Manfredi Lefebvre d'Ovidio has held the position of Director and Chairman of Silversea Cruises group of companies since 2001, as well as playing a key role in Lefebvre Investment. In addition to the above, Mr. Lefebvre d'Ovidio is associated with several other organizations, including: industry associate (partner) of the World Economic Forum WEF (Davos) and Travel & Tourism Governor, Member and Vice Chairman of the Executive Committee of the World Travel & Tourism Council (WTTC), and Chairman of the non-profit European Cruise Council. He has been awarded the recognition of Chevalier de l'Ordre de Saint-Charles and des Grimaldi from H.H. Prince Albert of Monaco.

## Moving to the global green economy

While individual countries are certainly not moving at the same speed or with the same conviction, faced with the potential implications of climate change, it seems clear that the global trend over the coming years will be towards a green economy. Many governments are already taking action to cut carbon emissions, create the conditions for green growth, and improve resilience to climate change. This will help to bring about the transition to a sustainable green economy. Such a transition is essential for delivering sustainable growth, not just in traditional environmental and low carbon sectors, but across the wider economy.

Businesses are the key to this transition. Businesses can create growth and jobs as well as contributing to a cleaner environment through taking action on climate change, the more efficient use of resources such as energy and water as well as minimising waste. T here will also be business opportunities for organisations of all sizes created by new and developing markets for more innovative green and low carbon technologies and processes that can help deliver the transformation.

Many businesses around the world have already recognised this potential and are actively and profitably involved in this new environment.

## The travel and tourism sectors

Travel and tourism continues to be one of the world's largest industries and can make a positive contribution to the creation of a global green economy. WTTC states that the total impact of the industry means that, in 2011, it contributed 9% of global GDP or a value of over US$6 trillion, and accounted for 255 million jobs. While the industry is currently challenged by considerable economic and political uncertainty, over the next ten years, it is expected to grow by an average of 4% annually, taking it to 10% of global GDP, or some US$10 trillion. By 2022, it is anticipated that it will account for 328 million jobs, or 1 in every 10 jobs on the planet.

In over 150 countries, tourism is one of the 5 top export earners and in some 60 it is the number one export. It is the main source of foreign exchange for one third of developing countries and one half of LDCs.

In the context of a future green economy, it is worth reiterating some of the key messages of the 2011 Report *Tourism Inventory in Energy and Resource Efficiency* developed by UNEP and UNWTO.

- *Green tourism has the potential to create new jobs and reduce poverty*. Travel and tourism are human-resource intensive, employing directly and indirectly 8% of the global workforce. It is estimated that one job in the core tourism industry creates about one and a half additional or indirect jobs in the tourism-related economy. The greening of tourism is expected to reinforce the employment potential of the sector with increased local hiring and sourcing and significant opportunities in tourism oriented toward local culture and the natural environment.

- *Tourism development can be designed to support the local economy and poverty reduction*. Local economic effects of tourism are determined by the share of tourism spending in the local economy as well as the amount stimulated in other economic activities. In greening the tourism sector, therefore, increasing the involvement of local communities, especially the poor, in the tourism value chain can contribute to the development of local economy and poverty reduction.

- *Investing in the greening of tourism can reduce the cost of energy, water and waste, and enhance the value of biodiversity, ecosystems and cultural heritage.* Investment in energy efficiency has been found to generate significant returns within a short payback period. Improving waste management is expected to save money for tourism businesses, create jobs and enhance the attractiveness of destinations. Investment in cultural heritage – the largest single component of consumer demand for sustainable tourism – is among the most significant and usually most profitable investments a society or tourism sector can make.

- *Tourists are demanding the greening of tourism.* More than a third of travellers are found to favour environmentally-friendly tourism and be willing to pay for related experiences. Traditional mass tourism has reached a stage of steady growth. In contrast, ecotourism, nature, heritage, cultural, and 'soft adventure' tourism are taking the lead and are predicted to grow rapidly over the next two decades. It is estimated that global spending on ecotourism is increasing about six times the industry-wide rate of growth.

- *Destination planning and development strategies are the first step towards the greening of tourism.* In developing tourism strategies, local governments, communities and businesses need to establish mechanisms for coordinating with ministries responsible for the environment, energy, labour, agriculture, transport, health, finance, security, and other relevant areas.

- *Government investments and policies can leverage private sector actions on green tourism.* Government spending on public goods such as protected areas, cultural assets, water conservation, waste management, sanitation, public transport, and renewable energy infrastructure can reduce the cost of green investments by the private sector in green tourism. Governments can also use tax concessions and subsidies to encourage private investment in green tourism.

## The global cruise sector

While tourism generally has grown over the past years and will continue to do so, the global cruise industry has also grown spectacularly. Over the 10 years from 2000 to 2010, demand for cruising has almost doubled from 9.7 million to 18.8 million passengers – globalisation is the single most promising development in the cruise industry.

It is significant that, worldwide, market penetration by the cruise sector is low. Even in the most mature US market, where over 10 million residents took a cruise in 2011, it represented only 3% of the population. In 2000, only 9% of passengers of the member companies of the two major cruise industry associations – CLIA and ECC – came from outside North America. By 2010, the percentage had tripled to nearly 27%. In Europe, with a population of 500 million, 6 million residents – compared to 3 million 10 years ago – took a cruise in 2011, representing only 1%.

The scope for growth is even more marked in Asia. In 2010, some 530,000 Asians took a cruise. With China alone having a population of 1.3 billion and with a rapidly expanding affluent middle class, there is massive potential.

The possibilities are equally good in Latin America, which could well become a year round cruise destination. In the 2010/11 season there were nearly 800,000 Brazilian cruise passengers on 20 vessels compared to some 140,000 passengers on six ships in 2004/05. With a population of 194m and also with a rapidly expanding affluent middle class, the scope for growth is enormous. The 2014 world cup and 2016 Olympics offer exciting opportunities in the short term. However, achieving continued growth will be dependent on effectively addressing infrastructure issues, high operating costs, and bureaucratic burdens throughout South America. The industry and governments will need to work closely to tackle these matters if the potential is to be realised.

It is the European market that has witnessed the most significant growth over recent years; it has experienced consistent double digit growth and is widely recognised as having considerable potential to make a significant social and economic contribution to Europe's recovery.

### Some key factors:

- In 2011 some 6 million Europeans booked a cruise. This has more than doubled in the past decade. It is estimated that some 5.7 million passengers embarked on their cruise from a European port.
- Each of these passengers spent an average of almost €100 when visiting a port and there are some 25 million passenger port visits per year.

- Crucially in the current economic climate, over 300,000 jobs have been created in Europe (with 55,000 employed directly by the cruise lines). This is an increase of 55% over 2005.

- In 2010 the industry generated over €35 billion of goods and services, with European bookings accounting for over 30% of the global market.

- 99% of the world's cruise ships are built by European shipyards that in turn buy 99% of all supplies from European manufacturers. While there will be fewer orders over the next few years than in the past, the cruise industry remains a key driver in maintaining a European shipbuilding industry.

As is evident from the foregoing, the cruise industry is experiencing strong growth throughout the world, with enormous potential for the coming years. This is clearly good for jobs and local communities. But strong growth brings increased obligations to act responsibility.

The cruise sector has always had a strong commitment to maintaining the integrity of the marine environment. This is increasingly reflected in a transparent way through the annual sustainability reports that cruise companies produce which, increasingly, shareholder groups are requiring. Cruise companies are working constantly to deliver ever higher environmental standards to ensure that the sector can grow sustainably. Indeed, almost uniquely in the shipping industry, the cruise sector operates in a 'business to consumer' model – a positive public perception of the industry is a fundamental part of the cruise product.

On a key issue, and reflecting its environmental commitment, the cruise sector fully supports efforts to reduce overall greenhouse gas emissions and is willing to assume its share of responsibility in reaching the overall reduction targets. Shipping is already a highly efficient means of transportation but further efficiency gains can certainly still be achieved through operational efficiencies, new technology and market based measures. To reflect the global nature of the cruise industry, a global regime to govern maritime greenhouse gas emissions – developed at the International Maritime Organisation – is the most effective approach.

As a second example, on the central environmental issue of sulphur limits, the industry fully supports the terms of the IMO Convention which offers an environmentally credible and far reaching way forward. Application of a truly global regime allows all to compete on a level playing field and introduces new opportunities for the industry to develop alternative compliance mechanisms to meet or exceed the higher standards, at a potentially lower cost to the industry and to society as a whole.

Having adequate and efficient infrastructure and waste reception facilities at ports are other crucial areas both for environmental sustainability and for offering customers an ever higher standard of service.

Overall, there is a shared goal of sustainable growth as between all stakeholders with an interest in the sector – industry, governments, NGOs and the general public. This includes of course safety, and while the industry has an excellent safety record and is highly regulated, the Concordia accident demonstrates that there is no such thing as perfect safety – only a perfect commitment to safety. As part of that safety culture the industry has made a far reaching commitment focused on identifying operational measures which can be further tightened and implemented immediately across the global fleet. It is fully recognised that the reputation of the industry must and will be, restored.

## Conclusions

In describing some of the characteristics of the cruise sector it is clear that it is an increasingly important part of global tourism with many similar characteristics as the rest of the sector, including the challenges and opportunities of environmental sustainability. As an industry, cruise companies are very much aware that it is in their own interests, as well as clearly those of the destinations they visit, that they pro-actively and constructively work towards sustainability. By doing so, the cruise industry can both secure its own long term future and continue to make a real social and economic contribution to the places and peoples they visit around the world as an integral and important part of wider tourism industry and, by extension, the future green economy.

# Chris Lyle

## CEO Air Transport Economics

## Aviation's role in green growth for developing countries

Chris Lyle is the Chief Executive, Air Transport Economics, and Representative of the World Tourism Organization to the International Civil Aviation Organization. Chris's career spans British Airways, the UN Economic Commission for Africa and ICAO where he led economic environmental and regulatory strategic programs. More recently his work has included development of essential tourism air services and policy aspects of the economic regulation of air transport; much of his focus has been on aviation sustainability and climate change. Chris has led delegations to meetings of international governmental and non-governmental bodies, participated in high-level negotiations on aviation environmental regulatory matters. Chris is a graduate of Cambridge University and a Fellow of the Royal Aeronautical Society.

*'Aviation sustainability is an oxymoron.'*

There is some substance behind this assertion in the context of aviation's impact on the climate. For example, air transport directly represents globally some 2% of anthropogenic carbon dioxide emissions but just under 1% of GDP, a ratio of about 2:1 which is presently rising. Growth in air transport is likely to continue to outpace technical and operational improvements for the foreseeable future, although biofuels should reduce the margin assuming the not inconsiderable challenges of full life-cycle assessment, scale-up and production sustainability can be achieved.

But therein lies a lesson of 'silos'. While air transport in isolation may not easily become sustainable, travel and tourism together, in which air transport makes a crucial contribution, may not only be sustainable but actually be a primary driver of green growth. In comparison with the above figures, 'travelism' (encompassing the air transport component) represents globally about 5% both of global carbon dioxide emissions and of GDP, a ratio of 1:1.

Air transport's value lies in delivering social and economic goods and services. Nowhere is this message more important than for developing countries. Take Seychelles for example. Tourism is the principal economic sector, predominantly dependent on (long-haul) international air transport. Tourism has enhanced the establishment of nature parks and marine protection areas. Partly in consequence, the country is a *net absorber* of greenhouse gases.

## Air transport and the three pillars

While sustainability is often equated with the environment, there are two other pillars of sustainable development, namely social and economic, in which travelism can produce a matchless payback, particularly in developing countries. The challenge is to find a balance amongst the three pillars of sustainability and the approach should be to position travel and tourism *collectively* as a strategic industry, with air transport as an interconnected core, not an isolated entity.

In this context, let's assess aviation in developing countries directly against each of the three pillars in turn and identify the challenges faced from the sector in making green travelism growth truly sustainable.

The first pillar is social. Here, of course, aviation's contribution is primarily as a catalyst for the considerable potential from tourism. For aviation in itself to be sustainable, however, it does require uncompromised commitment to safety and security, as well as to facilitation at airports. Aviation is in the vanguard of global safety and security by any measure and, thanks to the efforts of ICAO and IATA, the standards generally apply effectively in developing as well as developed countries. But air transport is struggling to cope with the security-driven facilitation requirements at airports. In a number of developing countries, inadequate quality of terminal infrastructure can also lead to a poor passenger experience. Facilitation of travel also has broader aspects (for example regarding visa availability and processing) which are having a substantially negative impact. Travel and tourism *collectively* need to address these issues.

The second pillar is environmental. The crucial issue here is aviation's contribution to climate change, although there are other aspects such as local air quality and aircraft noise which are also important and which continue to be addressed in appropriate contexts. On climate change, it is by now widely recognized that some form of market-based mitigation measures for air transport will be necessary. But exactly what form remains to be determined at a global level even after many years of consideration – one important reason is that thinking has been focused within the air transport 'silo'. This means that fundamental factors such as the following are not fully taken into account:

- Imposition of air transport levies in originating markets impacts not only airlines but can have a greater impact on destination economies (for example, the effect of the United Kingdom's Air Passenger Duty on tourism to Caribbean countries)

- Imposition of market-based measures only on airlines with principal place of business in major markets would still impact destination markets to which these airlines fly whether or not airlines from destination markets are exempted.

As stated in the Rio+20 zero draft, 'priority needs to be accorded to the special needs of Africa, small island developing states, least developed countries and landlocked developing countries'. Such provision should apply equally to air transport, but with aviation in its silo it has so far not been possible to find a widely acceptable formula. The time is ripe for a cross-silo conversation and for some lateral thinking, for example to differentiate by *route* or *route group* to exempt the above countries rather deal with them in the same way as the services of richer states or airlines.

The third pillar is economic. As with the social pillar, the predominant role for aviation is as a catalyst, and it is an extremely effective one. Figures from international aviation studies suggest the following multiplier effects for developing economies: every $100 of revenue produced by air transport triggers an additional average demand of $400; and every 100 jobs generated by air transport trigger an additional average demand of well over 500 jobs in other industries. Of course air transport and tourism are in a symbiotic relationship and it could be argued that tourism acts a catalyst for air transport rather than *vice-versa*, but the point is clearly made.

Perhaps the major contribution that air services can make to developing countries is through international tourism. Tourism facilitates poverty reduction by generating economic growth, providing employment opportunities and increasing tax collection, while fostering the development and conservation of protected areas and the environment. Green growth indeed!

At the present time there is a growing fiscal concern for air transport in the form of unsubstantiated levies. While the industry should contribute its due, there is an increasing proliferation of taxes and charges which can actually produce a net *disbenefit* to the general economy. Developing countries are often the victims of what can effectively be trade protectionism, but the situation is exacerbated when retaliatory levies or other action are applied which in effect targets their own tourism exports. This is killing the goose which lays the golden egg and needs to be addressed by collective positioning of the benefits of travel and tourism.

Air transport is a global industry whose maturity continues to be denied by arcane economic regulation. A key factor, for developed and developing countries alike, is the growing need for market liberalization. The concept of air service reciprocity, associated with protection of 'national' carriers, takes precedence in too many countries over a more rational assessment of net national economic and social benefits from tourism and trade. Separate sectoral policies on air transport and tourism in many states results in a fundamental and often conflicting disconnect which is a severe constraint on the development of travelism as a whole and thus of each of its components.

A primary concern on the regulatory front is that air carrier ownership and control is still vested in the citizens of single states or, in the case of Europe, a group of states. This puts severe constraints on access to capital (in a capital-intensive industry) and on market access (in a transnational industry). It has led to indirect and ultimately unsatisfactory means of obtaining market access such as alliances and code-sharing. Nowhere is this more of a constraint than in developing countries. But in Latin America, to some extent in Asia, and now potentially in Africa, innovative and pragmatic means have been found which not only overcome these constants but demonstrate leadership and benefits in liberalization.

Developing economies with high growth tend to be those where the tourist sector is key to economic activity. Many of the developing countries which have liberalised air transport continue to experience travel and tourism growth above the world average. At the same time there are quantum changes in originating markets and the South-South paradigm is changing the face of air transport as well as tourism.

Concern is raised by western carriers regarding the increasing global reach of rising airline stars from the Gulf and China. But if such airlines can bring in the tourists cheaper and more efficiently with net benefit to a country, why not let them? The host countries of these airlines offer a valuable lesson through seamless integration of trade, tourism and aviation policy. Attempts are being made to emulate this lesson in a few developing countries which are primarily tourism destination markets and, not incidentally, are a consolidator of 'green growth'.

Concerns about continuity of service in international air transport are a factor in the reluctance of many developing countries to embrace the liberalization process. In today's world, the risk of foreign carrier withdrawal is lessened since if one carrier withdraws there is often another to take its place, and through 'hubbing' even small markets can be made profitable as 'spokes'.

Furthermore, ICAO and UNWTO issued a joint study in 2005 on Essential Service and Tourism Development Routes (ESTDR). This important liberalization concept, originally developed as a safeguard, applies to international 'poor country' routes which are socio-politically equivalent to thin traffic domestic routes in developed countries currently supported by essential air service schemes, with associated subsidy and market protection. There is now a case for the concept to be applied more widely, for example in support of route franchising to reduce market fragmentation in Africa. Also of relevance is that the framework of regulatory and exemption/financial recompense principles and provisions set out in the study might well apply to resolution of the climate change impasse described above, since *inter alia* it is consistent with both UNFCCC and ICAO provisions; an example of fertilization across economic and environmental silos.

The conclusion regarding the economic pillar is that thinking beyond the silo provides synergy and positive results. It creates a larger box: an integrated, collective vision for travelism.

International tourism and air passenger transport are locked at the hip. International air passengers are predominantly tourists (business and leisure travellers). Over half of international tourist arrivals glob-ally are by air, with much higher proportions for long-haul destinations. International tourism and air passenger transport traffic and revenues tend to move in lockstep.

International tourist arrivals are forecast by UNWTO to reach 1.8 billion by 2030, compared with an estimated figure of 1 billion for 2012. Of particular interest is that emerging economy destinations will surpass advanced economy destinations by 2015 and have a 58 per cent share by 2030. Air transport market share compared with surface will continue to increase, if at a slower pace than in recent years.

But, as illustrated above, if all this is to be achieved, and particu-larly with the increasingly fundamental focus on green growth, some challenges have to be overcome, including institutional self-interest. Aviation will not surmount these challenges on its own. As stated in the January 2012 report of the UN Secretary-General's High-Level Panel on Global Sustainability, 'We must overcome the legacy of fragmented institutions established around single-issue "silos".'

On the travelism front, UNWTO has already taken some initiatives in the form of a *Global Leaders for Tourism* campaign (with WTTC), the *T20* (a Tourism Ministers forum leading into the G20), and a programme on *Tourism and the Millennium Development Goals.* Air transport now needs to be seen at the core of positioning travelism as a strategic industry. ICAO is in the early stages of an initiative on sustainable development of air transport and IATA is focusing on a value chain which not only encompasses airlines, airports, air navigation service providers, and manufacturers, but also plans to link up with travel and tourism, calling for a single voice on such issues as economics, taxes, liberalization, security and facilitation, and the environment. The time is now ripe for an overarching, collective approach, aimed at green growth, with developing countries and their institutions, both public and private, playing a key role.

# Francis McCosker

## Managing Director, International Organizations, Microsoft

## A global tourism transformation – sustainably connecting the unconnected

Francis (Frank) McCosker, Microsoft Managing Director International Organizations, handles the company's engagement with multilateral organisations, including the International Financial Institutions, Intergovernmental Organisations and the bilateral providers of Official Development Assistance (ODA). Frank joined Microsoft's East European Headquarters in 1997 and during his seven years with the company he successfully carried out key public sector related development projects. In 1999 he was promoted to General Manager of Microsoft Bulgaria establishing a subsidiary and assisting the Bulgarian government in initiating strategic public sector reform projects. He became General Manager of Microsoft's East European Headquarters in Munich, Germany, in 2000, and in 2004 promoted into his current role. Frank has also spent a personal life of public service with a focus on communities and people in need.

Tourism is one of the world's largest economic activities. In 2011, the United Nations World Tourism Organisation (UNWTO) estimated that there were nearly 1 billion international tourist arrivals – almost double the figure from 1995, with estimates of 1.8 billion by 2030. It is also amongst the top three economic drivers of nearly half of the world's least developed countries. Overall, tourism contributes about 8% of global GDP, and one in 12 jobs worldwide.

As such impressive figures show, tourism has become an increasingly vital contributor to economic growth for both developed and developing countries. The more this sector can grow sustainably, the broader the two-way economic benefit, particularly for the world's poorest counties, where the investment and foreign exchange boost can be a massive socio-economic driver.

This reality has been at the heart of UNWTO and Microsoft collaboration for several years, combining tourism knowledge and technical innovation to see how global tourism can benefit from the latest technologies. Our work together has focused on helping tourism managers and country authorities to better leverage the opportunities offered by tourism and address some of the challenges they face, using leading edge internet focused thinking.

Internet technology is enabling a revolution in how people travel – making it easier to do everything from researching destinations to booking flights and hotels to learning the local language to uploading pictures and videos after a trip. According to a study from travel industry research group PhoCusWright, of internet users in developed countries like the U.S., U.K. and Germany who travel for leisure, at least 98% planned their trip online. As internet penetration rates increase and global income levels rise, it is an exciting time for the travel industry as more people both come online and become business or leisure travellers.

Clearly in this transformation, the ability to access the internet cheaply and seamlessly is a key factor. The International Telecommunications Union (ITU) found that in 2011 of the world's seven billion people, one-third are online. Interestingly, for the first time, developing countries comprise a majority of internet users – growing from 44% in 2006 to 62% of all internet users in 2011. Impressive though these numbers are, the people that are not connected are particularly significant for the development agenda – where bridging the digital divide has long been recognized as a potential socio-economic game changer. Simply put, for many developing countries yet to reach a critical mass of connected citizens, the imperative to connect to increase education, capacity building and competitiveness is a national priority.

In the case of Africa, which contains 39 of the world's least developed countries (LDCs) expanding connectivity is a pancontinental priority that goes hand in hand with the expansion of tourism, boosting the infrastructure of travel – airports, high speed trains and superhighways.

According to a study by the World Bank, a 10% increase in broadband penetration can boost the GDP growth of low- and middle-income developing countries by 1.38% — more than any other telecommunication service. Even countries with higher internet penetration rates expect the demand for internet access only to increase, putting more strain on existing broadband networks and technology infrastructure.

These statistics show how the use of ICT tools is clearly becoming a key competitive factor for both tourism destinations and enterprises. There is agreement amongst many policymakers that expanding broadband access is a matter of national competitiveness – the challenge now is how to do so affordably and efficiently.

Fortunately technology is being pioneered that has the capacity to revolutionize internet access globally – ensuring that the billions of new internet users in the coming years will be able to leverage the benefits of being online in their everyday lives – and this includes travellers, host destinations and the companies in the delivery chain

Microsoft Research, in collaboration with many industry and government partners, has over the past several years been working on technology, sometimes referred to as 'Super Wi-Fi', which leverages unused TV spectrum to provide internet access at broadband types of speed.

With ever-growing demand for universal broadband access combined with the exponential mobile data growth we've seen in recent years, there is an urgent need to make more efficient use of usable spectrum. Super Wi-Fi technology uses unassigned TV channels to transmit data, which can be used for broadband-grade voice and video applications. And it does it in a way that does not disrupt existing TV broadcasts.

There are many benefits that both the developing and developed worlds can leverage from putting unused TV spectrum towards Super Wi-Fi technology.

First, the distances covered by such technology can be anywhere between three and ten times greater than those covered by existing unlicensed wireless solutions. Even greater transmission ranges can be achieved at higher power. Second, just like TV, the signal is much less impeded by obstructions like walls or buildings that tend to disrupt wireless signals. Using this spectrum non-exclusively in an unlicensed or 'license-exempt' manner will enable any entity – from the largest mobile operator to a single user or village – to take advantage of this technology.

Perhaps the most appealing feature of Super Wi-Fi for developing countries is the ability to provide wireless solutions at a much lower cost than traditional systems. Low-powered and low-cost TV spectrum-based wireless base-stations could connect entire villages, schools, and hospitals in impoverished rural settings, enabling much higher economic rates of return.

Microsoft is committed to showcasing the use of this spectrum in new and novel ways – including exploring how the next generation of wireless technology can help address critical broadband access issues for many communities who have traditionally been out of the reach of technology. Everyone from a rural community in Kenya to a densely populated urban metropolis in China can take advantage of Super Wi-Fi.

It is expected that the first products based on Super Wi-Fi will enter the US market this year while prototype products already have been used successfully in trials and demonstrations in the Africa, Asia, Europe, and the United States.

Microsoft, with several consortium partners including BT, BBC, and Nokia, is supporting one of the largest Super Wi-Fi trials to date in Cambridge, England. We've also worked with Scotland's University of Strathclyde which is conducting a trial project on the Isle of Bute. The combination of these two trials has tested two distinct but critical benefits of the technology. Cambridge's dense mixture of historic stone buildings and the Isle of Butte's rugged, remote terrain have traditionally presented both technical and economic challenges for wireless technologies. After implementing Super Wi-Fi solutions, we've seen incredibly promising results with Super Wi-Fi being able to better penetrate walls and other obstacles than current Wi-Fi technology and enabling connectivity spanning several kilometres.

The Cambridge trial, after 10 months of rigorous testing and analysis by Microsoft and the 16 other companies involved in the pilot, showed that in both urban and rural settings, Super Wi-Fi successfully helped extend broadband access and offload mobile broadband data traffic.

Base stations used in the Isle of Bute pilot were designed to run on wind or solar power creating a green and sustainable broadband solution. The ability to draw from either wind or solar energy sources will ensure these base stations are able to operate in a variety of physical settings around the world. The use of sustainable technology will be even more important as we look to connect new communities in rural or remote areas.

Since last summer, we've demonstrated Super Wi-Fi at several international forums, including the ITU Telecom World and annual meetings of both the Inter-American Development Bank and Asian Development Bank. Our demo is comprised of a base station and client device, provided by hardware suppliers like Adaptrum and Neul, and a prototype white spaces database developed by Microsoft Research.

A Microsoft XBOX, a Windows 7 PC, or another device is connected to the Internet through the client station allowing users to browse and stream videos and conduct video chats to other trial locations like the Isle of Bute.

Not only do the networks afford a better and more robust service, they are also envisaged to bring down costs and increase availability of access to consumers, helping to close the access gap in internet connectivity.

Meanwhile, cities around the world are struggling to manage the mass urbanization taking place at record rates – with access to technology and the promise of more opportunities key drivers of this movement. By using Super Wi-Fi technology in rural settings, we may now be able to provide access to technology previously unavailable to many communities and begin to offer substantially increased economic opportunities in rural areas. Sustainable rural access to the internet could also lead to new rural economies – providing a promising alternative to crowded urban environments.

Super Wi-Fi can also help to address the increasing consumer demand for internet-connected wireless devices, enabling more users to experience the benefits of always-connected devices many of us take for granted in the developed world.

By allocating this spectrum to Super Wi-Fi technology, we can dramatically increase the number of devices connected to the internet – helping more and more people to scan for a hotel on their next holiday, or research a restaurant for dinner on a business trip. The best news about this technology is that we should soon be seeing it reach its commercialization tipping point, enabling a new era of sustainable connectivity.

Super Wi-Fi will play an important part in ensuring that the underserved communities of today have access to the technology of tomorrow. It has the potential to make broadband technology incredibly more accessible and in a sustainable manner. Universal access to broadband will be one of the most important drivers of economic growth supporting the growth of both inward and outward tourism in the coming decade.

We believe Super Wi-Fi is one of the most important and disruptive technologies that is coming online. As policymakers and the technology industry start to implement Super Wi-Fi solutions in the coming years, global tourism will also soon start to see the first results as more and more people around the world are able to gain access to the online world.

Moreover in terms of the green growth agenda, any new technology that can accelerate the digital inclusion of the poorest countries and strengthen the capacity of industrialized countries will make a significant contribution to global transformation. Where that technology is also synergistically boosting the travelism capacity of those countries, with the employment, development and trade benefits, it's a socio-economic double whammy.

# Supachai Panitchpakdi

### Secretary-General of the UN Conference on Trade and Development

### Sustainable tourism development – a public-private partnership

Dr Supachai began his second four-year term as Secretary-General of UNCTAD on 1 September 2009. He received his Ph.D. in Economic Planning and Development at the Netherlands School of Economics in 1973 under the supervision of Prof. Jan Tinbergen, the first Nobel laureate in economics. He began his professional career at the Bank of Thailand in 1974, was later elected to the Thai Parliament and appointed Deputy Minister of Finance. In 1988, he was appointed Director and Advisor, and subsequently President, of the Thai Military Bank, later becoming Senator, and Deputy Prime Minister, entrusted with oversight of the country's economic and trade policy. He was active in the Uruguay Round and in shaping APEC and ASEAN regional agreements, A distinguished academic, he has authored books on globalization and trade policy.

R ecent UNCTAD research and technical co-operation activities have supported the view that tourism could make an important contribution to broad-based economic growth in least developed and developing countries, boosting income-generating opportunities, foreign exchange earnings and economic diversification. This is a relatively new view, as it was not so long ago that in many developing countries tourism was considered a less important or appropriate activity than more traditional activities such as manufacturing and agriculture.

This reappraisal of the potential benefits of tourism has come about in part because of the sector's dynamism: it has become a multi-billion-dollar-a-day global business. According to the UN World Tourism Organization (UNWTO), the worldwide contribution of tourism to gross domestic product (GDP) exceeds 5 per cent and is estimated to account for 6-7 per cent of the overall number of jobs worldwide (direct and indirect). Equally importantly, however, the reappraisal has come with a renewed appreciation of the need to have an engaged, 'developmental state' working actively alongside the private sector, to enable tourism to deliver more of the positive benefits that are desired and fewer of the negative ones. For tourism to be environmentally, socially and economically sustainable, it is essential to have a partnership between the public and the private spheres. Government's role includes ensuring that industrial policy, macroeconomic policy, investment policy and other regulations relating to the environment, to labour standards, and to training are in place and harnessed to serve national tourism and development goals, among other things.

The relative robustness of the sector in light of the recent economic and financial crisis has reinforced these new views. Despite having been hard-hit, the tourism sector continues to be extremely dynamic. Demand for tourism services fell abruptly in mid-2008, and from mid-2008 to mid-2009, all regions, with the exception of Africa, recorded declines in international arrivals. However, the UNWTO reported that tourism began growing again in the last quarter of 2009, and this trend continued in 2010 and 2011.  Growth has been especially fast in emerging and developing economies, where the share of international tourism arrivals accounted for 47 per cent of the world total in 2010, up from 32 per cent in 1990.

Least developed countries (LDCs) have not been excluded from this boom in tourism. International tourism is among the top three foreign exchange earners for as many as 23 of the 49 LDCs. For seven LDCs, it is their single largest revenue earner, inducing significant income-multiplier effects. By boosting per capita income, tourism has been a decisive factor supporting graduation from LDC status for countries such as Cape Verde, and Maldives. Three other small island LDCs (Samoa, Tuvalu and Vanuatu) are also regarded as potential gradua-tion cases in light of progress that has been, to a large extent, fuelled by tourism growth.

In part, the recovery of global tourism can be credited to post-crisis recovery measures that some countries implemented to stimulate their economies and restore growth – including fiscal, monetary or marketing support to the tourism sector. Moreover, tourism's resilience also owes much to a continuation of the trends of south-south investment and south-south tourism, alongside the more traditional north-south tourism of the past.

Another reason that least developed and developing countries are looking to tourism is that it can scale up very quickly, even from a low base. In the United Republic of Tanzania, where tourism is a relatively recent activity compared to some of its African neighbours, gross tourism receipts accounted for less than 10 per cent of total export earnings in the mid-1980s, but by the middle of the current decade had risen to become the country's top export earner, outperforming other services categories and accounting for over 35 per cent of total goods and services exports. In Tanzania, as with many other developing countries, tourism is promoted for its labour-generating and linkage-creating opportunities especially compared to mining, which offers markedly fewer employment possibilities.

Such linkages are not likely to emerge automatically and will require active government support. UNCTAD research conducted as part of a four-year project examining the development impact of foreign and domestic investment in tourism found many examples where tourism had generated significant linkages that boosted job creation and revenues for local enterprises and suppliers of goods and services, including agriculture. However we also found that much more could be done in terms of deepening and expanding these. In some cases, linkages had not developed at all, because of failures in the supply chain or in the necessary supporting infrastructures. The lack of a wholesale market, for example, or limited cool-storage facilities meant that hotels were unable to buy locally and relied on imported products instead, depriving local producers of the chance to participate in the sector and also requiring costly (and polluting) transport. In other cases, especially with very small scale enterprises, local suppliers were unable to guarantee regular deliveries or reliable quality. Sometimes the 'gap' was more one of information and perception. We found that tourism enterprises were unaware of the potential that could be offered by local communities, just as the local communities were unaware of the needs of the tourism enterprises. There was a clear role for government or an independent agency to help enable these linkages to be made, because they were unlikely to emerge on their own.

The need for an active role by government becomes even more evident with regard to the environmental impacts of tourism. Pressure on land use and waste generation can become significant problems especially for remote or island communities. This is also true for the high levels of water and energy use which the tourism industry is known for. Such use may exceed local sustainable limits and displace other economic and social uses of limited water and energy supplies. Again, strong regulatory and government support will be required to ensure tourism develops in a sustainable manner, consistent with local needs.

However this is achieved, it is clear that there will be a role for government to help chart this new course – including to guide the private sector. UNCTAD's Least Developed Countries Report 2010 argued that the State has an important role to play in guiding, coordinating and stimulating the private sector towards investment in national productive capacity, and this will be even more important if a transformative shift towards a more environmentally sustainable form of economic activity is to be realized. This may require large-scale investment in renewable sources of energy, for example, which the private sector is unlikely to achieve on its own; or the enforcement of new, more ecologically sensitive building practices and regulations, among many examples.

Evidence already exists to show that the redesign of tourism products can help to reduce the negative impacts of tourism operations and activities on environmental resources. For example ecotourism based on small-scale, community-led tourism operations, is now estimated to account for as much as 20 per cent of the international tourism market, and some LDCs, such as Uganda and Nepal, are already active in the ecotourism market. Governments have a role to play in setting a favourable policy and regulatory environment for eco-tourism. The private sector has also come to realize that community buy-in is essential for eco-tourism operations in ensuring the protection of natural resources, which most of these activities are based on.

Inadequate infrastructure remains one of the biggest impediments to developing the tourism sector, maximizing its benefits and minimizing its negative externalities. Private companies could be more involved in the provision of infrastructure, which should also benefit local communities. Attracting foreign direct investment (FDI) remains an important objective for the sector, particularly in LDCs where domestic resources are often limited, there is a lack of managerial know-how in the sector and connectivity with the network of international tour operators is generally weak. Investment promotion agencies (IPAs) can play an important role in attracting FDI into the tourism sector.

However, the private sector should not be relied upon for 'public good' types of investment. Also, the typical focus on foreign investment tends to neglect the essential role that is played by domestic investment. Domestic investors should be given an equally high priority, including by offering prospective entrepreneurs not only managerial training but also access to finance, because it is typically extremely difficult for small or new enterprises to access capital at internationally competitive rates, placing them at a further disadvantage compared to international firms. Encouraging the domestic sector is important in its own right, to contribute to national goals of job-creation, economic diversification and broadening the economic base. However it is also necessary as a complement to foreign investment and to help countries realise the benefits of FDI. UNCTAD research found that while many countries expend considerable efforts in attracting FDI, they are much less likely to put in place the flanking policies that will help them to get the fuller benefits from it, once it arrives (see UNCTAD 2007, 2009 and 2011 reports 'FDI and tourism – the development dimension').

The mainstreaming of tourism into national development and economic policymaking through a comprehensive national tourism strategy should include the involvement of all stakeholders, including local communities and the local private sector. The National Services Policy Reviews undertaken by UNCTAD, such as for Nepal and Uganda, assist countries in developing an integrated and holistic approach to tourism development.

International organizations are also committed to support States and the private sector through capacity building. Such activities are one of the steps towards local ownership of sustainable tourism development. One example involves UNCTAD and the International Trade Centre (ITC), which have joined forces to strengthen capacities in the tourism sector of Benin. Thanks to a pilot project targeting three communities, Benin can now count on a pool of tourism officials, from the public and the private sector, knowledgeable of sustainable tourism concepts, having benefited from concrete technical assistance activities. In another current project, UNCTAD and other UN agencies are working with organic agriculture producers and tourism enterprises in Laos to help promote more sustainable agriculture and strengthen the new sector's links with tourism. A related objective is to boost Laos's profile and tourism 'offer' in the increasingly competitive tourism market.  Bolstering the role of sustainable agriculture can even have wider macroeconomic effects on top of the obvious environmental benefits, including for example reducing the country's reliance on costly imported inputs such as fuel and petro-chemical based pesticides, all of which must be paid for in a foreign currency and which can have important implications for the balance of payments. This project is shortly to be rolled out in a series of other countries, and it reflects the way that the UN can 'work as One' to help developing countries put in place a more sustainable form of tourism.

P

# Jeanine Pires

President of the Tourism and Business Council at FECOMÉRCIO, Sao Paulo, Brazil

## Sustainable development of travel and tourism in South America

Professor Jeanine Pires, Director at Pires & Associates and President of the Tourism and Business Council at FECOMÉRCIO, São Paulo, Brazil. Jeanine was President and Director of Business and Events at the Brazilian Tourism Board, EMBRATUR, during President Lula da Silva's mandate, and Special Advisor of the Brazilian Minister of Sports for the 2016 Olympic and Paralympic Games. For 18 years, Jeanine was a teacher at the Federal University of Alagoas, Brazil. Jeanine is a professional with 16 years of leadership in the tourism sector, focusing on national and international marketing for destinations. She managed teams for the bidding and event promotion sector, coordinating marketing and communication platforms of Brazil as a tourism destination in more than 40 countries. Her leadership of multitasking teams focused on event management, marketing, sales and institutional relations created a new environment which led Brazil to improve confidence in the international tourism market.

Considered within its social, economic and environmental dimensions, sustainable development is an increasingly important topic in the global agenda and the travel and tourism industry is a major player in this field. Although the sector has not been seen to be in a leadership role, it is engaging more and more – green issues are central to studies, agreements and plans in tourism worldwide. Moreover, sustainable tourism programmes and practices, by definition, will have to involve both public and private sectors to seriously contribute to green growth – particularly initiatives that might be considered as replicable models.

The complex matters discussed at the Rio +20 Conference in June 2012 can be boiled down to four basic issues for our sector:

1 Reviewing responses and evolving challenges of the planet's sustainable development over the past two decades to assess the

impacts of policies, agreements and programs  for environment and development – including the pivotal climate change issues;

2   Identifying the revised Agenda 21 to include successful practices that can be shared, replicated and adapted to meet community specifics;

3   Assessing key public and private policies that have worldwide repercussions;

4   A better understanding of the level of importance that the 'green' agenda has in the global tourism industry's policies.

As regards the travel sector, a brief general assessment shows that several successful initiatives, both of policy and practice, have already become widespread. In fact, they have multiplied worldwide and are increasingly part of company culture and public policy in several cities, regions and countries. Yet, we are still a long way from establishing common sustainable policies and practices throughout all sectors of this industry, or from having most destinations and companies, that form this huge economic chain, adopt practices that reaffirm a broad and effective agenda geared towards balancing economic development, nature preservation and  social inclusion.

In the future, the travel and tourism industry has the capacity to further develop that green agenda – but it must be re-invigorated now if it is to be truly a part of the mainstream sustainable development agenda. My objective here is to point out some topics for discussion in this agenda for developing countries, or so called emerging countries, in Latin America.

Considering macroeconomic and social aspects around the world, Latin American countries can benefit from their current economic and social momentum as well as from international alliances and treaties. They can skip phases, leapfrog historic barriers and move on steadily towards a sustainable future, be it in social advances, poverty reduction, the level of destination and tourism product development, or from the authenticity of travellers' experiences. Emerging countries need to generate jobs, preserve their biological diversity as a tourism asset and appreciate their cultural heritage in order to gain more competitiveness in the tourism sector.

Latin America and emerging countries have their own peculiarities and distinct realities, but together they are increasingly important according to projections of growth in the sector. For example, in 2011, while average global travel growth was 4%, the South American continent alone grew around 10%. Whilst the direct impact of the GDP in the global economy should grow around 2.8% in 2012, in the BRICS, this growth should be of 8.7%, and in Latin America of 6.5%, according to latest figures for the World Travel & Tourism Council.

In Latin American countries, the impact of travelism on GDP, job creation, foreign exchange inflows and investments is a factor that makes this sector one of the most important for the development of their economies as a whole. Predictions made by UNWTO indicate that in 2015 emerging economies should overtake mature markets in the total percentage of travel around the world.

I consider the challenge of emerging and developing countries more adverse and intense than that of the tourism industry in mature economies. Of course developed countries still have many challenges to face but those in developing economies are bigger in scope and far more complex. Many Latin American countries have large social gaps, poverty, low levels of schooling, weaknesses in general infrastructure and the natural capital of these regions is often poorly preserved.

An illustration of this is in aviation, where significant emissions from our industry occur and are often cited by those lobbying for action on climate change. Here, the adoption of regional and global agreements would be more effective than the implementation of unilateral taxes and charges for curbing carbon emissions. Such unilateral taxes and charges on flying penalize faraway poorer countries in South America, creating cost barriers to increasing tourism which has such an important role to play in poverty alleviation.

To continue to increase visitation, many South American developing countries must overcome very basic problems such as inadequate sanitation where raw sewage is pumped into the ocean polluting beaches, or national heritage sites and protected areas which do not have really effective conservation frameworks.

Large numbers of high quality staff are required in all sectors of the tourism industry, which creates excellent job opportunities in many Latin American countries. However the tourism sector is constantly faced with unqualified staff resulting from low levels of schooling. In this same context, the training and preparation of staff and guides at historical and natural sites is a particular challenge, because many such sites do not have adequate conservation rules in place. Moreover in many places, there are poor public policies or private initiatives for preserving local identity and for protecting natural and cultural heritage within a planned, systematic and continuous framework.

What is now required are strong, long term coherent linkages with educational, professional training, health and employment policies in order to establish public and private strategies that optimize the use of tourism assets and resources, in the broader framework of green growth transformation. Furthermore, in order to ensure the sustainability of tourism destinations, the quality of visitors' experience and business profitability, public and private investments will need to be ramped up and more effectively coordinated for synergy.

These basic challenges must be tackled quickly and efficiency in order to cope with the pace of change of other existing policies that make the travel and leisure industry an ally in the construction of a more egalitarian, inclusive, and continuously innovative society.

The good news facing this complex scenario for many Latin American economies is that the tourism sector has a great capacity to generate jobs and to involve local communities in sustainable policies. Travel and tourism includes many economy sectors, big and small service providers, the appreciation of local assets, and it has a great capacity of recovery during times of crises. Moreover, there is increasing awareness among stakeholders, in both the public and private sector, that tourism will only be successful and have long term, sound economic returns if it takes into account its wider assets, natural wealth and local cultures, and if it provides quality service and uses well qualified, well trained labour. This needs to be at all levels ,with sufficient economic returns that allow innovation and investments aimed at transforming and building quality visitor experiences.

Ecotourism, nature and adventure tourism are important sub-sectors in many Latin American countries. Certification programs have contributed to transforming the way in which local destinations, tourists and operators behave in relation to natural resources, to the appreciation of biodiversity and to the preservation of cultural heritage.

In some communities in developing Latin American countries it is common for the tourism sector be in the forefront of arguing for public policies for preservation of natural assets. It is also common for business to create social inclusion programmes to employ people from local communities in hotels; to support environmental education programmes and to use local culture for visitors' experience. The awareness that both the present and long term survival of tourism's economic activities depends on environmental conservation and social inclusion is a major step towards change. In many places, these business practices have supplemented or even replaced public policies.

To give just three typical and replicable world class examples:

- Inkaterra, Peru winner of the 2012 Tourism for Tomorrow Conservation Award was judged to have made an outstanding direct and tangible contribution to the preservation of nature, including the protection of wildlife, expanding and restoring natural habitat, and supporting biodiversity conservation. It has been a pioneer in sustainable tourism, supporting scientific research for the Conservation of Ecosystems and Natural Resources from its ecotourism programmes. It designs replicable models for local communities and experiences for travellers which capture the culture and nature of Peru. Its comprehensive sustainability programs seek to exceed formal regulations and standards in terms of product quality, customer service, environmental impacts, staff remuneration and the like, and above all, with high positive impact on local populations.

- In 2008, The Marriott Corporation pledged $2 million in corporate funding to help preserve 1.4 million acres of rainforest in the Juma Reserve in the state of Amazonas, Brazil. Marriott partners and guests are encouraged to contribute. The Juma Reserve is the first Reduced Emissions from Deforestation and Degradation (REDD) initiative validated by the Climate, Community, and Biodiversity Alliance.

- The Cristalino Jungle Lodge in Mato Grosso State, Brazil began, as one woman's way to protect the rainforest and is today a global beacon of national park development. If the lodge didn't exist, most of the rainforest near Cristalino would have been cut down a long time ago. When something threatens the habitat, the owners pull together to find a way to purchase more land to conserve. They successfully recovered 26 of the 126 watersheds in the area, and they have preserved roughly 2 million hectares in under 20 years. They have been so successful that the government designated Cristalino as a national park.

The holistic vision in which all social, economic and environmental aspects are complementary to the development of the tourism industry is becoming more widely understood across the South-American continent.

To complement local and national initiatives, greater regional integration is required across the continent. This is particularly the case for creation of new mechanisms to effectively integrate policies and practices that benefit whole regions and allow rapid spread of technology and training. Tourism meetings and workgroups often have little effectiveness in practical green growth terms and suffer discontinuity with changes in public management. Last but not least many exclude private actors and NGO's from important deliberations and decisions – often perpetuating the status quo as a result.

Regionally, nationally and locally, provision of basic infra-structure, faster and more suitable public policies, investment in technology, education, research and innovation together with enhanced financing will be required for tourism to move towards balanced growth. Public planning and management of tourism destinations, together with the best and innovative private practices have to be incorporated in sector strategies if tourism is to increase its competiveness and sustainability. And increasingly, consumer demand for green products and experiences will imposes the use of renewable energy and the adoption of more sustainable practices for destinations and the businesses that operate in them.

Finally, a key element to consider is the balance between the different needs of visitors and the loading, or carrying capacity, of tourism destinations. It is necessary to reverse the paradigm that the more tourists a destination gets, the more successful it is. More important is the overall economic, social, cultural and environmental benefit to the whole destination. And at the end of the day, given the full facts, the choice is largely theirs as to the kind of tourism they want. Finding the economic, social and environmental balance is a key factor for the success of tourism today and in the future for Latin America. This industry, besides being the job creation, peace and happiness business, is also the sustainability business.

# Randy Powell

## President & CEO, Armstrong Group

## A sustainable train of thought

Randy Powell, President and CEO of Armstrong Group, was appointed to his current position in October, 2009 after spending two years as the first outside President in the company's 20 year history, second only to the founder. He joined Armstrong Group with 25 years of extensive consumer products and services business leadership. Prior to joining Armstrong Group in 2007, he was the Global President of Maple Leaf Fresh Foods, President & CEO of Second Cup, and President of S.C. Johnson and Sons. During his career, Mr. Powell has received a number of accolades, including the Financial Post's "Top 40 under 40" award and Business Hall of Fame recognition from Sheridan College. Randy currently serves on the Faculty Advisory Board for Sauder Business School – University of British Columbia.

Over the years, rail travel has been a preferred mode of transportation for those seeking a better pace and more intimate travel experience, where the journey itself becomes a fundamental part of the destination. With many of us striving to be more sustainably conscious in our everyday decisions, riding the rails has attracted another group of travellers, who plan their trips using 'greener' ways to see the world. In comparison to travelling by plane or car, train travel has been getting the green thumbs up as an eco-travel alternative. A recent CNN story suggested that, 'travelling by rail is on average three to 10 times less $CO_2$-intensive compared to road or air transport.' Even well-known Canadian environmentalist, David Suzuki recommends on his website to 'fly less' and 'consider greener options such as buses or trains' to reduce your carbon footprint.

As the Rocky Mountaineer train travels through some of the most stunning and naturally diverse areas in the world, we take great pride in our commitment to preserving and protecting the natural beauty of Canada's West.

Long before being 'green' was top of mind, Rocky Mountaineer was committed to environmental sustainability. In 1995, we became the first train company in North America to install sewage holding tanks on 100% of our rail cars, and before it was mandatory on Canadian railways, we implemented a 'no smoking' policy onboard all of our trains to minimize the risk of forest fires and littering. With the understanding that Rocky Mountaineer owes much of its success to the unspoiled scenery, fresh air and abundant wildlife found in Western Canada as well as a greater desire to protect the regions we travel through, our Caretakers program was born in 2003.

We designed the Caretakers program with the primary goal 'to promote the development and implementation of sustainable operating policies and practices throughout Rocky Mountaineer.' We wanted to be leaders in sustainable tourism and understood very early on the importance of developing innovative sustainable tourism programs that support all three pillars of sustainability: environmental stewardship, economic sustainability and social responsibility.

In the spring of 2006, Rocky Mountaineer enlisted the expertise of a leading consultant in environmental management and planning, to undertake a complete environmental audit of our operations. The study covered our rail services, the Rocky Mountaineer Station in Vancouver and the Kamloops maintenance yard. The report provided a comprehensive snapshot of the company's environmental management policies, programs and initiatives related to solid waste and energy management. Based on the audit, we began developing a series of action plans to address areas of concern and capitalize on opportunities for improvement.

Waste reduction has become a key focus for us on all Rocky Mountaineer trains. Following the environmental audit, we implemented new policies and partnered with recycling operators in various communities along our rail routes. Since 2007, we have recycled approximately 82% of the meal trays on-board, tested a composting program on our train to Whistler and on our Rainforest to Gold Rush route with the assistance of a local waste management company. And three days a week when the train arrives into Vancouver, all leftover food is donated to the local Food Bank. We have also removed disposable plates and cutlery in all crew cars. In 2012, we added yet another initiative by eliminating water bottles on board the train. This single initiative has reduced the use of over 60,000 plastic bottles every season.

Our diesel locomotives have been the biggest challenge and therefore opportunity in reducing our carbon footprint. We have made some strides with the cutting edge, ZTR Smart Start technology, which has been installed in all of Rocky Mountaineer's locomotives. This system automates the shutdown and restart of the locomotive engines, significantly reducing idling time which is an important ecological move towards reducing fuel consumption, exhaust emissions and noise pollution. We have taken our environmental initiatives a step further and in 2011, tested multiple generator set locomotives, which use three smaller engines rather than one big engine to power the train. Our overall goal is to create custom designed engines that meet our needs and lessen the impact on the environment. We aspire to one day be the first passenger rail service in North America to operate a hybrid locomotive.

In addition to our efforts to reduce waste and greenhouse gas emissions, Rocky Mountaineer is also focused on supporting environmental causes. Our trains follow some of the most important salmon habitats in North America and the largest runs in the world. With pressures of climatic change, warm water and unpredictable flows, some of these once abundant populations of salmon have declined to the point that they are swimming a fine line between survival and extinction. In a bid to help sustain and protect the natural environment along our rail routes, we entered into a long-term financial partnership with the Pacific Salmon Foundation, a not–for-profit organization dedicated to rebuilding sustainable and naturally diverse salmon stocks. The unprecedented eight-year commitment which began in 2007 is the equivalent of two salmon life-cycles.

The Pacific Salmon Foundation programs include support of the *Fraser Salmon Hero Awards* program, which recognizes regional stewardship of the waterways, individuals, businesses and corporations, ongoing fundraising and educational events within the many communities Rocky Mountaineer operates, and assistance in the *Gates Creek Recovery Effort*, an important watershed on the Fraser River. Through our work with the Pacific Salmon Foundation, we will continue to educate our employees and hundreds of thousands of guests about the importance of protecting our salmon population.

Another organization that we support on an ongoing basis is Tree Canada, a not-for-profit charity that encourages Canadians to plant and care for trees in rural and urban areas. To celebrate the annual anniversary of each of its employees, Rocky Mountaineer plants a tree along its rail routes. Since 2007, over 3,000 trees have been planted by the company. Additionally, Rocky Mountaineer donates more than $250,000 annually to support local charity fundraisers and community initiatives.

With our rail journeys travelling through several regions, we understand the importance of enhancing economic sustainability along our routes and are dedicated to building strong community partnerships. We promote regional tourism and encourage economic development, using local businesses and suppliers whenever possible. Rocky Mountaineer guests contribute to local economies through accommodation, dining, shopping and visiting local attractions. For example, the city of Kamloops, BC, which is the overnight stop on two of Rocky Mountaineer's rail journeys, has seen an economic benefit of approximately $20 million annually. The city of Quesnel, BC, the midway point for guests travelling on the Rainforest to Gold Rush route has also experienced a multi-million dollar impact to its economy. Rocky Mountaineer also employs many people in the communities it serves, to meet the needs of its guests or to service its trains.

We have always tried to lead the way with sustainable tourism and became one of the first members of the BC Sustainable Tourism Collective, which was founded on the vision that travels within BC can foster appreciation and stewardship for the natural environment, regions and communities. As a testament to our social, economic and environmental dedication, Rocky Mountaineer received the honour of Tourism British Columbia's first *Foresight and Sustainability Award* for leadership in sustainable tourism policies and programs.

Even after being acknowledged by our peers as a leader in sustainable tourism, we feel we have just touched the surface with our programs and initiatives and could always do more. It is our ongoing commitment to preserve and protect Canada's natural resources by eliminating as much waste as we can and continue to make a strong environmental impact by reducing our carbon footprint. Looking ahead, we strive to become carbon neutral through our ongoing environmental initiatives. Our goal is to provide our guests with life changes experiences on the Rocky Mountaineer, while preserving and protecting the environment and enriching the communities we travel through.

# Taleb Rifai

Secretary-General, UNWTO World
Tourism Organization

## One billion tourists ... one billion opportunities for more sustainable tourism

Taleb Rifai, Secretary-General of the World Tourism Organization (UNWTO), previously Deputy Secretary-General, has an extensive background in international and national public service, the private sector and academia. This includes Assistant Director General of the International Labour Organization (ILO), Minister of Planning and International Cooperation, Minister of Information and Minister of Tourism and Antiquity, Jordan, CEO of Jordan's Cement Company, and Director General of the Jordan Investment Promotion Corporation. Prior to public service, he taught and practiced architecture and urban design in Jordan and the USA.

By the end of 2012, international tourist arrivals will stand at a record one billion. This is an extraordinary achievement for our sector – and welcome news for the hundreds of millions who depend on tourism for their livelihoods – yet, it is also a moment to stop, step back, and assess where tourism fits into the global sustainability debate.

Tourism benefits many aspects of our lives – the economy, social progress, job creation and poverty alleviation. But it is becoming clearer and clearer that tourism's expansion cannot continue indefinitely the way it has until now. Let us use this year to reflect on our achievements and focus on the urgency of our challenges for the future. With the United Nations Conference on Sustainable Development (Rio+20) in June 2012, we have a crucial, perhaps unique, opportunity to review our strategy towards a more responsible tourism sector.

Today, the tourism sector faces mounting challenges – not least the economic situation which daily hits the headlines. But it is exactly now, amid growing economic concerns that we need to call for the right policies, the adequate investment and the proper business practices that can make tourism one of the most effective tools to generate a fairer and more inclusive growth.

## Tourism, one of the ten strategic sectors on the green economy agenda

The recent crises – financial, economic, food and energy – have high-lighted many of the failures of the current development models. Amidst the global economic crisis of 2009 the UN called for a new growth model – the Green Economy – a model 'that results in improved human wellbeing and social equity, while significantly reducing environmental risks and ecological scarcities'.

When this year in June, the international community comes together in Rio de Janeiro, Brazil, twenty years after the first Rio Earth Summit, to renew its political commitment to sustainable development and address new and emerging challenges, the green economy, in the context of sustainable development and poverty eradication, will be at the heart of discussions.

At the beginning of 2011, the *Green Economy Report* – a ground breaking UN study, led by the UN Environmental Programme (UNEP), on how to spur a green transformation while ensuring continued growth – identified tourism as one of ten economic sectors key to greening the global economy.

The *Tourism* chapter of the *Green Economy Report*, developed together with UNWTO, shows that investing in environmentally-friendly tourism can drive economic growth, lead to poverty reduction and job creation, while improving resource efficiency and minimizing environmental degradation.

The correct investment in green strategies would allow the tourism sector to continue expanding steadily over the coming decades, contributing to much-needed economic growth, employment and development while ensuring significant environmental benefits such as reductions in water consumption, energy use and $CO_2$ emissions.

Investment in green tourism would stimulate job creation, especially in poorer communities, with increased local hiring and sourcing and positive spill-over effects on many other areas of the economy. The direct economic contribution of tourism to local communities would also be increased, maximizing the amount of tourist spending that is retained by the local economy. Finally, a green tourism economy would ensure significant environmental benefits including reductions in water consumption, energy use and $CO_2$ emissions.

Given tourism's sheer size and reach, even small changes towards greening can have significant impacts. But to drive these actions, the sector needs the right policies and the right investment.

## Tourism in the global sustainable development agenda

It was not until the early nineties, and particularly since the first Earth Summit (1992), that the concept of sustainable tourism developed. The principles established in the Rio Declaration served as the basis for the progressive development of UNWTO's sustainable tourism programme, which in 1995 defined sustainable tourism as 'one that meets the needs of present tourists and of the host regions while protecting and promoting opportunities for the future. It is conceived as a way to manage all the resources so that they can meet the economic, social and aesthetic, while respecting the cultural integrity, essential ecological processes, biological diversity and life support systems'.

The World Summit on Sustainable Development (2002), also known as the Johannesburg Summit, emphasized for the first time the importance of the sustainable tourism for poverty reduction, the protection of the environment and of cultural heritage. It was in fact the first time that tourism's role in the global sustainable development agenda was made explicit with the inclusion of tourism in the Joint Programme of Implementation emerging from Johannesburg.

Since the Rio Summit in 1992, and particularly since 2002, significant progress has been made in a number of areas related to sustainable tourism, including environmental sustainability, climate change, social inclusion or gender equality. Nonetheless, much is still to be achieved.

## What will make tourism work for the economy, for society and for the environment?

As we position sustainability at the heart of the tourism development agenda, we need to understand that this is not only our responsibility; it is also in our interest.

People and profit should go together, people and planet should go together, and planet and profit should also go together. Advancing the sustainable agenda in tourism will strengthen the sector's capacity to generate economic growth and create jobs. Investing in green tourism can generate important return on investment and help differentiating businesses while answering market changes at a time when tourists' choices are increasingly influenced by sustainability considerations.

Yet, maximizing the opportunities brought about by a green tourism economy requires adequate action on challenges such as energy emissions, water consumption, waste management, biodiversity preservation and effective management of our cultural and natural heritage.

Governments, and the international community at large, have a key role to play in the move towards green tourism, namely through establishing sound regulatory frameworks, facilitating public investment and incentivizing private engagement. This is of particular importance to the development agenda given the opportunities generated by tourism for least developed and developing countries. Representing around 45% of the exports of services for least developed countries, tourism often provides them with one of the few competitive options to take part in the global economy. It is thus no surprise that tourism has been identified by most Least Developed Countries (LDCs) and Small Islands Developing States (SIDS) as a powerful engine for poverty reduction and development. The challenge before us is to ensure that the world's poorest countries – over half of which have tourism as a priority instrument for poverty reduction – continue to benefit from the income and social opportunities provided by the tourism sector, while tackling the environmental challenge in a win-win formula.

Today, perhaps the single greatest limiting factor for greening tourism is lack of access to capital, particularly at a global scale for developing countries, and at national level for all Small and Medium Enterprises

(SMEs), which represent the bulk of the sector. Public financing is essential for jumpstarting the green economic transformation. Governments and international organizations need to facilitate the financial flow to the tourism sector by prioritizing investment and spending in areas that stimulate greening. Subsidies and tax incentives are just some of the tools that governments can employ. Through public-private partnerships, governments can help to spread the costs and risks of large green tourism investments. At the same time, government spending on public goods such as protected areas, water conservation, waste management, sanitation, public transport and renewable energy infrastructure can reduce the cost of green investments by the private sector in green tourism.

On the business side, innovation should be top of the agenda together with productivity improvement through efficient equipment use, savings from fossil fuel substitution and local and global carbon markets. In joining the sector on these efforts, in 2008, UNWTO launched Hotel Energy Solutions, an initiative co-funded by the European Agency for Competitiveness and Innovation, developed with several international partners, which provides today's hoteliers across the world with access to free electronic software tool to assess their energy consumption and advise them on the most profitable investment alternatives in terms of energy efficiency and renewable energies.

Finally, on the side of the tourists, we need to create more global awareness of the negative impacts tourism can have. Education at all levels is key in this sense. This year, we will be celebrating World Tourism Day (27 September) under the theme 'Tourism and Energy – Powering Sustainable Development'. It is a great opportunity for all countries to reflect on how they can improve the use of energy in the tourism sector and raise awareness among all stakeholders and particularly the public at large to the importance of the rational use of energy.

## Growth and responsibility

By the end of 2012, one billion tourists will have travelled the globe in a single year.

Over the past two decades international tourist arrivals have more than doubled, from 433 million in 1991 to 980 million in 2011. By the end of 2012, one seventh of the world's population will be on the move crossing international borders for tourism in just one year. By 2030 this number is forecast to go up to 1.8 billion.

This is welcome news, given the economic growth and development opportunities generated by the tourism sector. Tourism represents today directly 5% of the GDP and over US$ 1.1 trillion in exports around the globe. More importantly, tourism employs 1 in 12 people worldwide and creates opportunities for decent jobs, particularly for women and youth.

Every tourist means more jobs in tourism and related sectors, higher income for families, increased investment in infrastructure and opportunities for development. Tourism – among the top three sources of export earnings for nearly half of the world's LDCs – is also proving one of the most effective ways to lift people over the poverty line and empower local communities.

At the same time, one billion tourists is a serious responsibility. Unplanned and poorly managed tourism development can cause serious harm. At the end of 2012, wherever the one billionth tourist arrives, and however she or he arrives, they will be part of one of the fastest growing sectors of the world economy. Acting responsibly and sustainably they will be injecting capital in national economies, protecting landmarks, funding natural parks and supporting the jobs and livelihoods of millions. Now is our opportunity to demonstrate tourism's value, not just as an economic force, but as one of the human activities best able to lead a new decade of fairer, stronger and more sustainable growth.

# Ignace Schops

Director, Regional Landscape Kempen
and Maasland

## Re-connecting with our planet: think globally, act locally, change personally!

Ignace Schops, Director of Regional Landschap Kempen en Maasland vzw, is a member of Europarc Federation and a non-governmental organization working on biodiversity, the natural and cultural heritage and sustainable tourism. Ignance is a landscaping expert and herpetologist, and honorary doctor of Hasselt University, Belgium. He is a recipient of the Goldman Environmental Prize 2008, an Ashoka Fellow (world leading organization on social entrepreneurship), and IUCN International Ambassador Biodiversity 2010. Ignace is also the Vice President of Natuurpunt Flanders, Member of the International Advisory Board Countdown 2010, Associate Member of Club of Rome, and Member of Board Natuurpunt Limburg. He has authored and co-authors several books and articles on herpetology, nature conservation and landscaping.

## Introduction

Globally there is a lot of information about the current status of the environment and much of this is rather negative. Continued loss of biodiversity will result in a rapid decline of the earth's natural wealth and a dramatic reduction of future ecosystem services. We are losing both the beauty and richness of our natural environment as well as destabilizing the very ecological processes on which we depend.

To tackle the environmental problems world leaders are trying to find sustainable solutions for present, and most importantly, for future generations. At the last world summit on biodiversity in Nagoya, Japan in 2010 (CBD, COP 10) political leaders and environmental organizations were emphasizing  the integrating of policies, the (local) implementation of global agreements, and the implementation of *The Economics of Ecosystems and Biodiversity* (TEEB).

We need to question ourselves if it is possible to find sustainable win-win solutions integrating various policies and implement those solutions into local situations. On the other hand we need to be aware there is still a gap between policy and practice. We urgently need to translate the environmental jargon into a language all people can understand.

At the Rio +20 Earth Summit the transformation to a green economy will be high on the agenda. Unexpectedly, in Flanders (Belgium), one of the most densely populated and prosperous areas in Europe we can find proof that the protection of biodiversity and the natural heritage can also be a tool for a green economy.

The development of Belgium's first and only national park, the Hoge Kempen National Park, was built on the (Re)connection model, a strategic vision that integrates policies, including policies on sustainable tourism.

In the framework of this letter !e will focus on how sustainable travel and tourism can tackle the problem of biodiversity loss and contribute to the transformation to a green economy.

## Ecosystems and biodiversity loss

Due to the global growth of the human population and the increasing demands for food, fresh water, timber, fibre and fuel humans are changing ecosystems more rapidly and extensively than ever before. Future climate change will also increasingly degrade ecosystems and resultant ecosystem services. The Millennium Ecosystem Assessment pointed out that approximately 60% of ecosystems are being degraded or being used unsustainably with important consequences for human wellbeing. In some parts of the world the transformation of ecosystems brought prosperity, in other regions – often least developed countries – it brought the opposite. The degradation of the ecosystem services are already a significant barrier in achieving the agreed Millennium Development Goals.

The diversity of life on earth is also rapidly changing. Genetic diversity and biodiversity loss – the number of species and genes within species on the planet is declining. Some 10%–30% of mammal, bird and amphibian species are currently threatened with extinction and many species living in freshwater ecosystems are threatened. WWF stated recently that every 13 minutes a species is going extinct.

Isn't there any good news to report? Of course there is! Nature conversation works! For instance, the EU-policy on biodiversity – with the implementation of a nature network across Europe (NATURA 2000) – shows the resilience of nature when it is well managed and maintained.

## Sustainable travel and tourism and sustainable destinations

Tourism is an important and increasing sector. Often whole regions and countries depend on the revenues gained from tourism. The last decade has seen two interesting trends. Firstly, people are seeking for a 'sense of stay' which is more sustainable and healthy. People want to have authentic experiences. Tourist destinations need to adapt to this new approach and one means of supplying such authentic experiences is by conserving and restoring biodiversity. Secondly, trend watchers predicted that LATTE destinations will become more in demand. LATTE is an acronym standing for: Local; Authentic, Traceable, Trustworthy, and Ethical. Tourist destinations which are LATTE-proof will become successful in the future. And again, these places can be found often near biological hot spots. So the smart development of (more) national parks is one important means to stimulate green growth while at the same time tackle the problem of biodiversity loss.

Globally, the success of national parks, biosphere reserves, nature reserves and other protected areas in attracting visitors is increasing. Millions of people are hiking in or having their holidays in protected areas. This overwhelming success causes its own problems: often visitor facilities are located within the parks resulting in overcrowding including traffic jam in peak use time, and visitor impacts on local ecosystems from trampling, waste disposal and resource use. Sometimes species are disappearing due to this constant pressure. And although the related revenues obtained from visitors to protected areas are high, it is almost never enough to cover the costs for maintenance and conservation.

One way to address this problem is to integrate the natural heritage (national parks) into the broader society where a win-win situation can occurs. People would not only visit the national park but the sustainable region, where the national park is located. Regions with an industrial history and a beautiful natural heritage could then transfer into a sustainable tourism region.

## Value is in the eye of the beholder

The restoration of ecosystems and the protection of species have of course financial costs. For a lot of sectors, stakeholders, politicians, corporations and even the general public the financial costs are too high. So, even though the problem of degrading ecosystem services and biodiversity loss is recognized, the willingness to pay for the solutions is often absent. The (protection of the) intrinsic values of our natural heritage aren't convincing enough. The need to come up with additional and convincing arguments is key.

*The Economics of Ecosystems and Biodiversity* (TEEB-report) is drawing attention to the global economic benefits of biodiversity conservation and the growing costs of biodiversity loss and ecosystem degradation. Moreover, the TEEB-report is an interesting tool with practical actions for moving forward.

Raising general awareness is key! If we want to succeed we urgently need to 'translate' policies into a language people can understand. In other words: a polar bear or a tree frog does not know how valuable it is in dollar terms. But if we human beings become aware of their dollar value, we will make sustainable changes and ensure their preservation.

## The (Re)connection Model, finding local solutions for global problems

In order to achieve the dual outcome of green growth and biodiversity conservation, the (Re)connection Model was developed by a Belgian NGO, the Regionaal Landschap Kempen en Maasland (RLKM) and has been repeatedly copied internationally. The (Re)connection Model tries to (re)connect society with nature. The model is built upon 4 main key-elements: (re)connect nature with nature; (re)connect people with nature; (re)connect business with nature and (re)connect policy with practice.

By integrating the natural heritage (often national parks, biosphere reserves, etc.) into communities, it is possible to tackle the problem of biodiversity loss, raise awareness for sustainable solutions, generate economic benefits for the region and create extra (green) jobs. The direct economic benefits are often related to sustainable tourism. A fantastic opportunity for a new type of travelism. Sustainable travelling to sustainable destinations.

## The Limburg case, an interesting example

The Limburg region is located in the northeast of Belgium (Flanders) and is one of the most densely populated areas in Europe. Since coal was found in 1901, the province became prosperous and over 40,000 people were employed by the coalmining company. But time changed and the collieries closed in the final decade of the last century. Luckily the natural heritage of the Limburg region was still beautiful with headlands, forests, lakes, etc.

The RLKM NGO believed strongly in the idea that protecting biodiversity could be a tool for green economic growth. In 1995 RLKM developed a cycling network giving access to the region's natural heritage. The development was combined with a significant investment into conserving the natural heritage. In the past 15 years, an average of over 750,000 cyclists per year visited the region (consisting of 12 municipalities) with an economic benefit of 16.5 million euro each year. Following this success the cycling network was increased to cover the whole Limburg region with an annual average of 2 million cyclists and an annual benefit over 45 million euro. The concept is now copied in several countries in Europe.

The next step was to create the first national park in Belgium in 2006 based on the (Re)connection Model. The Hoge Kempen National Park consisting of 6000 ha and containing over 7000 species was established. The focus of this development was not contained within the borders of the park, but on a much broader region of 25,000 ha, covering six municipalities. The development was funded with money allocated to revitalize the region after coal mining rather than money earmarked for biodiversity, but could be converted to a green goal. A real example of investing in green growth.

All visitor facilities are located outside the national park near to the local communities. The advantage is lower pressure on the species in the national park, a higher concentration of tourists in the community centres and an increasing awareness for biodiversity of citizens.

Over 120 million euro has been invested in the Hoge Kempen National Park project. The travel and sustainable tourism outcomes are remarkable.

Tourism to the region has increased by 32% with over 725,000 people visiting the park in 2010. The overnight stays increased 26% over the 5 years since establishment of the park. The number of hikers increased 85% and annual revenues from park visitation averages 24 million euro a year. In 2010, a TEEB-study was made of the national park project which estimated annual turnover over related to the park of 191 million euro and over 5000 (green) jobs created.

Plans are in place for light-rail and, together with improved public transport and cycle paths, a sustainable travel system will be soon be in place. This will enable both locals and visitors to travel as sustainably as possible. As well, a new research campus, consisting of an international field research centre and a sustainable tourism unit working on green growth and travelism, will be developed with the University of Hasselt and the support of the Limburg Region.

The (Re)connection Model has shown that the protection of biodiversity can be a tool for green growth as well. Limburg is showing that a region can become a sustainable region where it is good to live, to work and to enjoy a fantastic natural destination. A place where tourists want to spent their holidays.

Recently all politicians of the Limburg region, mayors, aldermen and regional ministers, have agreed for the region to become carbon neutral by 2020. This will add further stimulus to the biodiversity conservation and green growth objectives that the (Re)connection Model aims to achieve.

# Daniel Scott

## Canada Research Chair in Global Change and Tourism at the University of Waterloo

## Towards climate compatible travelism

Dr. Daniel Scott is a Canada Research Chair in Global Change and Tourism at the University of Waterloo (Canada). Dr. Scott has worked on the human dimensions of climate change for over a decade and has been a contributing author and expert reviewer for the United Nations Intergovernmental Panel on Climate Change Third and Fourth Assessment Reports. He was the lead scientific author of the special report *Climate Change and Tourism: Responding to the Challenges* commissioned by the United Nations World Tourism Organization (in 2007) and the tourism sector White Paper on *Weather and Climate Information for Tourism* commissioned by World Meteorological Organization for the World Climate Conference 3 (in 2009). Dr. Scott has provided expert advice to a number of international and national government agencies, tourism businesses, and non-governmental organizations, and is currently on the Advisory Committee to the *Global Partnership for Sustainable Tourism*.

## The new realities of global climate change

In its 2007 report to the UN, the Intergovernmental Panel on Climate Change (IPCC) presented compelling evidence from every continent of the world indicating that the global climate system has changed compared with the pre-industrial era. The IPCC declared the warming of the global climate system unequivocal and mostly attributable to human activities that are increasing greenhouse gas (GHG) concentrations in the atmosphere. These conclusions have been reinforced by more recent reports on the state of the global climate system by UNEP (2009) and NOAA (2010). Critically, the IPCC emphasized that human-induced climate change has only just begun and that the pace of climate change is 'very likely' to accelerate with GHG emissions at or above current rates. The impacts of human-induced climate change are not consigned to some distant future, but are increasing a strategic reality that leaders of government, business, and indigenous populations must confront.

In 2009, UN Secretary General Ban Ki-moon declared that, 'Climate change is the pre-eminent geopolitical and economic issue of the 21st century … (it) rewrites the global equation for development, peace, and prosperity.' Resolving the dual challenges of reducing GHG emissions to slow climate change and adapt to the future climate change that the planet is already committed to, is at the very heart of the new Green Growth paradigm.

## Tourism's climate change vulnerability and the adaptation imperative

As one of the most prominent challenges to sustainable development in the decades ahead, global climate change will have far-reaching consequences for all countries and economic sectors. With its close and complex relationships to climate and the natural environment, tourism will be no exception. The salience of climate change for the future development of global tourism was aptly recognized in the 2007 *Davos Declaration on Climate Change and Tourism* and the subsequent Tourism Minister's Summit (London, England) that endorsed it, which concluded that climate change must be considered the greatest challenge to the sustainability of tourism in the 21st century.

All major components of the global tourism system will be impacted by climate change and climate policy. Climate change is already affecting investment and operating decisions in tourism, and accumulating evidence indicates greater warming scenarios associated with current emission trajectories would have extensive impacts on sustainability and competitiveness of tourism destinations. Furthermore, global climate change and climate policy is expected to alter regional weather patterns, ecosystems and biodiversity, security and personal safety, as well as travel costs; these will transform geographic and seasonal patterns of tourism demand.

The integrated effects of climate change will generate both negative and positive impacts in the tourism sector and these impacts will vary substantially by market segment and geographic region, creating highly differential vulnerability at the business, destination, and country scale. Differential regional vulnerabilities are particularly noteworthy. A number of independent assessments have indicated that small island developing states and developing regions in Africa, Asia and Oceania appear to be at greatest risk because of potential shifts in demand favouring higher latitude countries, large impacts on natural tourism assets, heightened security risks, relatively lower adaptive capacity, and greater distances to major markets. This has significant implications for the many developing countries that look to tourism as a key future development strategy, and must be more thoroughly considered in national development plans, official development assistance programmes and international climate adaptation finance.

While our understanding of the impacts of climate change has continued to improve over the last decade, a number of experts have emphasized that major regional information gaps remain with regard to the impact on natural and cultural resources critical for tourism. These information gaps are particularly acute in the developing countries of Africa, the Caribbean, South America, the Middle East, parts of Southeast Asia, and the Islands of the Pacific that are anticipated as being the most vulnerable to climate change. The large information gaps related to losses and damages of climate change have limited the place of tourism in major international climate change assessments, and as a prerequisite to successful adaptation, must be a priority for the tourism research community. Over the past decade university scholars have dedicated less than 2% of tourism research to climate change (as measured by the proportion of climate change focused publications in the top four international tourism journals) – a level of investment highly inadequate to the challenge.

All tourism destinations will need to adapt to climate change, whether to minimize risks or to capitalize on new opportunities associated with local impacts of climate change or impacts on competitors and across the broader tourism system. The UNWTO, UNEP and WTTC have all emphasized the important role of the tourism sector in developing strategies to assist local communities and SMEs to understand climate change vulnerabilities and increase their adaptive capacity. Positively, the dynamic nature of the tourism industry and its ability to cope with a range of shocks, including SARS, terrorism attacks, major natural disasters, and the recent global financial crisis, suggests a relatively high adaptive capacity within the sector overall.

Assessments of the state of climate change adaptation by destination and regional tourism stakeholders in very diverse tourism regions have consistently found low but improving levels of climate change awareness, relatively low perceptions of climate change risk, and substantial optimism about the capacity of adaptation to overcome the challenges of climate change. With very limited knowledge of the capacity of current climate adaptations of tourism operators and tourism dependent communities to cope successfully with future climate conditions and little evidence of long-term strategic planning in anticipation of future changes in climate, there is some concern that tourism stakeholders may be overestimating their capacity to adapt cost-effectively and sustainably. Furthermore, because international tourists can hold different expectations for services and environmental conditions, this can impose unique adaptation challenges in communities with visitor-based economies. These tourism specific challenges have not been adequately explored.

The adaptation imperative that has emerged within the scientific literature and policy agendas over the last decade has yet to translate to the tourism sector. Mainstreaming of adaptation will require government and business leadership to overcome several key barriers to adaptation at the enterprise and destination level, including: scientific uncertainty on climate change and its implications for tourism, incompatibilities between business and climate change planning timelines, inadequate financial and technical capacity (especially among SMEs), concerns that early adapters could be penalized by changes in adaptation legislation, and financial assistance. The broader business case for climate change adaptation that has been made extensively by the World Business Council for Sustainable Development and others needs to be better translated to the tourism sector.

## Carbon management: decoupling tourism growth and greenhouse gas emissions

The complex two-way relationship between tourism and climate change has been recognized for over a decade. While the tourism sector has become increasingly aware of its vulnerability to climate change it has also recognized its non-negligible contribution to anthropogenic climate change and expressed an unequivocal commitment to being part of the solution.

The seminal report commissioned by UNWTO, UNEP and WMO for the *Second International Conference on Climate Change and Tourism* in Davos, Switzerland in 2007 provided the first estimate of the contribution of global tourism to climate change, at approximately 5% of $CO_2$ emissions in 2005. With strong growth in international tourism projected by UNWTO through to 2030, business-as-usual $CO_2$ emissions were also projected to grow 135% by 2035. Such a trajectory is at stark odds with the ambitious emission cuts sought by the international community and the Davos Declaration set out voluntary emission reduction strategies for all tourism stakeholders to consider seriously.

The World Travel and Tourism Council signalled the intentions of its members to act in 2009 when it specified 'aspirational' targets to cut carbon emissions 25–30% by 2020 and 50% by 2035 (from 2005 levels). With projected emissions growth over the next 10 to 25 years, such reductions are the equivalent of making the entire current tourism sector carbon neutral. This indeed represents a bold vision for the future of tourism.

The three watershed reports, *Climate Change and Tourism: Responding to Global Challenges* (UNWTO-UNEP-WMO 2008), *Towards a Low Carbon Travel & Tourism Sector* (WEF 2009) and *Leading the Challenge on Climate Change* (WTTC 2009), reveal that much is possible to decouple future tourism growth from GHG emissions. What is now required is to translate the green innovation and carbon management possibility vision set out in these documents into a technologically, economically, and socially credible road map to decarbonise the tourism sector over the next three decades.

## Transitioning from the 'danger zone' to the 'green economy'

Despite a steadily improving information base and increased engagement of the tourism sector in, recent years the critical question remains – how prepared is the tourism sector for climate change? One answer comes from the business community itself. KPMG's (2008) assessment of the regulatory, physical, reputational and litigation risks posed to 18 major global economic sectors versus the level of awareness and preparedness, found tourism to be one of six sectors in the 'danger zone' (along with aviation, transport, health care, the financial sector and oil and gas). A similar answer comes from the 2011 OECD and UNEP assessment of tourism sector adaptation and mitigation preparedness in 18 countries, which concluded that, 'The inescapable conclusion is that current [national tourism] policy, with few exceptions, is inadequate to the scale of the challenge, both on mitigation and on adaptation.' Can tourism afford to continue to be among the global economic sectors least prepared for one of the most important development challenges in the decades ahead?

The international community has agreed to negotiate a successor to the Kyoto Protocol by 2015, which will stabilize atmospheric GHG concentrations at levels necessary to avoid exceeding the +2 °C global warming threshold that represents dangerous climate change and address the adaptation needs of the most vulnerable nations. These next four years represent a crucial window of opportunity for tourism to secure a meaningful place in the Green Economy and our response must be equal to the challenge – a *Tourism Leaders Roundtable on Climate Compatible Travelism.*

# Vanessa Scott

## Director of Strattons Hotel

## Never too small to make a difference

Vanessa Scott, Director of Strattons Hotel, Swaffham, Norfolk, the first hotel in the UK in 2000 to win the DTI's Queen's Award for outstanding Environmental Performance. Before entering the hospitality industry, Vanessa came from a construction background with a special interest in period buildings, which brought the environment to her business model at Stratton's Hotel. She believes that operating from a listed building within a conservation area in a unique landscape has a special responsibility. This is to continue to demonstrate how man has interacted with his natural surroundings to produce food and shelter for thousands of years and to serve as a reminder that humans are never owners, simply caretakers of our places and environments.

There was a story that appeared at the beginning of a tourist board 'Green Tool Kit' for small tourism businesses during the nineties which went something like this: There was an old man walking along the seashore throwing back into the ocean washed up starfish from a receding tide. A young boy approaches him and says, "What difference will that make there are millions of starfish washed up?" to which the old man responds, picking up another throwing it back into the sea and saying, "It makes a difference to that one". I always liked that story because it was a time when you needed a clear message to engage small and medium businesses (SME's) in the sustainability issue. And the clear message was that however small you were you could make a difference. That theme is a reoccurring one in my methodology in engaging staff to come with us on that mission to reduce our environmental impact. Looking at one action and then multiplying it by times in a day, by days in a year; simplistic but the sums are effective and very compelling.

It was that story that also answered a question which might have swayed us in feeling 'too small' to engage in a partnership project that was headed up by the University of Hertfordshire and Professor Anne Smith in 1997. The 'Waste minimisation project in the food and drink industry in East Anglia' aimed to improve the competitiveness and environmental performance of participating companies in the Food and Drink Industry. This was achieved through a programme of site support, training and consultancy in waste minimisation. The Project was the first in the UK to focus on the regional economy of the northern and north-eastern areas of East Anglia with the food and drink sector being the second largest contributor to the Gross Domestic Product (GDP) of East Anglia. The areas targeted were significant in that they had a 5b rating for European funding under the Social Regeneration Budget and eligibility for business competitiveness funding; in a nutshell areas suffering from social and economic deprivation within Europe. A total of 115 implemented opportunities gave rise to annual savings of £1.1m per annum among 13 member companies. This was combined with savings in raw material use (1,390 tonnes), water abstraction (69,900 m$^3$) and energy use (1,170,000 kWh). The project results were to be taken to the rest of the industry to effect change for the better. If you couldn't appeal to a business's emotion to engage in waste control you could through its bottom line.

Participation for Stratton's Hotel was a real turning point in our story. As directors whilst we had good intentions, all our initiatives were brought from our domestic habits and life before becoming hoteliers and, therefore, somewhat ad hoc. Our decision to run a hotel was made, quite literally, from a throw away comment made by my father reacting to the fact that my husband and I filled our house prior to Stratton's with guests. My father quipped 'Why don't you stick up a sign saying hotel and start charging!' The rest is – as they say – history but the environmental commitment was also in a way formed in our consciousness by messages, as young children, from our parents who had grown up with the spirit of managing waste during the later years of the last World War. These messages were not always totally understood; my father's description of the house on his return home from work, managed by myself and three siblings, could be that the house resembled the Queen Mary. I was an older teenager before I found out the reasons for the analogy. Suffice it to say it simply meant we had more illuminations in use than were possibly called for. When we opened the hotel, we had light use firmly under control, a compost heap, chickens, a recycling habit and a passion for great food which we looked to the back garden or our locality to provide. When we joined the 'Waste Minimisation project' we felt a little smug that we were already there but it would be good to be amongst like minded people.

We were soon to realise how inadequately we were dealing with our Green Growth scenario. Lots of ideas were in our heads, no formal policy had been written, no monitoring, no targets or vision to cope with the expansion of the business and most importantly (like most small businesses) we had missed bad practise. It had become part of the wallpaper, because we were tired and outstretched constantly working at the coalface. The consultants who informed us as part of that project were fantastic from pointing out the low hanging fruit or easy gains, to helping us form solutions to larger problems. The first comprehensive environmental policy was written as a result, looking at the good and the bad; the good built on and the bad tackled – not always perfectly to begin with but there was now a process. Most importantly I remember that time as a catalyst which completely reignited our interest in the business and informed us of our way forward. We realised that auditing was the key and that our green approach did not stop at the garden gate but led us out into the local community where we could make a serious difference to a town that had grossly suffered with the decline in agriculture. Most significantly, though, we realised that the Green policy we had written, this way of thinking, sat at the very core of our business and informed our every decision. Nothing was discarded until it had gone through that process of 'What else can we do with it?' and this was applied to reports and legal obligations as well as inanimate objects. If we had invested resource in EH for example could we use that information to generate a PR story; everything was and is expected to have more than one life.

There are tough decisions to make in order to respect our green brief. The guest toiletry issue was one such 'tricky' problem. Prior to the University of Hertfordshire we had stocked our guest bathrooms with the perceived 'luxury' toiletry miniatures of 25gram bars of soap wrapped in tissue and boxed, shower gel, bath foam, shampoo and conditioner in 30ml bottles and a body/hand lotion. We swapped to Body Shop 1000ml pump dispensers and the toiletry bill immediately reduced by 83%. In the ensuing months a few guests would ask for bar soap and with old stocks in our store it was easy to accommodate their wishes but as the old stocks dwindled we knew we had to face the inevitable decision of how we were going to cope post bar soap. Engaging our guests in the soap facts seemed the way to achieve buy in, using the data we had collected that had informed our decision to use refillable pump soaps. We rewrote all our guest room information and under toiletries we stated the facts that every year we accumulated kilos of little used bar soap (last year it would have been 164kg under the old system), that use of the 30 ml bottles averaged only 30% before being discarded and that we had swapped to a better quality product from an ethical company who would refill our bottles thereby reducing the volume of plastic bottles we sent to landfill by 97%. We never again got asked for a bar of soap. The following year Body Shop ceased making 1000ml sizes; 250ml was now their largest size and we went back to the drawing board! Our green policy is rewritten every year and improved upon taking audited information to set targets for reduction and use to engage guests and staff.

Over the years the toiletry procurement brief has been refined to incorporate: ability to purchase in bulk sizes, not tested on animals, and from a local company. But we have never swayed from using a liquid product which gives us zero soap waste despite the fact that our business sits within the 'luxury' end of the market where profuse amount of product and large bars of soap are still 'de rigueur'. Several years ago our marketing director went out to all local soap makers with a brief; a one product liquid soap to wash hands, hair and body, it had to be organic and the essential oil ingredients sourced from Norfolk, it had to be 'no tears' baby friendly and available in large bulk containers of 35litres. Simply Soaps of Norwich fulfilled the brief and created our own bespoke soap; to me it is the new definition of 'luxury' as years of refinement and thought went into creating the spec for it and it being born! Likewise decisions such as removing orange juice from our menu owing to large quantities of citrus pulp going into our composting streams and the environmental impact of growing and transporting citrus fruit per se have been difficult. The fact that we have a wonderful local fruit farm on our doorstep to us makes it a no brainer but informing the guest and training the staff are a challenge.

Having tackled and formed a natural resource reduction policy, audited every bit of our waste stream in detail for all the ensuing years post University of Hertfordshire, we look to the minutia of our business running to improve. In recent years, this has increasingly involved perfecting our approach to engaging stakeholders. One innovative way is to remove spent coffee grounds from our waste stream by naturally drying them and bagging them back up in the packaging they arrived on site in as a horticultural compost to hand out to our guests. This removes the packaging from our waste stream as well as clearly indicating to the gardener the purity and provenance of the beans that this fabulous nitrogen rich compost has. The new system of disposing of grounds started in January after restaurant manager Charlie Cousens and Head Chef Sam Bryant were brainstorming ideas on how to reduce the hotels waste compost as part of the hotels campaign to involve all stakeholders.

The initiative has gone from strength to strength since then, taking on a life of its own! When coffee compost bags started to mount up, the local allotments were contacted to take the surplus the hotel guests were not. The allotment association SCALGA were so impressed with the researched properties of coffee grounds that Charlie had provided them with that they wanted more. So head of the compost association, Christine Wright, went to other cafes in the town to see if they were willing to pass their grounds on also. Since February over 800kg have been collected from Swaffham. Strattons may be a small hotel and restaurant but with a little lateral thinking and lots of enthusiasm it hopes it can influence a change in behaviour for the better. Charlie decided to take this further and has contacted the CEO of Whitbread and Costa coffee to explore the possibilities of the scheme being rolled out.

Possessing no formal background in the hospitality sector has been in the main a positive influence; when we started our journey we were naively romantic about what we were about to do, never realising the steep learning curve we would be faced with. We were unencumbered with any preconceptions of what was the norm in the industry so we just did what we felt was right. When I was asked in 1997 by an inspector for the Business Commitment to the Environment Award how different we were to the rest of the industry regarding our green approach I honestly did not know. A week of research later heartened my hopes for a BCE award, but seriously dismayed me that it seemed like it was only the big players like Whitbread and Marriott who had engaged in the Green agenda. We went on to win Green Globe's 'Best Small Global Hotel' and then the first hotel in the UK to win the DTI's Queens Award for outstanding environmental performance. I found myself in London addressing fellow Queen's Award winners talking in terms of making hundreds of pounds worth of green savings and wishing I had converted them to percentages as Jaguar cars trotted sales figures out in their millions!

Small businesses comprise the vast majority of tourism enterprises. In England alone of 31,980 serviced accommodation providers, 57% are micro enterprises and the 33,525 non serviced providers are in the main SME's. These businesses often lie at the heart of their communities as standalone businesses without a corporate strategy but playing some part in those communities. Last year Stratton's Hotel spearheaded the first annual Food & Drink Festival for the Brecks in Swaffham; a celebration of the wonderful local food, farming and countryside of the area staged by those that live and work within it. In celebrating local food and drink we hope to reconnect people with their surroundings and show how what they choose to buy not only tastes better but can have a positive impact upon the countryside and local rural economy. The Brecks is one of the largest areas in the country for root crops such as onions and carrots and we acknowledge the importance of farming in the rural economy and its contribution to the landscape and wildlife. The Brecks is a nationally recognised landscape covering almost 400 sq miles across Norfolk and Suffolk of open heaths, forestry, farmland and rivers with a varied natural, built and cultural history reaching back to Neolithic times; a landscape that has been produced by how we have interacted with our natural surroundings to produce food and shelter for thousands of years. In interacting with it today as a tourism business we should be aware that great environments are the key to a sustainable future.

# David P. Scowsill

**President & CEO, World Travel and Tourism Council**

**Travel and tourism leading the way towards green growth**

David Scowsill is President & CEO of the World travel and tourism Council. Prior to joining WTTC in November 2010, David worked for six years in private equity and venture capital, completing deals in technology and travel. David was CEO of Opodo, a pan-European online travel company from 2002 to 2004, building the business from start up to a €500million transaction turnover, before it was sold to Amadeus. He joined the board of Hilton International in 1997 as senior VP sales, marketing and IT, leading the brand re-unification programme between the two Hilton shareholder companies. David rejoined British Airways from 1993 to 1997 as regional general manager Asia/Pacific. He established the Joint Service Agreement and global alliance with Qantas. He joined American Airlines in 1991 as managing director sales for Europe Middle East and Africa.

---

Travel and tourism is a growth industry. Despite the many crises and challenges experienced over the past decade – terrorist attacks, health scares, natural disasters and economic crisis – travel and tourism has continued to grow by around 4% a year. Over 11.3 million jobs have been directly created by the industry since the Rio+10 (World Summit on Sustainable Development) in 2002; a direct testament to its resilience and adaptability. According to latest WTTC forecasts, this rate of growth is expected to continue over the next ten years, generating a further 20 million jobs. To ensure that the industry's potential is maximised, and to ensure on-going stability in the wake of increasing risks and challenges, future growth needs to balance the needs of economics with people, cultures and the environment.

The pursuit of a green economy has grown in prominence in recent years. Its concept and values represent a more sustainable economic system for individuals, business and the planet based on long-term economic foresight, facilitating safe and efficient development.

The travel and tourism industry is intrinsically linked to the preservation of natural resources and cultural heritage. It is also heavily reliant on a dedicated workforce and high calibre of business management and leadership. As one of the largest industries in the world, directly and indirectly generating 9% of global GDP and 255 million jobs, and responsible for the 980 million people who travelled internationally in 2011, the travel and tourism industry has the opportunity and responsibility to lead green economic growth. Ensuring the sustainable future of the environments and cultures in which we operate is fast becoming a business imperative.

The pace of change in the 21$^{st}$ century is massive and we are seeing global shifts which will fundamentally impact travel and tourism. Increasing global interconnectedness and demographic change will require new areas of investment and innovation. We will need to cater for more people travelling more often, but at the same time we know we cannot simply scale up current levels of activity. Environmental limits will also have a profound effect on the way that tourism functions, with intense competition for resources such as land, water and food, as well as the depletion of wildlife and marine resources which require protection. While the industry needs to harness the growth opportunity of expanding demographics, its long-term viability depends on balancing people's desire to travel with the resources which enable travel. How the industry as a collective force tackles these transformations will be the making of its long-term success.

Travel and tourism is by no means a newcomer to the sustainability agenda.

Transformations from the industry first were transferred into action in 1996 by *Agenda 21 for the travel and tourism Industry*. A collaborative effort between UNWTO and WTTC, this was a ground-breaking moment for travel and tourism, followed up by several progress reports raising awareness of this agenda within the industry, and raising the bar of sustainable business practice.

Since then industry leaders have harnessed the challenges and opportunities presented by more environmentally focused issues such as climate change. Sustainable development strategies, eco-planning and responsible operations are becoming increasingly commonplace. WTTC Members share a vision of sustainable mobility and growth for the industry as a vital part of modern life. Through the initiative Leading the Challenge on Climate Change in 2009, Members set the aspiration for reducing their $CO_2$ emissions by 25% by 2020, with further aspirations to achieve no less than 50% reduction by 2035. Their progress and challenges have been showcased by WTTC. Additionally, our Tourism for Tomorrow Awards recognise and promote the achievements of travel and tourism businesses with incredible sustainable practices from all over the world.

Nevertheless, the fragmented nature of the industry means that good practice is not uniform, with varying levels of commitment across companies and geographic areas. Travel and tourism continues to receive bad press in the sustainability arena, and is often the target of punitive eco-taxes. The Rio +20 conference presents an opportunity to reflect on the significant progress that has been made by the industry, as well as the challenges which lie ahead. As an industry we are always striving to do better, and in the sustainability arena there is still work to be done.

The challenge is for industry to leverage its core competencies of economic growth, job creation and as a conduit for cross cultural understanding, to deliver greater benefits for local communities and society, while 'future-proofing' the businesses through which these benefits are channelled.

As consumer preferences evolve to demand greater sustainable performances by the companies from which they buy their travel, there is not only the opportunity to influence and educate the consumer further but also to set the mould which others can follow. In addition, business has the opportunity to influence local and international supply chains by demanding more sustainable products. This in turn creates a ripple effect as these suppliers demand better products from their suppliers. The potential global outreach is immense, making travel and tourism well placed to lead the green economic revolution.

On a destination level there are many opportunities for innovative and mutually beneficial schemes. Tourism is part of and reliant on the success of a destination. It is an investment in business and livelihoods. Community benefit can come from employment training and transfer of skills to get the very best out of our local staff, to enhancing and protecting the cultural experience for the traveller. There is business logic to such an approach. Cultivation and respect of local identities and cultures benefit not only the host country and its people, but also responds to the customers' desire for authenticity. Forward-thinking entrepreneurs are carving out lucrative new prospects in the market – from eco-hotels to purpose-built, carbon neutral convention centres, with holiday packages encompassing community payback opportunities.

The industry's fragmentation has been an obstacle in the past. Now is the time to celebrate diversity and create meaningful collaborations, through which networks can be built to facilitate and strengthen progress beyond the competitive interests of individual players.

## WTTC's focus for the future

At WTTC we believe there are *three priority areas* for action which the industry must take in order to leverage its influence.

First, we must recognise and understand those global trends which will impact travel and tourism in the future, and devise *solutions to ensure that our industry's growth* continues in a sustainable way.

Secondly, these solutions, many of which are already available, need to be *mainstreamed into everyday operations*. They should become normal business practice rather than 'optional extras', and fully integrated into company reporting systems. This does not require a radical, one time change, but developments should be integrated over time as they become available.

Third, it is only through *real collaboration and co-operation* between the vast number of stakeholders which make up travel and tourism, that our industry can fully realise its potential. And the industry must be open with our struggles, lessons learnt and experiences to help others become more sustainable.

Actions stemming from these key areas are a vital aspect to true leadership in creating a more sustainable travel and tourism industry. This will ensure a strong coordinated effort towards a global green economy.

# Sonu Shivdasani

## Founder of Six Senses, CEO of Soneva

## Luxury and sustainability – natural partners for delivering green growth

Sonu Shivdasani, Founder of Six Senses and Chairman and CEO of Soneva, together with his wife and Creative Director Eva Malmstrom, have dedicated their lives and business activity to driving positive sustainability change. Sonu has created a pioneering vision for green tourism, coining the concept of barefoot and intelligent luxury which recognizes the ability for luxury holiday making and care for the environment to co-exist with perfect ease. Having recently sold the Six Senses Group, he is now focusing on a total sustainability operation at Soneva with the idea of creating positive environmental and carbon impacts. His goal of luxury with sustainability covers total ecosystem management and local community engagement. His initiatives include reforestation (with PATT, Plant A Tree Today), marine ecosystem preservation (with the Blue Marine Foundation). Sonu is an alumnus of Eton College and a graduate of Oxford University, where he received an MA in English literature.

I was recently challenged on whether it was actually possible to create a truly sustainable luxury holiday experience. As the CEO of the Soneva group of resorts, it is a question that gets thrown at me at regular intervals. The simple truth of the matter is that luxury and sustainability are compatible concepts, and we are reaching a point at which it will be impossible to enjoy one without the other.

What do I mean by that? A generation ago, it was relatively straightforward to visit a resort in the midst of a wonderful, unspoiled ecosystem. Fast-forward to today, and the pressure of tourists on the last untarnished parts of the world has never been greater. On this express train to environmental ruin, resort companies that do not take radical steps today to protect the ecosystems in which they operate will not have a business in 20 to 30 years – such is the degradation that we are witnessing.

So what can be done? There are no straightforward answers to the question, and solutions will vary from destination to destination. But with determination, a long-term commitment to renewable energy investment and some clever thinking, it is possible to avoid an environmental catastrophe. In fact it is quite possible to become a part of the solution to global environmental and social issues.

Some countries are already making impressive commitments to address green growth issues. Ex-President Nasheed of the Maldives, for example, had pledged to lead his country to carbon neutrality by 2020. I hope that despite the recent political uncertainty in the country, that commitment remains intact regardless of who wins the next election. At Soneva, we are also working on the carbon agenda and hope that all our resorts will become decarbonising (i.e. actually take carbon out of the atmosphere) by 2015. There is no roadmap or manual to achieving this goal, so we are learning as we go along and we will be delighted to share our experiences with anyone within the industry who wants to follow suit. It is a mammoth project and we can't leave any stone unturned if we are to achieve our goal.

We are making our sustainability commitments because we care about the environment (and that is reason enough). But we are also making them because they make good business sense. I don't mean just grabbing a market opportunity or delivering cost savings (although these are important). It is good business sense because we know that protecting the environment and communities of destinations is fundamental to our license to operate.

So what are we doing to make our resorts truly sustainable?

Soneva Fushi in the Maldives is the testbed for all our efforts. As we make our sustainability journey, we are prepared to make mistakes, try things that may not work and be bold in our decision-making processes.

Addressing energy related emissions requires two disciplines: one is reducing our energy needs, with a focus on building and appliance performance and on demand management; the other is cleaning the power supply.

In the Maldives, diesel has been increasing in price by about 2 per cent a month. At Soneva Fushi our monthly diesel bill exceeds $100,000. If we carry on consuming diesel at our current rate, the bill is forecast to exceed $250,000 within three to four years. We believe we can shave at least 30 per cent off current energy use by employing demand management strategies. These can be applied in three main target areas: 1) energy performance of buildings; 2) appliance efficiency, and 3) user education.

Reducing energy wastage and inefficiency in demand gives a double dividend. Our 30 per cent target (140 kilowatts each hour) would yield annual cost saving in the region of $400,000 to $600,000. We estimate that each kilowatt of capacity from the sun delivered during the six peak solar hours costs $2,800 to build. But delivering solar capacity at night via batteries requires a capital spend of roughly $4,000 per kilowatt. Thus the cost of installing 140 kilowatts of clean energy capacity incurs a $1,000,000 capital spend. These figures mean that it is much better for us to reduce consumption in the first instance rather than simply to swap diesel for renewable capacity.

Given the tropical locations of our resorts it is not surprising that space cooling is the dominant energy service – accounting for between 40 and 60 per cent of resort load and more than 60 per cent of villa energy use. Improving our buildings ability to resist ambient heat gain and to retain internal air conditioning cooling is, therefore, a priority target.

To identify the building performance measures that deliver the greatest energy saving return (in minimizing air conditioning load) per dollar of investment we have conducted side-by-side monitored tests. These tests revealed that roof insulation alone yields a potential energy saving of 50 per cent. With an installation cost of about $6,000 per villa and annual energy saving of 6 Megawatt hours ($2,000) per villa the cost recovery period is a mere three years.

However, optimal test conditions differ from real life. Guests are likely to leave the air conditioning on and windows and doors open as they enjoy the freedom and privacy of their beach access, so additional supporting measures are needed to capture those potential cooling savings. Sensors in the doors and windows can be programmed to switch off the air conditioning unit after a few minutes of being open and these technologies are an integral part of our strategy to reduce carbon emissions.

In our Maldivian resorts, solar photovoltaics is the natural choice for clean electricity supply. Complete diesel independence at Soneva Fushi, for example, could be achieved with 2.5 megawatt peak of photovoltaic capacity. However, following the targeted 30 per cent demand reduction, a full solar photovoltaic solution would require about 1.8 megawatt peak – with panels covering 3 per cent of the total island.

In phase one of implementation, we plan to install 1 megawatt peak photovoltaic capacity at Soneva Fushi. This is sufficient to meet all our daytime needs and some carry-over capacity to the solar morning and evening hours. We have recently undertaken a rigorous procurement process to identify our technology and consultancy partners for implementing this array. And if there are still resort owners in tropical parts of the world that doubt the business case, we estimate that we will get a return on investment of roughly 20 per cent, meaning that the whole cost of the project will be recouped in just five years.

The compelling financial rationale is not just confined to energy use. At present about 50 per cent of our hot water needs at Fushi are met by drawing waste heat derived via heat exchangers on our diesel generators' radiator system. In the future, following the switch to renewables, we will need another source for this supply. We are looking at a phased approach to implementing solar thermal solutions for removing electric hot water boilers from the energy load. In phase 1, due to commence shortly, we will install solar thermal collectors to serve 35 villas that are currently served by electric boilers. This measure is projected to cost $45,000 and will yield an energy saving of 240 kilowatt hours per day or $29,000 per year fuel saving. The return on this investment is therefore even shorter than for installing solar photovoltaic (electrical) capacity.

Water – something we all take for granted – is another area where we have taken huge steps. You will not find an imported bottle of mineral water on any of our resorts.

We began the Wellness Water Initiative in 2008 when the properties banned imported water. Instead each resort serves their own locally produced drinking water. This groundbreaking initiative was in recognition of the considerable and unnecessary carbon emissions resulting from the shipping of drinking water great distances – often by air – and supports Soneva's move towards a greater use of local and seasonal produce to reduce carbon footprints while adding value to community partnerships.

But we felt that it was not enough just to stop imports of water and wanted to help tackling water related issues. Since October 2009, therefore, we have dedicated 50 per cent of our water sales at the Soneva resorts to provide clean water for people in communities who lack access to safe clean drinking water or basic sanitation. The main partner organizations for this activity are Water Charity and Thirst-Aid. As of this April, 582,506 people have been helped through 454 projects in 52 countries.

In the current economic environment, some resort owners are inevitably uncertain about spending large sums on big ticket items. For these businesses, there are lots of options that cost nothing but that still make a difference. For example, instead of plastic straws, why not introduce biodegradable paper straws? Instead of incandescent lamps, why not introduce low energy LED lightbulbs that use 90% less electricity. Why not implement some staff training that can deliver a 6 per cent reduction in energy consumption? There are lots of small steps that any business can introduce tomorrow.

These numbers should demonstrate beyond any real doubt that the business case for investing in sustainability is obvious. But it is not enough simply to make the switch to a carbon-free future without educating consumers about what we are doing. We are fortunate in this regard. The guests who visit the Soneva resorts tend to be those that are already environmentally minded. The sustainability of our resorts and our unceasing efforts to reduce our impact on the planet is already a unique selling point for the resorts.

That being said, it would be counter-productive to lecture our guests at Soneva Fushi, but there are other ways of getting our message across. These go back to my original point about luxury and sustainability being intrinsically linked. At Soneva Fushi we have a wonderful garden that grows fruits, vegetables and herbs on permaculture and organic principles. The rocket grown in the garden is served in our restaurants and is quite simply the best anyone has ever tasted. Once a guest has experienced the rocket, they want to see the garden itself. And in doing so they find out how the resort is turning food waste into compost and woodwaste to biochar that both are enriching the soil on the island through careful crop rotation.

The Soneva resorts are a big supporter of marine protection. Soneva worked with EcoCare Maldives for many years on a campaign to protect sharks, which lead the government to implement a ban on export of shark products. As a result, we are already seeing more baby reef sharks around Fushi. To further protect this Soneva are supporting the Baa Atoll Marine Conservation area in the Maldives that has received UNESCO Biosphere Reserve status to ensure the area remains pristine and is used in a sustainable matter. A pristine environment adds value to the guest experience and increases the sense of luxury. This is just another example of how prioritising sustainability provides for a better, more luxurious experience for guests.

Although carbon emission from energy consumption on the resort is the main factor we can influence, it only counts for 15% of Soneva Fushi's total annual carbon footprint of 22,000 tons. We, therefore, have a duty to consider other carbon emissions. When we look at our carbon footprint, we find that guest flights account for 75% of total carbon emissions. To manage this impact, we have created a Carbon Sense Fund to mitigate against those emissions that cannot be directly controlled. The Fund is capitalised by a 2 per cent levy on room rates. This capital is then invested into our carbon mitigation projects through our foundation, The Soneva SLOW LIFE Trust.

The Soneva SLOW LIFE Trust funds a number of innovative carbon-reduction projects around the world, including the Darfur Stoves Project, working with an NGO that provides energy efficient stoves to women in Darfur, Sudan. The Darfur Stoves Project aims to distribute more than 150,000 energy efficient cook stoves over seven years to residents of the internally displaced person (IDP) camps in the area. The stoves dramatically reduce the amount of time women must spend collecting firewood in an unprotected area – an activity that can take up to 25 hours per week.

They will also reduce the carbon emissions resulting from cooking fires by an estimated 300,000 tonnes over a seven year period which in turn reduces pressure on the local biosphere and deforestation in surrounding areas by reducing demand for wood-fuel.

The Soneva SLOW LIFE Trust is also working with the PATT Foundation in Thailand and, in celebration of 2011 UN International Year of the Forest, launched a large forest restoration project linked to existing forest areas. In total 200,000 trees, covering 200 acres, are planted annually. Not only does this mitigate 160,000 tonnes of carbon per year, but it is also creating wildlife corridors, preventing erosion, restoring biodiversity and generating local jobs.

Important though carbon and climate change are, sustainability for us is about much more. We strongly believe that ultimately the will to push through positive environmental change has to come from local communities. And sometimes these local communities need help in addressing the range of issues they face. In response, Soneva Fushi has joined forces with EcoCare Maldives, a non-profit environmental NGO to organize the Soneva Nature Trip. This is an annual environment education field trip aimed to create environmental awareness among school children in the Maldives.

In June last year 80 students from nine primary schools in Male and the local Godhood School participated in the latest trip. This project runs in Baa Atoll, the home province of Soneva Fushi, about 96 miles to the north of Male. National and international experts give lectures on environmental issues to the participants. The scheme is now in its 13th year. School children from Malé and islands in Baa Atoll work as colleagues to study environmental issues such as mangrove ecosystem, coral reefs, beach erosion, biodiversity, natural vegetation and waste disposal in the atoll. The Soneva Nature Trip is now an active component of the country's official education calendar and has received PATA Gold Award for Environmental Awareness.

So let me end with an upbeat message: it is possible to make a tangible, real difference to the environment. No matter how many gloomy headlines you read, please do not feel powerless.

I continue to make my business as sustainable as possible – because I believe it's the right thing to do and because it makes financial sense. The benefits are tangible, rooted in practical solutions and make a hugely positive difference on people's lives. The alternative is doing nothing and that is definitely a luxury we cannot afford.

# Alain St. Ange

## Minister for Tourism & Culture, Seychelles

## Seychelles Sustainability Framework

Alain St.Ange, Minister for Tourism & Culture, Seychelles, was formerly the Seychelles People's Progressively Front (SPPF) directly elected Member of the People's Assembly for the La Digue Constituency (1979) and the Seychelles National Party (SNP) directly elected Member of the National Assembly for the Bel Air Constituency (2002). He led the SNP to victory in the 2001, 2002 and 2006 elections in the Bel Air Constituency. In 2009 he was promoted to the position of CEO of the Seychelles Tourism Board. Alain St.Ange has authored or co-authored a number of books including *Seychelles, What Next?* (1991), *Seychelles, In Search of Democracy* (2005), *Seychelles, The Cry of A People* (2007), *Seychelles, Regatta 2010* (2010) and *Seychelles, Enters The World of Carnival* (2011). Alain studied hotel management and tourism in Germany and France. He has worked in hotels and restaurants in Seychelles, the Channel Islands and in Australia.

**S**

In a recent speech, the President of Seychelles, James Michel, high-lighted the importance of pursuing Seychelles' brand of tourism. 'The unique way in which we must, each and every Seychellois, contribute towards ensuring that we make the very best of all that Mother Nature has bestowed upon us, but in a well-thought through, visionary and sustainable manner which will create prosperity, not only for today, but for tomorrow as well.'

The President asked us not to forget that it is tourism that creates the wealth necessary to protect our biodiversity and our unspoiled natural environment. Also, that it is our contributions, both collective and indi-vidual which provide the impetus to our industry. Indeed, there has never been a better time for Seychellois who dream of a future in our tourism industry, to seize the moment and play their part, whether it be in the opening of a small hotel, guesthouse or self-catering enterprise, providing an invaluable service to the industry or training to be a part of that industry. It is an appropriate time, also, for Seychellois to 'raise the bar' with a 'Quality Tourism Seychelles' label to ensure that tourism industry players, across the board, provide the welcome, courtesy, professionalism, honesty and value for money that will do our tourism proud and make our beautiful islands among the most sought after destinations on the planet – today *and* tomorrow.

Seychelles has indeed been blessed with a grand diversity that includes not only the wonderful, and in many cases, unique, physical attributes of our islands, but also the varied ethnicity, cultural vibrancy, social harmony and the distinctive, island-style way of life that helps to make us everything we are.

In a world that is becoming busier and grimier by the day, much of what our islands have to offer is a refreshing departure from the norm; a far cry indeed from the processed, look-alike experiences on offer in other places. The Seychelles way of life is time honoured, our customs and traditions authentic, our environment pristine and the activities and services we offer, full of promise and potential.

We, in Seychelles, are seated on a treasure-trove of natural wonders, riches and delights that have made Seychelles one of the most aspirational destinations on earth. It is time to harness our energies to ensure that we capitalise to the maximum on all that we are and all that we possess. All the while, doing all in our power to ensure that we protect what we have and maintain that fragile balance between our tourism and our biodiversity that is the key to our present and future prosperity.

The Seychelles archipelago belongs to one of the major biodiversity hotspots in the world. Approximately 47% of the country's landmass, and some 228km² of its ocean territory, are under some form of protected status. However, Seychelles' biodiversity remains at risk from a variety of human induced pressures, this makes the conservation and sustainable use of biodiversity of vital importance for the country's sustainable development.

The beauty of the natural environment and the friendliness of the Seychellois people form the core of the Seychelles' tourism product. Careful stewardship of these key tourism assets is essential to the sustainability of tourism and to the integrity of the island's beautiful, yet fragile, ecosystems.

The concept behind the development of the Seychelles Sustainable Tourism Label (SSTL) originated from the Ministry of Environment in the preparation of *Vision 21*. The Seychelles Ministry of Tourism (now through the Seychelles Tourism Board) adopted the SSTL project.

SSTL has been developed over the last three years through research, stakeholder discussion, and local piloting. The criteria used in the assessment are based on international standards, but their development has drawn on local knowledge.

SSTL is a sustainable tourism management and certification programme designed specifically for use in Seychelles. It is voluntary, user-friendly, and designed to inspire more efficient and sustainable ways of doing business. SSTL is presently applicable to hotels of all sizes.

The vision of SSTL is that every hotel enterprise in Seychelles integrates sustainability practices in their business operations

The mission of SSTL is to encourage hotels in Seychelles to mainstream sustainability practices into their business operations and to safeguard the biodiversity and culture of Seychelles by assisting operators in improving the sustainability of their operations. This is done with useful tips and advice and motivating operators to improve the sustainability of their operations via the certification process

SSTL seeks to encourage and guide improvements in sustainability outcomes and as such the project is as much an educational process as an examination process.

The rationale behind SSTL is that there exists an inextricable link between tourism and the biodiversity which underpins it. In an age when, according to the United Nations Environment Programme, uncontrolled land conversion, climate change, pollution and other unsustainable human activities are causing biodiversity loss at many times the rate of natural extinction, it is time to take stock and reflect upon how, in so many ways, our civilization is energetically sawing through the ecological branch upon which it is seated.

Biodiversity is important for its own sake and it is clear that large areas of unique, natural beauty worldwide are attracting rising numbers of visitors, demonstrating how biodiversity is not only one of tourism's greatest assets, but quite fundamental to its long-term, sustained growth. However, biodiversity is far from being just a simple attraction and we must never permit ourselves to lose sight of one simple fact of paramount importance: our eco-systems also sustain us by providing food, energy, health and some 40% of the global economy. It may, therefore, be claimed that our biodiversity is our lifeline – one that needs to be nourished and protected because, when it becomes impaired, so will we.

Tourism and biodiversity are natural partners; each one in need of the other and with each partner contributing invaluably to the partnership. However, that synergy is a very delicately poised balancing act, requiring us to ensure that our tourism is sustainable. Also, that it contributes positively to biodiversity conservation and the quality of life of local populations while, at the same time, minimising negative environmental and social impacts. This is the juggling act that we, as custodians of our nation, must continually and successfully perform if we are to ensure, not only the continued prosperity of our tourism industry but, also, the survival of the extraordinary natural beauty and myriad riches with which Seychelles has been blessed.

Seychelles is a country whose economy and, therefore, prosperity is very much based on the health, both present and future, of its tourism industry.

Safeguarding the interests of that industry and, at the same time, those of the environment and local community is a delicate balancing act the outcome of which will very much determine the future prosperity of this nation.

Sustainable tourism is definable as an industry committed to making as low an impact as possible on the environment while helping to generate income and employment for the people of that community. The overall aim of sustainable tourism, then, must be to ensure that development is a positive experience for local people; tourism companies; and, of course, the tourists themselves.

In order for this to happen, it is of prime importance that we as a nation take *ownership* of our tourism industry and, through that ownership, find ourselves in a position to charter its course through sometimes turbulent waters created by the exigencies of the industry itself and, also, by external factors such as the recent global recession. The more our people buy into the industry at every level, the more they will find themselves taking the level of ownership required to become sensitive to the impact of tourism on the environment and the community and, therefore take steps to ensure that it remains a positive one – not just for today but also in the future.

The role of government in sustainable, community based tourism is also critical: in addition to providing a stable economy, government needs to ensure a market friendly business environment with appropriate regulation and oversight to ensure that social policy, environmental and safety concerns are adequately dealt with. Governments also need to ensure that the necessary physical infrastructure is in place, that the schools are producing sufficient numbers of trained men and women and that the workforce is healthy.

In the case of Seychelles, in particular, conservation of our unique marine and terrestrial biodiversity is key to maintaining tourist interest in the region and needs to be brought to bear in such a way that the long term interests of these assets are not sacrificed for mere short term gains.

Here, again we come to the question of ownership: communities are more likely to protect their environment if they share in the rents or profits accruing from tourists who appreciate their unique heritage, flora and fauna etc.

It is only through such an integrated approach that Seychelles' tourism industry will flourish as a balanced enterprise – one that takes into consideration the many requirements of tourism but also those of its host – the Seychelles islands, their fragile ecosystems and their communities.

# Lyonchhen Jigmi Y. Thinley

## Prime Minister of Bhutan

## Gross national happiness as an alternative development paradigm

The Honourable Lyonchhen Jigmi Y. Thinley is the first democratically elected Prime Minister of Bhutan. As founding President of the Druk Phuensum Tshogpa (DPT), he won a landslide victory in Bhutan's first ever national elections in 2008. Prior to this, he served the previous government as Minister for Foreign Affairs and Minister for Home and Cultural Affairs. He was Prime Minister from 1998-99, and again from 2003-04, when the post rotated annually. He is a strong global advocate for the Gross National Happiness development model and a committed conservationist who promotes eco-literacy in the school system. Lyonchhen is presently the Chairman of the National Environment Commission and of the Ugyen Wangchuck Institute of Conservation and Environment. He is also an International Counsellor for the Asia Society, New York; Member of the SNV International Advisory Board, and President of Maha Bodhi Society of India. He has received many awards for his strategic vision linked to practical community and individual based sustainability action.

I wish to express my deep appreciation and gratitude for the Honourable Maurice Strong's lifetime of commitment to promoting development in harmony with nature. As the world gathers at the Rio +20 Summit, it is an appropriate moment to pay tribute to one of the foremost pioneers of sustainable development. As Bhutan's Honorary Consul in Canada, Maurice Strong promoted a very special relationship between the Kingdom of Bhutan and his great country, for which we remain profoundly grateful. It is indeed an honour to contribute to this book dedicated to his lifetime of service.

As Secretary General of the United Nations Conference on the Human Environment, as the first Executive Director of the United Nations Environment Programme, as a Commissioner of the World Commission on Environment and Development, as Secretary-General of the first Rio Earth Summit, and actively involved today in pushing for a genuinely successful Rio +20 Summit in 2012, Maurice Strong's powerful advocacy of environmental responsibility has been unwavering.

To achieve the vision and goals propounded by Maurice Strong, I believe we now need to re-define not only the structure and practical workings of our economic system, but the very definition of an economy. Indeed, I would argue that an economy is not an economy if, at the very least, it does not promote sustainability, community welbeing and social harmony. It ought to encourage prudent use and management of scarce resources to make life stable and secure.

The GDP-led development model that compels irresponsible growth on a planet with limited resources no longer makes economic sense, and is the cause of our present immoral and self-destructive actions.

- This present economic paradigm is irresponsible, because we extract, produce, consume and waste ever more, even as natural resources are rapidly depleting.

- It is immoral and unethical because having consumed far beyond our share of natural wealth, our reckless profligacy amid unconscionable inequities comes at the cost of what belongs to generations unborn.

- And it is ultimately self-destructive, because, aided by technology, we are rapidly bringing about the collapse of our ecological life support systems.

Having far outlived its usefulness, our fundamentally flawed economic arrangement has itself become the cause of all our deepest problems. Within its framework, there lies no solution to the economic, ecological, social, and security crises that plague the world today and threaten to consume humanity.

Mankind is like a meteor, blazing toward self-annihilation along with all other innocent life forms. But this course can be changed if we act now.

Bhutan's role in the global search for a rational economic system has to do with the growing acceptance of our Fourth King's idea of GNH (Gross National Happiness) as an alternative development paradigm. Founded on the belief that happiness can be achieved by balancing the needs of the body with those of the mind within a peaceful and secure environment, this understanding requires that the purpose of development must be to create enabling conditions through public policy for the pursuit of the ultimate goal of happiness by all citizens. In short, GNH is a sustainability based, wellbeing centric, inclusive economic model.

Here it is important to acknowledge openly that, contrary to what many mistakenly believe, Bhutan is not a country that has attained GNH and it is not from a pedestal that Bhutan recently served as a humble facilitator of a remarkable and historic event at the United Nations aimed at launching a new economic paradigm. Like most developing nations, we are struggling with the challenge of fulfilling the basic needs of our people. What separates us, however, from most others is that we have made happiness the most fundamental of human needs as the goal of societal change.

The growing interest in GNH, discontent with the existing metrics, understanding of happiness as a measurable good, and the present multiplicity of natural and manmade calamities, compelled Bhutan to take the initiative that led to the consensus adoption last year of the UN resolution on *'Happiness: towards a holistic approach to development'*. This resolution called on Bhutan to convene a discussion *"on the theme of happiness and wellbeing"* while *"acknowledging the need to promote sustainable development and … the MDGs"*.

I was awed, humbled and, indeed, inspired by the extraordinary response to our call for a gathering on the new economic paradigm under the auspices of the UN General Assembly. In the presence of the United Nations Secretary General, the General Assembly and ECOSOC Presidents, the President of Costa Rica (who gave the keynote address), the UNDP Administrator (Helen Clark, former PM of New Zealand), cabinet ministers and ambassadors from throughout the world, and more than 800 distinguished participants including Nobel Laureates, top economists and scholars, and spiritual and civil society leaders, the gathering launched a global movement to create a new wellbeing and sustainability based economy aimed at furthering human happiness.

The extraordinary constellation of great minds, nations, civil society, business and industry, spiritual leaders and concerned citizens gathered on 2nd April at United Nations headquarters has given me tremendous hope. It has rekindled my faith in humankind; in its goodness and innate wisdom; and in the enormous potential to build a sane, secure and happy world. Together on that day, we began to share the vast knowledge, wisdom and the will to break away from the tenacious grip of mindless consumerism.

There was an overarching sense among participants, reflected in their statements, that, given the combined ecological, economic, and social crises the world faces today, this gathering could not have been more timely or appropriate. There was also basic agreement on a shared vision: Instead of simply pursuing growth for its own sake, too often at the expense of our fragile earth, the new economy will respect planetary boundaries, ensure fair distribution of our limited resources, and use those resources with care and efficiency, to serve human happiness and the wellbeing of all life.

And we are committed to continuing on that path with determination. To that end, and at the request of the 2nd April gathering at the United Nations, an expert Commission has now been convened to elaborate the details of the new economic paradigm over the coming year, in time for consideration by the UN General Assembly session in September 2013. Greening the tourism industry — the theme of this book — is clearly an essential component of what the new Commission must examine.

In all this, our shared need and purpose are clear: we desperately need an economy that serves and nurtures the wellbeing of all sentient beings and the human happiness that comes from living life in harmony with the natural world, with our communities, and with our inner selves. We need an economy that will serve humanity, not enslave it. It must prevent the imminent reversal of civilization and flourish within the natural bounds of our planet while ensuring the sustainable, equit-able and meaningful use of our rapidly depleting resources.

Business as usual cannot go on, and tinkering with the existing system will not do. We need a fundamental transformation that the Tellus Institute calls *The Great Transition*.

Our goal on 2nd April was not simply to launch the initiative for such a transition in a theoretical or rhetorical way, but to move towards concrete outcomes and action steps that begin to create the new economy in practice. To that end, I was deeply moved that more than

200 participants at the UN gathering stayed behind for two more days of follow-up meetings to synthesize the 2nd April deliberations into clear outcomes and implementable processes.

These actions include:

- A report submitted in June 2012 to the UN Secretary General for distribution to all UN member states.

- Policy recommendations I sent in May 2012 to all Heads of State, which their governments may consider adopting to move towards the new economy. Of direct relevance to this publication, I wish to note that these recommendations specifically include 'greening' the tourism industry.

- Creation of a commission of eminent experts to elaborate the details of the new economy.

- Carrying this process forward to Rio +20, and thence to UN General Assembly deliberations to succeed the Millennium Development Goals after 2015 with a collective vision of a holistic, sustainable, and inclusive economic paradigm.

- Initiatives to promote a global citizen based movement for the new sustainability based economic paradigm, and to communicate the initiative widely.

Challenging as these aspirations may appear to be, and not without obstacles, I am confident that we will, in the coming months and years, find reasons for pride and satisfaction in having contributed to the crafting of a new and bright chapter in human history.

My deep appreciation goes to Maurice Strong for the inspiration he has given me, and for all he has done in his lifetime to create the ground and lay the foundation for the historic endeavour on which we have now embarked. May this book strengthen and further our shared vision.

# Valere Tjolle

## Principal of TotemTourism.com

## Tourism – towards a green economy

Valere Tjolle is the Principal of TotemTourism.com, publisher and editor of TravelMole.com *Vision on Sustainable Tourism* weekly newswire, and editor of the annual *Sustainable Tourism* suite of reports. Valere is an authority and key proponent of direct and alternative marketing and product creation in the travel and tourism industry with over 40 years in-depth 'hands on' experience at every level. He has singlehandedly created one of the most significant and thoughtful information bases on sustainable travel and tourism and is a vigorous advocate of the role the sector can play in green transformation.

The tourism industry is very young and extremely resilient. Although it took until 1950 to reach 25 million international tourists a year, the figure for 2012 is expected to be 1 billion. Add to this the unseen part of the iceberg, the domestic tourism industry, which is said to be some five times larger than international tourism, and you have a gargantuan multi-faceted, multi-sectoral global activity.

Phenomenal growth indeed, and phenomenal potential too; currently the international part of the tourism industry alone is said to provide around $1 trillion in export earnings and some 8% of global employment.

Moreover, the industry now pulls together a broad range of participants including transportation suppliers, hotels and restaurants, and provides both a virtual and actual showcase for local agriculture, viniculture, crafts and other products. The industry embraces all sizes of business from self-employed guides and traders through SMMEs (small, medium and micro enterprises) and billion-dollar global organizations.

These facts and figures are dramatic enough, but when one understands the challenges that the tourism industry has overcome in its short but driven adult life, the power of demand and the ingenuity of the industry is palpable.

Although tourism had already existed for hundreds of years, the 1960s really provided an incubator for its dramatic growth. Governments and NGOs had spotted the opportunities for tourism-fuelled economic growth, substantial airplane manufacturing industries had been established during the world wars, and low cost fuel was plentifully available. World airlines had gotten together with governments in 1945 to establish the global ground rules for air travel in the form of the Chicago Convention, which established airlines' international freedoms to fly and outlawed tax on fuel or spare parts. The market in Europe and the US was waking up with ready cash and it only needed entrepreneurs to blend the tourism mix of lower cost transportation and accommodation and put the resultant product to a willing marketplace. The industry took off.

The first hurdle that the industry overcame was the massive hike in fuel costs of the 1970s. In retrospect it is surprising that this emerging industry managed to deal with a tenfold fuel price rise from some 11c a gallon of kerosene in 1971 to over a dollar in 1980; but it did, and carried on growing.

How did it do it? Simply by waking up to the smell of coffee, understanding the true position and dealing with it. Before the fuel price rise, to those managing and marketing tourism (airlines and operators), tourism had been a numbers game: the more tourists you had, the more power you had, the more money you made (or appeared to make). After the fuel price rise, those that survived had recognized that the only relevant sustainability criterion was profit, and the critically important management skill was revenue management reflected in the profit and loss account.

Moreover, the industry's hardware, largely airplanes, got much more efficient, as did the industry's software; management, pricing and reservations systems. Efficient enough to take the massive fuel price rise into their stride, brush themselves off, pick themselves up, and carry on growing.

It's a truism that tourism needs marketing. Tourism wholesalers and retailers find market needs and they fulfil them. But what happens when there is economic trauma?

Fuel prices are only a product of general energy (read 'oil') prices and they affect national and international industries and economies just as much as they affect the airlines. The effect of high energy prices is usually high unemployment, reduced disposable income and crippled demand. In the 1970s, although there were fears to the contrary, tourism source markets demonstrated that travel and holidays were not up for grabs and the general public just carried on buying travel and tourism.

And through terrorism, wars, the fall of the Soviet Union and the economic disasters of 2008–2010, tourism growth has barely missed a beat; after a short hiccough it's now on a growth path again, continuing to be an industry full of opportunity and chock-full of real potential for world economic, social, cultural and environmental development.

And now, in 2012, we face another set of challenges that both affect, and are affected by tourism. Fuel prices are again spiking. Whereas the oil price per barrel from 1980 to 2008 remained within the $12 – $64 range, it is now hovering around $130 and likely to increase as world economies come out of stagnation/recession.

Man-made greenhouse gas (GHG) emissions are hastening global warming and world governments are gradually moving to cap these. The effect of this cap is certain to be an increase in the end-user price of travel. The effect of global warming itself will be to change the geography of tourism and the destinations key assets (e.g. ski tourism will not be feasible without snow; island tourism unfeasible without islands)

The call is for mitigation (of GHG emissions) and adaptation (to a changing world). Clearly we will move towards less-emitting transportation and less-emitting activities. In the same way that the outbound tourism industry dealt with the rising price of fuel (a combination of skilfully focused financial management and technical change), it will certainly deal with these new challenges and probably carry on growing. But will the travel and tourism industry become truly sustainable? Can it assist in a global move towards a sustainable economy?

The fact is that tourism can bring tourists and economic development to communities; it can bring tourists and effect social change; it can bring tourists and affect cultures; it can bring tourists and change environmental awareness and effects.

But can tourism be a sustainable activity and influence these areas in a positive way; can it assist in coping with the coming massive environmental and related economic and political challenges that now face us?

First of all, there appears to be no question that tourism will carry on growing. An industry that can deal with a tenfold cost rise in its primary raw material, in its infancy, and still grow is clearly endowed with such a massive market franchise that in the foreseeable future it is unstoppable.

But will it deliver on its opportunities for sustainable growth and become a major driver towards the sustainable and equitable green economic model envisaged by the Rio Earth Summit of 1992 and Agenda 21?

The key is the speed that tourism can adapt, how it will mitigate its affects on climate change, and its ability to maximize its positive sustainable local destination benefits. If it achieves this successfully, it will lay the foundation for its leadership industry position. Tourism will roll out a green carpet to a new sustainable world.

The airline industry will certainly respond to the challenge with a variety of technological changes and advances, including low emission biofuels, new ways of managing routes, higher load factors and enhanced engineering.

The rail industry is already beginning a global expansion of high-speed routes, taking advantage of its opportunity as a low emission carrier and opportunities for current technology to regain a large proportion of the short and medium haul market.

One can be sure that other surface transport operators such as shipping and bus transport are not far behind in the drive to maximum efficiency and emission management. And accommodation operators are quickly recognizing that energy and waste mean money and are reducing their costs and their consequent emissions. Tour operators, travel agents and global travel distribution networks, aware of the inherent marketing advantages in efficient systems will foster this growth in fuel and waste economy and low emission growth and promote these new products.

So the challenge of fuel prices and GHG emissions will be engaged, but what about the remainder of the Earth Summit Agenda 21 hopes; delivering local economic, cultural, environmental and social benefits?

Tourism is comprised of a partnership of three major stakeholders; this triumvirate comprises market, transportation and destination. The first two partners have their interest in generating and moving tourists for profit, usually for their shareholders. As part of their flexible business model, they are involved in the sustainability of the destinations to which they operate.

The third tourism stakeholder, the destination, has its interest in receiving tourists for a profit, usually for its residents who are reliant on the sustainability of their home location. A destination is a country, region, city, town or village community that naturally attracts tourists because it has a specific range of assets, or, indeed, has been created specifically to attract people.

The world's destinations range from key tourism countries such as France or Spain, iconic city venues such as the Cote d'Azur, New York, Rio de Janeiro, Cape Town, Benidorm, London, Paris, Rome, New York, Venice or Amsterdam, and world heritage sites, through to a massive range of other places large, small and tiny, all with a kaleidoscope of features and all who see tourism as an opportunity.

Whether managed by ministries of tourism, tourist boards, convention and visitors bureaux or local initiatives, it is fundamentally necessary for destinations to take responsibility for the overall sustainability of their inbound tourism-flow and exact from it the inherent benefits of local sustainable economic growth, local social and cultural advantages and local built and natural environmental stewardship and protection.

In the same way that that the outbound tourism industry woke up to the smell of reality in the 1970s when fuel prices escalated, and recognized that tourism is not a numbers game, but a revenue management game, destinations need to do the same now.

To create true sustainable tourism, destinations need to assert the key management role in the tourism triumvirate. Why? Because, whereas the marketers are answerable ultimately to their shareholders and their domicile legislators, destinations are responsible to their taxpayers and residents who are practically affected by inbound flows of tourism.

It is a fact that, apart from the environmental issues embodied in inbound transportation, the vast majority of social, environmental, cultural and economic opportunities and challenges of tourism take place in destinations and it is therefore their responsibility to manage tourism in a sustainable manner.

In this context, success for a destination will not be judged by numbers of tourists but by what beneficial effects tourism will have on the social, cultural, economic and environmental health of their destination.

This is the tourism challenge for the next 50 years. Which destinations will manage tourism to generate profit for their communities, economic profit, social profit, environmental profit and cultural profit, thus empowering their stakeholder residents?

Those destinations that understand their community's needs and manage tourism to fulfil them; engage in tourism revenue maximization; integrate destination branding incorporating locally produced products and services; use volunteer tourism to assist local development; reduce the energy, waste and carbon footprint of each and every tourism service; create integrated low energy local transportation systems; use training and interpretation to add maximum value and gain maximum revenue from each tourism visit. In short, it is those that see tourism in terms of a profit and loss account, take charge of it and manage it for their own benefit. These destinations will create a global industry that can rightfully be called sustainable.

# Tony Tyler

## Director General and CEO, IATA

## A green economy: the contribution of travel and tourism – the aviation viewpoint

Tony Tyler, Director General and CEO of the International Air Transport Association. Tony Tyler built his career at John Swire & Sons in Hong Kong starting in 1977. From 1978 he moved within the Swire Group to Cathay Pacific Airways, eventually serving as its Chief Executive from July 2007 to March 2011. Internationally, Tyler served on the IATA Board of Governors from 2007 to 2011 and was its Chairman from June 2009 to June 2010. Tony Tyler became the sixth person to lead IATA when he took on the role of Director General and CEO from 1 July 2011. He has broad international working experience in Australia, Canada, Hong Kong, Italy, Japan, the Philippines and the United Kingdom. At IATA, Tony works from both its main offices in Montreal, Canada and Geneva, Switzerland. He is a graduate from Oxford University in jurisprudence.

T

Connectivity is a crucial element of a modern, resource-efficient global green economy. Aviation is a good example of a key driver in the development of sustainable travel and tourism.

Let's start with some numbers. In 2011, 2.8 billion people flew safely. By value, over 35% of goods traded internationally were transported by air. By volume, that is approaching 50 million tonnes of cargo annually. A recent Oxford Economics study concluded that aviation and aviation-related tourism supports 56.6 million jobs worldwide. This, in turn, contributes $2.2 trillion to global GDP. If aviation were a country, it would have the 19th largest economy in the world. Aviation connectivity directly links some 35,000 city pairs. With a couple of kilometres of runway, even the most remote region on the planet can be globally connected.

Aviation is a force for good in our world. Every aircraft that takes off carries with it almost infinite possibilities—connecting people, facilitating trade, supporting journeys of discovery, and linking cultures to name just a few of the aviation's most important roles. Without aviation's connectivity, today's global economy simply could not function.

Regardless of the importance of aviation's economic and social benefits, like all industries, it must account for its environmental footprint. The Intergovernmental Panel on Climate Change (IPCC) has long said that aviation contributes about 2% to manmade carbon emissions. Despite the industry's phenomenal growth, this is as true today as it was a decade ago. Using aviation's global fuel uplift, which is carefully measured, we can calculate that it produced 676 million tonnes of $CO_2$ emissions in 2011. That is slightly less than 2% of the global total of man-made emissions, which is 34 billion tonnes. Looking ahead to 2050, the IPCC forecasts aviation's carbon footprint growing to about 3% of the global total.

## Commitments on carbon reduction

Regardless of the small relative size of its contribution to global carbon emissions, aviation is committed to constantly improving its environmental footprint. In 2009, the airlines, airports, air navigation service providers and aircraft manufacturers, agreed three sequential targets to reduce carbon emissions:

1. Improving fuel efficiency by an average of 1.5% annually to 2020
2. Capping net carbon emissions from 2020 for carbon-neutral growth
3. Cutting net emissions in half by 2050 compared to 2005 levels

Aviation remains the only global business sector to commit to such ambitious emissions reduction targets. Agreeing to these targets demonstrated how important this issue is for our industry: setting aside commercial rivalries to cooperate together for the greater good. This value chain approach has played an important role in aviation since its very inception. For example, by working together with governments and guided by global standards, aviation has become by far the safest mode of transport.

Green business is also good business. At 2012 prices, fuel accounts for well over 30% of an airline's operating cost. For an industry that has struggled to eke out an historical net profit margin of less than 1%, anything that can be done to reduce the fuel bill is of critical financial importance. And if we look back over the last five decades, industry fuel efficiency has improved by over 70%. At the same time, jet aircraft have become 75% quieter.

Aviation's carbon emission targets will be met by implementing a four-pillar strategy. First, technological advances in new engines, fuels and aircraft design. Second, improved operational efficiency aims to fly aircraft more directly point to point, or to cut weight onboard. The third strand, infrastructure, is all about tackling air traffic management inefficiencies (by up to 10% per flight in Europe) and improving the use of airport capacity. Finally, positive economic measures, such as emissions trading or offsetting, are a temporary medium-term bridge to help us meet our carbon-neutral growth commitment.

## Market-based measures

Governments have placed much emphasis on economic measures. And many environmental activists have mistakenly propagated accusations that international aviation's protection from tax on fuel uplifted for international operations has meant a free-ride for the industry. If we conservatively estimate the impact of just three of the many taxes that aviation faces—the UK's Air Passenger Duty, and departure taxes in Germany and Austria—we come to a bill of well over EUR 4 billion annually. All three taxes were introduced specifically as environmental measures, even if over time governments have re-purposed them. At today's prices for UN issued Certified Emissions Reductions that would offset all the world's aviation $CO_2$ emissions about one-and-a-half times.

Positive economic measures are the fourth pillar of our strategy. But a global industry such as aviation needs such measures to be globally coordinated to be effective and not just an excuse for yet another tax. For example, economic measures for a coal burning power plant in country A can be dealt with domestically as a matter of national policy. But an uproar among governments has arisen over the challenge to sovereignty presented by Europe's extra-territorial approach to including international aviation in its emissions trading scheme. This illustrates the critical need for states to come together through the International Civil Aviation Organization to agree a global framework.

## The prize of sustainable biofuels

But I should stress that rather than just pay for emissions, aviation believes we must reduce them. That is why the industry has invested so much in the development of sustainable biofuels. If we took a short-term hard-nosed economics approach, sustainable biofuels don't make a lot of sense. Fuel is already among the biggest cost item for an airline. Biofuels are currently much more expensive than traditional jet fuel. And our financial performance over the last 11 years has seen the industry post a global loss of over $26 billion on about $5.5 trillion in revenues.

But, with the promise to reduce aviation's carbon footprint by up to 80%, biofuels have the potential to be a key component of aviation's license to grow. Biofuels themselves emit about the same amount of carbon as traditional jet fuel. Emission reduction comes from the fact that the source crops or biomass has absorbed carbon as they have been grown or produced. Second generation sustainable biofuels do not compete for land or water with food-crops and they do not threaten bio-diversity. With test flights and over 1500 commercial flights already completed, we have proven that sustainable biofuels are safe to use in the current fleet of aircraft and they can be mixed with existing jet kerosene without problems.

This is a game changer. Five years ago there was no alternative to jet fuel. The challenge now is to make sustainable biofuels commercially viable by increasing production volumes and reducing their cost. To do this, governments must help. There are six ways governments can offer concrete assistance:

1. Foster research into new feedstock sources and refining processes;
2. De-risk public and private investments in aviation biofuels;
3. Provide incentives for airlines to use biofuels from an early stage;
4. Encourage stakeholders to commit to robust international sustainability criteria;
5. Make the most of local green growth opportunities; and
6. Encourage coalitions encompassing all parts of the supply chain.

Alone, biofuels are not the answer. And we are not putting all our eggs in one basket. But sustainable aviation biofuels and reformed air traffic management, together with the new generation of advanced aircraft (which cut emissions 20% compared to their predecessors) will provide the bulk of the emissions reductions the industry has committed to in the coming years.

Aviation is putting its house in order. And with the right policy framework from governments, it will continue to be in the forefront of environmentally responsible industries. That is important because an ever-more sustainable aviation industry is an indispensible tool for driving environmental development. Human expertise, specialist materials, hi-tech equipment, and essential drugs – all of these need air transport. The green economy is founded on technological solutions to our most pressing challenges. Disseminating technology and ideas with great speed is what aviation does best.

## Aviation drives productivity and development

A key tenet of sustainable development is producing more by using less. In other words, we must become ever-more efficient in our processes. Air transport is a proven stimulator of greater productivity, through the benefits of better connectivity to markets. The direct effect of improved connectivity between nations is hard to quantify, but a conservative estimate is that a 10% improvement in connectivity relative to GDP equates to around a 0.07% per annum increase in long run GDP. This means over the last two decades the growth in air connectivity has added around $200 billion to global GDP.

Aside from its role in generating productivity, aviation plays an important role in directly facilitating the green economy. Two such examples from Africa concern national parks in Namibia, and organic produce in Ghana.

In Namibia tourism generates between $160 and $300 million each year. Many of these tourists are coming to view the country's remarkable variety of habitats and ecosystems, to the extent that the government has created a single Ministry of Environment and Tourism to align these two important issues. The government actively protects the land and wildlife, and has attracted UN and US grants, creating 6,500 jobs and safeguarding these fragile habitats for generations to come.

Ghana is an important example of the trade in fresh produce between Africa and Europe. Fresh fruit and vegetable exports from Ghana to the UK supports 50–60,000 small-scale producers and larger farms, and across Africa as a whole, trade with the UK alone is worth around $320 million to rural economies. An organisation dedicated to the development of sustainable agriculture, Blue Skies Ghana, is providing training and support to over 150 farmers, over half of them organic smallholders. The company's fresh-cut fruit factory employs 1,700 people and accounts for 1% of Ghana's total exports.

Without aviation, the eco-tourists bringing investment to Namibia's national parks, and the exports which sustain Namibia's economy, would not be possible. And the future growth opportunities of this kind to developing economies are multiplying. According to Oxford Economics, of the 57.6 million jobs supported by air transport, 35.9 million are in developing countries and contributing $490 billion to their GDP. With aviation-related industries set to grow faster than the wider economy, these numbers will grow in absolute and relative terms.

## A foundation of the knowledge economy

Globally, the future green economy will be a knowledge economy, and aviation is a driver both of knowledge exchange and knowledge creation. In addition to the connectivity advantages described above, aviation directly stimulates research and development into new materials, products and manufacturing techniques. Airframers invest billions of dollars in finding more efficient materials, with spin-off benefits far beyond the industry itself. Every $100 million of aviation R&D spending is estimated to generate a further $70 million in additional GDP year-after-year.

The industry also fosters educational and technical opportunities for people in the workforce. Aviation requires skilled workers, whether they are pilots, designers or technicians, and the training they require gives a boost to universities and technical colleges. Aviation jobs are also 3.5 times more productive than other jobs on average.

When you put together the tremendous economic development opportunities facilitated by aviation with the positive strides the industry is making in reducing its environmental footprint, then it is clear that aviation is an integral part of the developing green economy.

Aviation is a fantastically positive story. And when combined with tourism, with which it is integrally linked, it becomes even more compelling.

Of course a story, no matter how compelling, is only effective if it is communicated. It is clear to me that 'tax and restrict' policies towards aviation are misguided. I am sure that it is equally clear to every partici-pant in the value chain – from the manufacturers who create aircraft right through to the airports, hotels and restaurants that receive travellers.

The Rio +20 Summit is a great opportunity for aviation and tourism to tell its common story. The world will gather in Rio to explore two themes:  a green economy in the context of sustainable development and poverty eradication; and the institutional framework for sustain-able development.

The economic and social benefits of aviation and tourism are already key drivers for sustainable development that is lifting millions from poverty. And the aviation industry's challenge to governments to support its agreed global approach to emissions reductions is a model for effective global cooperation.

Of course there is always something to learn. And we must welcome and encourage a partnership with governments that will supportively challenge our collective efforts to make this key component of our modern world—aviation and tourism—ever more sustainable. At the same time, the Rio +20 Summit offers policy-makers the chance to seize the positive example of our industry. I hope they take that opportunity for the sake of continuing to enrich and develop the global community that connectivity has created.

# Marthinus van Schalkwyk

## Minister of Tourism, South Africa

## Breaking out of the silos

Marthinus van Schalkwyk, Minister of South Africa. He is a lawyer and political scientist by profession. His academic qualifications include a B Proc degree as well as a Bachelor of Arts Honours degree and Master of Arts degree in Political Science from Rand Afrikaans University (now the University of Johannesburg). Minister van Schalkwyk has served as a Member of the National Parliament since 1990. He later, in 2002 to 2004, also held the helm of the Western Cape Province when he took up office as the Premier of that Province. In 2004 he assumed the role of South Africa's Minister of Environmental Affairs and Tourism and in 2009 he became the Minister of Tourism, an office which he currently still holds. He was Chairperson of the Aviation, Travel and Tourism Industry Agenda Council of the World Economic Forum (WEF) for the 2010-2011 period.

## Travel and tourism is a force for good

The travel and tourism sector is a significant contributor to gross domestic product (GDP) and job creation. The sector creates one in every 12 jobs globally. If travel and tourism were to be a country, it would rank 11<sup>th</sup> on the list of G20 countries for its direct contribution to GDP, or third if we had to count its total economic contribution. Given the volume of tourism activity in developing and emerging-market destinations, travel and tourism also presents an opportunity for more equitable global economic growth, which would promote social inclusion at a global level.

However, the sector's impact extends much further. This is something that was highlighted in the report produced by the commission appointed by President Nicolas Sarkozy three years ago. In this report,

Prof Joseph Stiglitz reminded us to look beyond narrow GDP metrics and also consider the sector's significant contribution to quality of life and sustainability in the broader context of societal well-being.

The travel and leisure experience goes to the core of the aspirations of people worldwide. It fosters an improved understanding between people and cultures, thereby promoting global peace and harmony. Just imagine how many people-to-people connections will be established by the one billion international tourist arrivals expected in 2012. Not surprisingly, tourism is often also one of the first industries to be rebuilt in post-war or post-conflict reconstructions, and tourism promotion has also emerged as a key foreign policy strategy in the transformation of many previously closed societies.

## The 'dark side' of travel and tourism must be managed

An honest assessment requires that we also recognise the indirect drawbacks associated with travel and tourism. The rapid expansion of our sector goes hand in hand with increased greenhouse gas emissions, escalating waste streams, increased water consumption, and sometimes even permanent damage to terrestrial and marine biodiversity as well as local cultures and traditions.

As a sector, therefore, we also have a responsibility to deal with these critical sustainability challenges; to deal with the so-called 'dark side' of tourism. We need travel and tourism with a social, ethical and environmental conscience.

## Breaking out of the silos

I am a firm believer in the need to break out of silo-based thinking about tourism and aviation. These two sectors have, for historical reasons, been institutionalised and regulated in silos. Yet, they both face many cross-cutting policy challenges, which require coordinated action between different government line functions, United Nations agencies and industry bodies. For example, the two sectors are equally exposed to global economic shocks; restrictive travel barriers and the slow uptake of e-visas; archaic legal frameworks, such as those created by the Chicago Convention; global health pandemics and security scares; volatile oil prices, and so on.

The two sectors also share a responsibility to address the growing carbon footprint of aviation and long-haul tourism..

## The decoupling challenge

On the one hand, the aviation industry is extremely vulnerable to climate change response policies, especially when these involve the pricing of carbon emissions. On the other, the industry has to contribute its fair share to efforts to limit the global temperature increase to below 2 °C. This will be no easy task. The growth expected in international tourism and trade flows over the next four decades, the superiority of air transport as enabler of long-haul travel, and the dependence of aviation on fossil fuels all render this a huge challenge.

Slowing down aviation and tourism growth simply to reduce carbon emissions will be in no-one's interest. It will destroy jobs and undermine our efforts to reduce poverty. Aviation is not only a key enabler of tourism, but also of trade, investment and global integration. However, as much as 'slowing down' is not an option, sitting back and 'doing nothing' isn't one either. Business-as-usual growth of emissions will simply not be environmentally, economically or politically sustainable in decades to come. It will contribute to irreversible damage to our ecosystem and the livelihoods that depend on it.

Therefore, the challenge is to decouple aviation growth from emissions growth. If decarbonisation of aviation does not accelerate, this industry will not remain competitive in a carbon-constrained world.

## Government and industry both have important roles to play

The travel and tourism industry cannot be expected to tackle this multi-decade challenge on its own. The intolerable status quo is the result of both a massive market *and* governance failure.

The International Air Transport Association (IATA) has consolidated the industry around a common set of targets for 2020 and 2050. Of course, a comparison of these targets with what is required by science will follow in due course, but, for now, the 'in principle' commitment is an important start. That being said, words on paper can never become an end goal. The aviation industry should take these targets more seriously. In saying this, we should recognise that we are dealing with a long supply chain, and those that need most prompting are often not airlines, but the oil companies that control the production and distribution of kerosene jet fuel. I believe they need to take their environmental stewardship much more seriously. Their lack of investment in developing second-generation drop-in aviation biofuels is of great concern.

The immediate challenge is much broader, though. All players in the aviation industry will have to do more to realise the potential of operational and infrastructural improvements, and to accelerate the uptake of market-ready technologies. Many of these efficiency improvements do not require government intervention, but simply make good business sense: they reduce fuel bills.

However, governments also have a critical role to play. This includes their contribution to research and development, airspace redesign, optimised flight routes, freeing up the skies for competition as well as the provision of more modern airport and air traffic management infrastructure. Also, given that we are faced with market failures of global proportions, introducing stringent carbon dioxide ($CO_2$) standards as well as benchmarks for green certification may soon become unavoidable. In addition, the aviation sector is looking to Europe and the United States of America to make substantial progress with the implementation of the SESAR (Single European Sky ATM Research) and NextGen (Next-Generation Air Transportation System) initiatives.

## Biofuels and market-based mechanisms

Once the near-term carbon abatement opportunities are optimised, only two long-term options remain, namely the drop-in of sustainable, second-generation biofuels and a global cap-and-trade scheme. This is not an 'either/or' situation: both a market-based mechanism *and* the drop-in of biofuels are required. It will be irresponsible to place all our eggs in the biofuels basket. The scalability is simply too uncertain. Therefore, an emissions trading scheme must provide offsetting opportunities for unavoidable aviation emissions, but, even more importantly, must create a price incentive for new investment in low-carbon technology.

Governments have a critical role in de-risking the substantial investment that will be required to kick-start an aviation biofuels industry.

Besides research and demonstration partnerships, public policy has to create the framework conditions for feedstock production. Governments also have a responsibility to introduce globally harmonised sustainability standards, and to level the playing field with the automotive industry. In time, this may require the phased introduction of fuel-blending mandates.

Ultimately, policy signals must be *loud,* in that they should be ambitious and create a viable market; they must be *legal,* in that they should provide market certainty, and they must be *long-term,* given the long lead times involved in the aviation technology life cycle.

## A price on carbon

A global price on carbon is a potential game changer. This is a transnational industry requiring global solutions. The creation of a global, sectoral cap-and-trade emissions trading scheme for aviation is long overdue.

Such a scheme should be underpinned by an ambitious long-term target and mid-term pathways. It should be legally binding, in other words there should be consequences for non-compliance, and, in time, the cap should become more stringent. Carbon pricing would have to be progressive yet foreseeable in order to allow the industry to plan over long time horizons. There are of course also important caveats, including that aviation's burden should not be disproportionate to that of other economic sectors – aviation cannot become the 'cash cow' of the climate regime. Also, to avoid double-counting and double-taxing of emissions, such a global scheme should replace the current patchwork of unilateral emissions trading and green taxation schemes that are spreading like wildfire in Europe.

Take for example the United Kingdom's air passenger duty (APD). What started off as a green tax has now become a pure revenue-raising mechanism. Its green credentials are long gone. The tax started off at a low level, but has now grown into a substantial levy on international tourism. And for those of us in the developing world who depend on eco-tourism, it is a tax on our green services exports.

## European Union emissions trading scheme (EU ETS)

Another issue with global ramifications is the European Union emissions trading scheme (EU ETS). Without necessarily questioning the underlying principles of this market-based mechanism, it would be fair to say that the aggressive unilateralism associated with its introduction leaves a fairly bitter aftertaste. The strong reaction that it has triggered from across the world, including threats of a trade war, was not a surprise.

From a tourism and aviation vantage point, the potential competitive distortions as well as the potential supply chain disruptions that may result from this kind of unilateralism, counter-threats of a trade war, retaliation and an uncoordinated proliferation of equivalent measures are rather disconcerting – and remain so, whether you represent an airline with narrow operating margins or a long-haul developing-country tourism destination that depends heavily on international airlift to create jobs and reduce poverty.

The EU's frustration with 15 years of intransigence and doublespeak in the International Civil Aviation Organisation (ICAO) has been clearly stated. Progress with negotiations has been too slow, and too many vested interests have frustrated the political process. Ultimately, though, multilateralism must prevail. Aggressive unilateralism and extra-territorial measures are not the way to go in an increasingly globalised world. These may look attractive in the short term, but will reap the whirlwind of confrontation in the medium to long term.

It is in this context that I have previously proposed that, given the EU and the rest of the world's commitment to a global solution, the EU should suspend aviation's inclusion in the EU ETS for two years. The EU should go the extra mile and give the negotiating parties in ICAO a fair chance to conclude negotiations on a global, sectoral emissions trading scheme by the end of 2013. The multilateral negotiating options have not yet been exhausted and it is still possible to capture our commitment to clean up our act in a negotiated agreement under a stronger, forward-looking ICAO.

## A global ICAO deal is in the interest of travel and tourism

With stronger leadership from all sides, it is possible to resolve the outstanding issues in ICAO, including the seeming clash of principles between the climate change and air transport regimes. One way to resolve the impasse could be to agree that any market-based mechanism would have 'zero net incidence' for developing countries. In the design of an emissions trading scheme, provision could be made for the ICAO principle of equal treatment to apply at an operator level when revenues are raised. However, when the resources from a multilaterally managed fund are allocated, differentiated disbursements could be made, for example towards decarbonised infrastructure and sustainable-biofuels industries in developing-country markets. This assumes that a significant portion of revenues from carbon pricing will be re-invested in green growth.

It is in the tourism sector's best interest that the negotiations on a global cap-and-trade regime for aviation emissions in ICAO take a quantum leap in the next year – not only because of the additional costs imposed on tourists due to uncoordinated taxes and levies, but also because of our firm belief that aviation and tourism should contribute its fair share to the prevention of dangerous climate change.

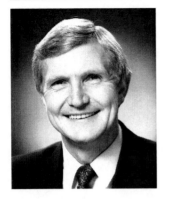

# Dawid de Villiers

## Special Advisor to the UNWTO Secretary-General on Ethical Matters

## Responsible tourism, local communities and ethics

Previously Deputy Secretary-General of the World Tourism Organization, Dr. de Villiers is presently the Special Advisor to the UNWTO Secretary-General on Ethical Matters, and has been the Chairman of the World Committee on Ethics in Tourism since 2008. He also chairs the World Tourism Network on Child Protection. Prior to joining UNWTO, Dr. de Villiers was South Africa's Minister for Environment and Tourism in the Government of National Unity under President Mandela. Dr. de Villiers further played a key role in the negotiations that facilitated South Africa's transition to democracy. Drawing on his background in philosophy and theology, he was instrumental in drafting the Global Code of Ethics for Tourism, a roadmap for responsible tourism development. He captained South Africa's national rugby team 'the Springboks' for many years.

People often ask, what is ethics? A seemingly simple but enormously challenging question, because it is not easy to define, and in a complex world facing enormous social, economic and environmental challenges that need ethics based directions, there is no place for intellectual debate. The origins of the ethical debate, are, of course, rooted in history. Aristotle is one of the first authors to consider the meaning of ethics, considering it to be the study of how individuals should best live. Over the intervening generations, strangely little has changed. In my mind, 'ethics' refers to a set of standards and values that an individual, or a group of individuals, have about what is right and what is wrong, what is good and what is evil.

A person's ethical standards are first absorbed as a child from parents, family, friends, and other influences such as religious organisations, school, television, magazines et cetera. Later, as people grow up and experience more of life, their intellectual development or cultural norms may lead them to question and change some of these early developed ethical standards.

There are many different kinds of standards – quality standards, environmental standards, educational standards – and many more. Moral and/or ethical standards, however, are different. Moral standards deal with behaviour that we judge to be of a serious nature, with bad consequences (such as theft, rape, murder, child-abuse, fraud, and so on). Moral standards are based on sound values and good reason developed over mankind's 'civilization evolution' and not simply decisions by governments or any other authority (unlike laws or rules created by official public institutions). Moral standards should also override non-moral values, such as self-interest. Moral transgression is associated with feelings of guilt and shame when moral those standards are broken.

The definition of ethics, then, is the discipline that examines one's moral standards or the moral standards of a society. It asks how these standards apply to our lives, guide our behaviour and whether these standards are based on good reason. A person starts to practise ethics when he or she takes the moral standards absorbed from family, religion and friends and asks: What do these standards imply for the situation in which I find myself? Do these standards really make sense? Why should I continue to believe in them and behave as they prescribe? And so on.

The *Global Code of Ethics for Tourism* is a document and associated process in which a number of moral issues – rights and wrongs – in the tourism industry are stated. The Code is, in essence, an ethical road map to guide tourists and the various key-players through the tourism landscape. The Code recognises tourism as a vehicle for individual and collective fulfilment; for mutual understanding and respect between peoples and societies; and as a driver of sustainable development. In nine articles the 'rules of the game' are outlined for destinations, governments, tour operators, developers, travel agents, workers and travellers: for all of us.

Tourism has grown dramatically into one of the biggest economic activities in the World. It has become a major economic force and a driver of economic growth and development. It constitutes 30% of the world's export of services and employs between 7%-8% of the world's workforce. Travel and tourism is the primary source of foreign exchange for the vast majority of developing countries. However, in its success lies its biggest challenge. The mere size and growing volume of the tourism industry has a huge positive, but also a negative, impact on the social, cultural and the natural environment. The environment – the very product that forms the basis of most tourism activities and provides much of its profits – is in danger of being harmed irreparably.

As tourism activity continues to grow, every facet of the sector has become increasingly intertwined with environmental sustainability. Industry leaders are acutely aware of the challenges we face. They have made remarkable progress in many sectors to reduce the carbon footprint of the Industry and to introduce new and cleaner technologies. The fact is that responsible tourism can be a major driver of the 'green economy' in providing sustainable infrastructure, green business-models, opportunities, jobs and income.

The case for sustainable development has been made convincingly over and over again – it is increasingly recognized over the past two decades that our planet and its resources are being rapidly eroded by unsustainable policies and practises. We depend on the resources of the Earth to sustain our lives – from the most basic requirements such as air, water and food, through to the materials we use for shelter, transport, work and recreation. Some of these resources – like minerals and fossil fuels – are finite and hence not renewable. However, most of the Earth's resources are infinitely renewable – if, and it is a big IF – they are utilised in a sustainable manner.

The problem of sustainability is fundamentally an issue of values – it is a moral issue. Moral issues can be dealt with in two ways: from the perspective of impersonal impartiality, in other words, from a cold, objective and intellectual analysis, or from the perspective of caring – caring for persons and relationships. The great philosopher Martin Buber wrote about the three fundamental relationships that define the identity of every person. The first is 'I – you' (the relationship between people), then 'I-it' (the relationship with things) and finally 'I-Thou' (a relationship with the unknown). But it is through the 'I-you' relationship, that I become 'I'. Buber said: 'Ich werde am Du'. Through you, I become myself. It is through people, fellow human beings, family, neighbours, and friends that I become what I am; that my identity is developed. That is a very powerful vision, and it places human relationships at the heart of the discussion of questions such as: 'who am I?' and 'how should I care for others and for our planet?' That is why I believe that the ethics of 'caring' and of taking responsibility for others, for our world, for the future of society and our planet, is an approach with more feeling, more heart, and is, therefore, more effective.

Through interaction with people and the discussion of moral issues, we can develop our ability to move beyond the simple acceptance of moral standards and turn them into action-driven objectives. And the exchanges become guidelines of what ought to be, of what I can do to promote sustainability and responsible tourism: in my business; in our village; in our community; and in our country.

Doing business in a specific place is not an isolated exercise. It is linked to an interrelated network with the people of a geographical area and all the activities that take place in it. My business is linked to the people, nature, culture *and values* of the place where I do business.

Local communities can play a central role in advancing the principles of responsible tourism and sustainable development. Most countries have a history in which the views of communities on matters that affect their lives are seldom seriously considered at governmental levels. Decisions are handed down from the top and they begin to resent this attitude. Communities want to have a direct say in matters that affect their lives and futures. Communities have a crucial role to play in creating a sustainable environment with sustainable tourism products. The expression 'think globally, act locally' is a particularly relevant principle for communities. Real sustainability will come from the villagers, the communities, and from the people – or not at all. After all, tourists come and go but destinations and communities remain.

I have thought about a conceptual framework that would facilitate the implementation of sustainable tourism with clear ethical guidelines. A framework that appeals to me is one based on the concept of environmental 'embedding'. It is the concept that all our activities are rooted in the surrounding natural, cultural, political environment and have knock-on effects on that environment. All our relations and actions are inter-connected and establish a framework in which we can formulate our policies. The point I raised earlier was that sustainability is fundamentally an issue of values – it has to be dealt with at the cultural and political level. Solutions must be explored and tested through a process of continuous learning and application. Because there can be no permanent solutions in an ecologically dynamic world; choices will have to be made again and again as circumstances evolve.

I am convinced that the tourism industry can play a key role in establishing sustainability as the guiding principle for economic activity and development. It can help to provide the income and means to care for our world by generating money and energy for conservation. It can stimulate a process of responsible planning and good management of our scarce resources. It also reaches out to people by redistributing wealth and income and provides opportunities to improve the quality of life. There is a fine balance between development and sustainability – we walk a tightrope – but, at the same time there are many exciting opportunities.

I would like to conclude my contribution with a question about the application of some of the principles contained in the *Global Code of Ethics for Tourism*. Would it be possible in your business, in your job, in your trade to turn those aspects of the *Global Code of Ethics* that are relevant to your activities, into a personal code of responsibilities? Would it be possible to phrase the relevant sections as goals that you set yourself or the company, or the community, and actively aspire to reach those goals? I think it is possible to phrase the goals in such a way that you can monitor, and over time measure, your progress or regress; that you can audit your actions? And adjust them to be more ethically responsible. That is our next big challenge. To walk the walk; not just talk the talk.

Paul (the apostle) wrote to the Romans and advised them that they should overcome evil by doing good. But how to do that? Well, he wrote, by not being lazy, sluggish, and inactive. The application of that advice to our reality and our problems is that we can overcome bad situations of environmental degradation or resource depletion, if we are willing to act decisively, to work hard and purposefully and be prepared to make personal sacrifices. Things can go desperately wrong and awfully bad when good people choose to do nothing. But we can turn the tide if we act decisively.

Responsible tourism challenges us to take action, to implement our moral convictions and help to turn the tides that rise against us. And at the core must be the cultural values of tourism communities. It is our challenge and responsibility as travellers, as businesses and as policymakers to understand them and to ensure that our own behaviour respects and enhances them. In the process we will strengthen our own ethics.

# Gordon Wilson

**President and CEO, Travelport**

**Green growth and travelism – a technology company's commitment**

Gordon Wilson is President and CEO of Travelport, one of the world's leading providers of critical travel content aggregation, search and booking services for the global travel industry. Mr. Wilson was appointed to his current post on June 1, 2011, having previously served as Travelport's Deputy CEO since November 2009 and as President and CEO of the Travelport GDS, the largest division of the company, since January 2007. Mr. Wilson has 20 years' experience in global electronic travel distribution, in various senior positions, including CEO roles with Galileo and Cendant Travel Distribution Services. During his career, Mr. Wilson has lived and worked in the United Kingdom, the U.S.A., South Africa and Portugal. Gordon Wilson holds a Masters Degree in Law from the University of Cambridge.

I run a leading global technology company which every day enables on-line and off-line travel agencies, as well as corporations to search, price and book travel itineraries to enable leisure and business travel to virtually everywhere in the world. Last year we transacted over $83bn in ticket sales and hotel nights alone and our technology was involved in the reservation experience of every passenger carried by airlines such as Delta, United and Emirates Airlines - for whom we run some critical systems.

So although Travelport doesn't operate the airplanes, rental cars or railways, or build or service hotel rooms, or directly sell to travellers – we are involved in and therefore have a connection with the impact the literally billions of travellers who make trips can have on the environment. Not that we are in any way apologists for travel or the travel economy – which in my opinion is a force for economic and social good. By travelling to other nations and understanding other people, much more environmentally destructive activities can perhaps be avoided. By engaging in global commerce, wealth can be created that enables everything from irrigation of unfertile regions, to being able to afford to feed the world's hungry mouths. Travel and tourism creates jobs and jobs are good things.

That said, it would be madness if the very business of travel – from which I and my co-workers earn a living – was allowed to destroy the actual asset which underpins the reason for that business in the first place. Since we intend to be in business for at least another 40 years beyond the 40 we have already chalked up, the wisdom of our ancestors is worth paying attention to and doing our part to deliver upon. As the Native American proverb says: 'We do not inherit the earth from our ancestors, we borrow it from our children.'

So what can a company such as mine do to play our part?

First, our operating mantra is that we are all about providing technology which enables the ultimate consumer of travel – the person who flies in the plane, or stays in the hotel – to make an informed choice. Increasingly, that informed choice is about many factors in addition to price and convenience of schedule. Customers want to know what impact their activity has on the environment and what choices they can exercise accordingly – which can include adding to search parameters the relative carbon burn of one type of aircraft used on a route versus another. Choice can also include adding into the search criteria for a hotel in the destination city some form of green credential to understand which hotels use best recycled products, operate 'green clean' establishments, or have an active policy to put something back into the environment for everything they take out. Choice can be checking whether a car rental company offers electric vehicles as an alternative to petrol, or diesel powered options, or if there is a rail alternative to get between these two cities? Travelport has, and continues to invest in, letting people make their own choices through bringing together a wider range of travel options, of which rail would be a key example, and improving our search options to include the sort of additional filters that a customer of the travel agency might want to see before finally deciding the route, airline and hotel to which they want to give their business.

Secondly, there is what we do in our own world. And as you might imagine, running systems that process well over a billion transactions a day and operates on a 24 × 7 basis across over 170 countries, requires a pretty sizeable and secure facility of state of the art computing power.

Today my company deals in multiple petabytes of information per second. A petabyte is approximately 1,000 terabytes or one million gigabytes – a mind boggling number. It is hard to visualize, so it easier to imagine that one petabyte could hold approximately 20 million four-drawer filing cabinets full of text; the equivalent of around 500 billion pages of standard printed text; or, there again, about 500 million floppy disks' worth of data. So there is good news for the environment in that all this data is not on paper – but potentially less so in the sense that the power footprint we have to run the systems to store and process this size and scale of data is quite large. We do this through a fully backed up major league data centre facility in Atlanta in the USA and of course run our own generators as a back-up.

Over recent years, Travelport has invested millions of dollars in upgrading the computer hardware on which our applications run and in which our data is stored. And, while we have clearly done this to make our business more efficient, we have also done it because each new generation of servers and mainframes has a significantly improved power footprint in terms of lower consumption than the last. This power consumption is not just the electricity to run the machines themselves, but also the cooling and air conditioning required, since older equipment in particular tends to run 'hot' and needs to be cooled down.

Travelport will continue to work with the manufacturers of large scale computing equipment to continue to pull down the environmental footprint this equipment has, requiring on-going investment into our infrastructure. This includes greater use of battery power back up – not your average AA battery for sure, but industrial strength batteries which, whilst not a complete alternative to diesel generated back-up power, do mean that we would have to use diesel less.

Finally, in my company, in addition to what we are doing in our data centre, we are reducing our own energy consumption, increasing recycling and purchasing more green products in our office locations around the world. To give you just one example, when we moved one of our major offices in Kansas City in 2010 we worked with the building owners and architects to make our new home as green as possible. Together we made sure we used low VOC paint, that other wall coverings were PVC free and Greenguard certified, we used cork flooring which is material that regenerates, our bioglass counter tops were made from 100% recycled glass and so on. Interestingly, this does not actually cost more in total than less environmentally sensitive décor, but it does require careful thought and planning. Other initiatives include energy-saving lighting and sensors that automatically turn lights off in unoccupied rooms, which we have rolled out to all major offices, adjusting heating and cooling systems by a degree or two to save energy and recycling all of our waste paper, aluminium and glass containers. We provide bike stands and encourage the use of car-pooling and environmentally-friendly cars, while ensuring a greener supply chain. Paper-based employee communication has been almost entirely eliminated – in much the same way that we pioneered electronic ticketing for airlines and paperless itineraries.

But we are just one company and all of us can do more. We just need to give what can be fairly simple initiatives – either cost neutral, or in some cases cost reductive – the air time, priority and commitment from the top. Once it becomes engrained in the company culture that we are about 're-covering', 're-cycling', 're-ducing', 're-using', and encouraging the discussion of ideas for a greener workforce, it is quite amazing what momentum can be achieved.

As we all know, big though the world is, it is made up of little things and it only takes all of us to individually or collectively do some of these little things to make massive change. This is one of the reasons that Travelport serves on both the Working Committee and the Steering Committee for the World Travel & Tourism Council's efforts on leading the challenge on climate change – subjects particularly close to my heart. This is a 'little thing' in terms of additional commitment in my working life – but for a big outcome. Similarly, for the past five years Travelport has been one of the two proud sponsors of the Tourism for Tomorrow Awards at the World Travel & Tourism Council Summit. This award recognizes destinations, resorts, hotels and other players in the travel space who are leading by example in developing their business of tourism and travel in a manner which mitigates the environmental impact of such business. It ensures that the earth we have borrowed from our children is returned to them in at least as good as state, if not better, than we received it.

The great thing now is that if you have children I am sure that you have seen what I see with my own – the set of filters through which they engage in informed choice absolutely includes consideration of the environment impact. This next generation of consumers is going to demand that freedom to travel and experience the world will not be compromised, or come at the cost of the planet. As business people, as well as responsible world citizens protecting the asset from which we earn our living, we need to be totally tuned into this.

The Rio Summit this June with one of its principal objectives to – secure renewed political commitment to sustainable development – is absolutely something that has to be a responsibility which is totally shared with the business community and anyone who earns their living from travel.

And together, we can ensure the earth we have borrowed from our children is returned to them in at least as good as state, if not better, than we received it.

# Reto Wittwer

## President and CEO, Kempinski Hotels

## Harnessing people power to secure green growth

In July 1995 Reto Wittwer was appointed President and Chief Executive Officer of Kempinski Hotels, Europe's oldest luxury hotel management company, which operates internationally. Over the past 30 years he has gathered extensive experience in the international hotel industry and is considered one of the leaders in luxury hospitality. One of the industry's longest serving CEOs since the 1990s, Wittwer previously held the position of President and CEO of Ciga S.p.A. and prior to that, he was President and CEO of Swissair Nestlé Swissôtel Ltd. Reto Wittwer was born in Switzerland and has lived and worked all over the world. He is a graduate of the renowned Swiss Hotel Management School in Lausanne. Wittwer has received many honours for his contribution to the Hotel and Tourism Industry, including the 'Freedom of the City of Paris' and the title 'Knight of Honour of France'.

## The sustainability of our business depends on people

W

The hospitality industry is unique in many ways. But what makes me most passionate about it is that our industry, with all the people we hire across the world, is not only a melting pot of different cultures from whom we can learn, but is also an important platform for sharing and conveying knowledge and improving understanding between peoples. Cultural diversity, exchange and unleashing potential within people inspires me personally and greatly influenced my aspiration to be in a position where I could drive change within a people oriented company.

It's the people that really make the difference in our industry. As a hotel management company, our obligation is to provide management know-how to manage hotels on behalf of our owners. The quality and sustainability of our business depends therefore on who they are and what they have learned. Since we are constantly growing, we must ensure a sustainable flow of management talent to our hotels at all times.

To successfully operate hotels, we need managerial and technical know-how. But this alone is not sufficient for us. Kempinski is Europe's oldest independent luxury hotel brand. As a 5-star company, which offers its guests a particular European guest experience, expressed through caring and individualised services, we need employees with the right attitude (considerate, efficient and caring). This is especially important as we do not want to provide our guests with a standardised experience. That's what makes us different from other hotel management companies. That's what makes our guests keep returning.

In 2011, we had about 19,000 employees in more than 30 countries serving around 4 million guests. By 2015, we'll need a further 17,500 new members of staff, but most of all new talent to ensure the renewal of hotel leaders. This brings me to today's biggest challenge – the war for talent. 'War for talent' – an expression used by a lot of companies. However, I'm not sure to what extent the gravity of the situation has been realised and even less, translated into the action needed.

## War for talent – the challenges of providing a sustainable flow of talent

*'Men use their full resources only in tasks of war'* (John Foster Dulles).

It seems that more employees are leaving our industry than joining us! We have noticed that a significant percentage of graduates from renowned hospitality management schools prefer to pursue career opportunities outside the hospitality industry. This decreases the probability of finding qualified talented people who have the right attitude to deliver 5- star services and who are willing to become hoteliers with all the challenges that the job implies.

Personally, I believe there is a mismatch between the academic models used by hotel schools, expectations created and the evolution of the business in reality. Today's graduates expect to become general managers within a couple of years, and are neither willing nor flexible enough to work their way up through operational roles. This conflicts not only with what we as an employer can offer, but also with the steadily rising expectations from our guests for highly individualised service. Especially in Europe, this has also been influenced by the promotion of new concepts such as work-life balance, which is difficult to translate in an industry and segment where 24 hour service is the norm.

In other geographic areas, the challenge is the same but the reasons are different. For example in Africa and in the Middle East, which has become a focal point for growth for many companies, the willingness to work in our industry is not the problem. In these areas it is the availability of skilled labour that is the key challenge. Visa restrictions are already strict in Europe and are increasingly becoming a barrier in developing countries as well.

I do not have the answers to today's challenges as yet; but it is our responsibility to generate a sustainable flow of talent. Therefore, I spend 50% of my time on talent management: on identifying and developing talent.

## How to face the war for talent – evolving needs of tomorrow's leaders

To effectively fight in the war for talent, it is important to understand how the new generation ticks and to acknowledge their expectations. Today's young talent want to be empowered, they want to be given the opportunity to grow in a role that pursues meaningful objectives, within a company that has a bigger purpose than just producing services or that focuses solely on shareholder returns. This involves a shift in the traditional hotelier's autocratic leadership style. Today's young talent refuses the 'comply & obey' model, which may work from time to time in the short-term but won't serve staff retention. Within Kempinski, we try to foster a participative leadership style that promotes collaboration and team work.

I also noticed that social and environmental sustainability principles are integral to the expectations of our young future leaders. They are more likely to feel attracted to and stay within companies which have a positive impact on the environment and that have a business purpose which goes beyond producing guest facilities.

In my role as a CEO, I have to steer the company with a clear strategy towards the upcoming needs of our employees as well as our guests. To ensure long-term success, we need to shape Kempinski to ensure that it meets these needs and to feed those values that can be shared not only by our current and future employees, but also by society. Having shared values is crucial for achieving a sustainable success for our company. This is where I can contribute today to help my successors to find solutions for tomorrow.

## Shared values, the starting point for sustainability

A few years ago, I found out that most employees joined our company because of our 'individuality'. People sensed a strong company culture, although our values weren't explicitly defined. It became obvious that we had to treasure our company culture and to protect it from dilution by our rapid growth. Therefore, together with the University of St. Gallen, we gave a face and a name to our values by conducting a bottom up company survey in 2009. Hundreds of interviews were carried out, and five company values emerged. They were so implicit to our operation that they surprised no-one. The five values were: people oriented, straightforward, entrepreneurial performance, creating traditions and passion for European luxury.

Over the last two years, we have provided training and seminars for our employees at all level to emphasise and underscore the importance of how these company values support our company strategies and sustainability. Today, our employees refer to these values in their daily work, in their relations with colleagues and guests. Empowered by management and inspired by our values, I want our people to think outside the box and to achieve meaningful objectives both for the company and the environment we operate in. We provide our employees with the platform to live these values beyond their daily responsibilities.

For example, health is a shared value between Kempinski and society. We consider health to be vital both for guests and employees. This is particularly the case because the hospitality industry is a people business. Over the last four years, Kempinski Hotels has been a member of the Stop TB Partnership (part of the World Health Organisation) that is committed to combating tuberculosis. Every year, a new awareness raising campaign is launched for our employees and guests. Our employees are encouraged to share their knowledge with their families and friends as the workplace is a remarkable springboard from which to reach the local community.

Being straightforward, people-oriented and entrepreneurial is part of our company culture, which explains why we went a step further last year on our quest to fight infectious diseases. Together with three business partners, Kempinski founded an independent non-profit health organisation called BE Health Association. BE pursues one goal: to prevent the spread of infectious diseases, in particular HIV/Aids, tuberculosis, and malaria. In collaboration with public and private healthcare partners, BE fights to spread health.

We also want to be straightforward when it comes to reducing our impact on the environment. Kempinski's latest partnership KREEN (Kempinski Renewable Energies) offers hotel owners consulting, planning and project management in the field of renewable energies. We are, to my knowledge, the first company that has its own energy consultancy, which perfectly integrates economic and environmental needs. And that's a big step forward to support the sustainable development of our company and its environment! It is thanks to the entrepreneurial spirit of our employees, in this case our general managers, that we found this innovative approach to tackling rising energy costs while becoming more environmentally sustainable. This initiative reflects my belief that a company which integrates sustainability within its strategies and operations will create environmental and social value through its daily work.

Promoting values that people can relate to helps, but is not sufficient, to generate a sustainable flow of talent and to ensure that our company's values survive our growth. I don't believe in the success of the traditional Human Resources model. We have, therefore, invested a lot of time and resources in finding the right structure to support us in finding and retaining the right talent. We have moved from the one-pillar HR approach to a holistic three-pillar people management strategy. Talent Development, People Training and People Services are the three pillars. The responsibilities for making progress under each of these pillars are split between Management Board Members.

- Talent Management supports corporate and hotel top management to identify, select and develop talent.
- People Training makes sure they acquire the right skills.
- People Services provide the working environment in which staff can flourish.

Identifying, selecting and retaining talent has thus become a shared responsibility, and a key condition for generating a sustainable flow of talent.

As CEO, I still have some years ahead of me and it's up to me and my team to show the way to the new generation. My capabilities to solve the challenges of today's talent war are limited; it is now up to the new generation to find the necessary answers. My generation has the duty to build the right nurturing ground to ensure that the organisation is prepared and hires the right people who are driven to find the needed solutions to social and environmental as well as business needs. My vision is to ensure that Kempinski's values continue to be met. In my capacity as CEO I have planted the seeds to find solutions to the challenges ahead; the harvest will hopefully be reaped by my successors.

# Ian Yeoman

## Associate Professor, Victoria University of Wellington

## Our sustainable future – looking back from 2050

Dr. Ian Yeoman, Associate Professor, Victoria University of Wellington, New Zealand, is the world's leading futurologist specializing in travel and tourism. Ian was scenario planner for VisitScotland, where he established the process of futures thinking within the organisation using economic modelling, trends analysis and scenario construction. Today he is a leading academic researcher at Victoria University of Wellington and the European Tourism Futures Institute, Netherlands. Ian has published widely on the future of tourism, including *Tomorrow's Tourist* (Routledge 2008), *Tourism and Demography* (Goodfellow 2011). His forthcoming book, *2050: Tomorrow's Tourism*, addresses the three main factors influencing and shaping the future of tourism: wealth, technology and resources with scenarios from Shanghai to Edinburgh, Seoul to California encompassing complex topics such as hotel design, conferences, transport, food tourism or technological innovation. http://www.tomorrows-tourism.com

W e know that by 2050 the world will be different compared to 2012, 10 billion will live on the planet, the average citizen will be older, oil will be a thing of the past and the world will be warmer.

But it all depends how the world behaves in relation to these changes. For a sustainable future, that behaviour must be co-operative – a world of scarcity of resources drives policy to focus efficient resource use, waste minimization and collective responsibility

What does this all mean for tourism? In the spirit of this book I have tried to reflect on this from the perspective of three leaders writing to their constituencies, the President of the USA, the Prime Minister of New Zealand and the leader of New Zealand's tourism industry.

## Our sustainable future – a retrospective look: a letter from the President of the USA

Dear all,

The landscape, the environment and climate change are the key issues in 2050, just as they were in 2011. Reading the newspapers of the time there were resource shortages in society. In Australia it was water, in Africa it was food, in Asia it was floods and in the Pacific it was rising sea levels.  It seemed that the world couldn't agree on climate change, short term behaviours prevailed and no one was a winner. Today without doubt as a consequence of rising populations, new middle classes and climate change we face a situation of scarcity of resources. When I speak to tourism leaders, they agree that  access to the environment, the beauty of the landscape and authenticity is luxury because of its scarcity. The world has come together to tackle the problem of climate change. I feel that we live in a world of altruistic values, ethical behaviour and cooperation. When I speak to President Lin Deng of China there is a realisation that taking a global perspective is the only way to deal with this situation.  The power of the UN World Trade Organisation has been paramount. Without the world working together for the benefit of humankind the situation would have been a lot worse. A sustainable future has meant everything from ISO standards for architecture, personal carbon allowances for travel and severe punishment to those who operate an unsustainable future.

I do know there have been many conundrums on the pathway to a sustainable future. The debate about food supply and science based alternatives has been a heated one, and we have seen limited success within this field. Where we have seen improvements, it has been about increased yield, better fertilisers and sustainable communities, like the City of Bend who have taken a vertical a farming perspective. Some of the changes have been exceptional such as the advancement of green technologies and in particular Saudi Arabia's ability to export solar energy technologies; under the leadership of Professor Mohammad Dali at the University of Riyadh and the work of the UN Compliance Board with technological tracking. The key in scientific applications has been resource efficiencies and new ideas.

All of this has changed the consumer perspective. Consumers' behaviours and attitudes have fundamentally shifted over the last 40 years. We have a respect and a relationship with the landscape which some call spiritual. Resources today are more expensive and consumers spend a higher proportion of their income on such things as fuel, food and other essentials. There is a noticeable divide in society; the rich have got richer at a faster pace than the middle classes of the world. We still have substantial levels of poverty in Africa and Asia. As demand hasn't equalled supply inflation is now a problem. I would say life is a bit more frugal and simple.

So to summarise the world has become more sustainable because of:

■ Growing national, regional and international agreements
■ Good science relating to pollution impacts, human health and ecological systems
■ Increased regulation
■ Market demand for green and clean energy, safe foods, efficient transportation and green buildings
■ More effective and active NGOs

On a final note, my children keep reminding me I am responsible for their future so let us hope it is an everlasting future.

Yours

Carolyn Adams
President of the USA
30th June 2050

Y

This letter represents a number of trends in society. These include:

• The world's middle classes are being squeezed as resources become scarce, price inflation erodes consumers level of disposal income, squeezing disposal income for out of home expenditure i.e., dining, tourism and leisure activities.

• Prioritisation and incentive for resource substitution is driven by entrepreneurship and severe penalties for bad practice. Sustainability is the only business model.

• The environment and natural products are perceived as the new luxury in a crowded, urban and metropolis world.

## Our sustainable future – a retrospective look: a letter from the New Zealand Prime Minister

Dear all,

In the 2025 election the issue was New Zealand's green future. Across the political spectrum the only debate was about the degree of resources and commitment. The elected government's first piece of legislation was the passing of the 100% Pure New Zealand Act which establishes New Zealand's low carbon economy based upon a controlled pathway motivated by resource maintenance and economic stability. The Act was necessary given the world's problems of climate change refugees, wars over food supply, and the post peak oil economy. The Act formulates a number of policy levers and instruments that incentivise a Green Economy for business and consumers, educates for change, accelerates investment in Green technologies, facilitates adoption, and penalises 'ungreen' behaviour. New Zealand's real priority is to protect and develop its resources and land economies which are viewed by most of the world as the new gold. In spite of some dissenting voices, New Zealand has come to realise its only future is this Green pathway, to the extent that people talk more about the environment than they do about rugby these days. Green is the kiwi psyche.

Post 2025, New Zealand exports its agricultural produce, mineral resources, environmental intellectual property and tourism. Because of the scarcity of resources in the world New Zealand is a beneficiary. According to the latest OECD tables New Zealand is ranked 8th in the world in terms of wealth per capita and purchasing power. New Zealand is a nation of strong political and economic force in Oceania, a place which advocates human rights, a liberal culture which has an open door and promotes cooperation. New Zealand over the last 40 years has seen a number of changes because the country has significant energy resources including oil, hydro and geothermal. This has funded high levels of education attainment which in turn has driven investment in research and development. The Universities of Auckland and Victoria are ranked in the top 100 with particular emphasis on carbon chemistry, technological compliance, digital mediums and the liberal arts. Some of the big issues in 2050 have been the dilution of Maori ethnicity and an increase in Pacific and Asian economic and climate change immigrants to this country.

The price of this environmental success is the erosion on individual liberties. In order for the government to bring about change, individuals and businesses have set carbon allowances which are monitored via an extensive ubiquitous network of data and mind reading technologies. These technologies allow the government to know what you do, when you do it, how you do it, when you are thinking about it and for how long. Even babies are chipped at birth to monitor their environmental life span. Eco priority principles mean that individual liberty has had to be sacrificed for the benefit of the planet. As a consequence, New Zealanders are morally self-regulating when it comes to the environment.

Yours,

The Rt Hon John Smith,
Prime Minister of New Zealand
30th June 2050

This letter represents a number of trends in society. These include:

- The kiwi psyche is green whether it is government, business, society or the individual. However in order to attain this position, individual rights are being sacrificed for the collective good through ubiquitous networks.

- New Zealand is a successful nation in a world of scarcity of resources, and is deemed a plentiful society due an abundance of resources that are well managed. The country's diverse economy is based upon intellectual property, a natural resource base and agriculture products, with a strong knowledge research and development attitude.

- New Zealand has a liberal attitude but strong environmental values which is comparable to Nordic countries. Smallness allows uniqueness and specialisation in a global environment.

**Y**

## Our sustainable future – a retrospective look: a letter from the Leader of New Zealand Tourism Industry

Dear all,

According to the Lonely Planet New Zealand is a microcosm of an eco-paradise. In a world of scarcity of resources New Zealand's uniqueness is an abundance of land, water and food in a temperate climate. Although the glaciers have shrunk the impact of climate change has been less compared to many other countries in the world. Now that the Mediterranean fringe is a desert, California is no longer a wine region and there is no reliable snow coverage on the Alps, New Zealand is 'the destination' and the winner of the Condé Nast world sustainable travel award every year since 2038.

In order to preserve this eco-paradise the New Zealand Government operates a variable tourism tax for international visitors with a range from \$50 to \$5,000 per visitor, per day, in order to manage demand. The policy operates in a number of ways; for those tourists involved in community projects and volunteering the tariff is low whereas the top end tourists have a minimum spend per day equating to a high tariff. In addition there are a number of schemes that combine these elements.

The tax, although controversial, is the cornerstone of New Zealand's sustainable tourism policy. Revenues generated have been reinvested into tourism in order to position the industry as the First and Everlasting Industry of the nation. According to Prime Minister Theo Coy tourism is a significant contributor to our economy. New Zealand is the first country that people across the world think of in terms of where to holiday. Tourism is the first industry in terms of professionalism and career choice. The tourism industry has set the standard for others to follow. Its pursuance of an everlasting strategy in which the guardians of the present have set out to secure the environment has enabled the industry to be one of New Zealand's sustainable industries. Those guardians have protected our children's future.

New Zealand has had to position itself as an aspirational eco tourism paradise because of a shortage of resources. Although the world has seen improved transport efficiencies over the last 40 years aviation is still a problem. The eco paradise tourist represents approximately 10% of all tourists providing 25% of the revenue. The remainder of the market is dominated by New Zealand's domestic tourists and those tourists who advocate a more sustainable life style. All tourism providers comply with an assurance scheme for green businesses which includes sustainable architecture, community involvement, professional practice and energy efficiency. The assurance scheme extends to customer service in which the 100% guarantee policy offers tourists their money back if their experience doesn't meet their expectations. Many in the industry laughed at such a proposition when it was first introduced in 2025, but New Zealand only targets and attracts visitors who have an affinity with its environmental outlook and way of life. The country is marketed as 'the slow holiday place'. According to the Visitor Attitudes Survey, enrichment, solace, space and an abundance of natural products are the reasons why tourists holiday in New Zealand. These are attributes many countries don't have these days!

Yours,

Wendy Liu
Chief Executive, Tourism Association of New Zealand
30th June 2050

This letter represents a number of trends in society. These include:

- The impact of climate change globally has been dramatic, but New Zealand is an oasis as climate change here hasn't been as dramatic as in other countries. The environment is temperate and favourable. New Zealand's 'green' credentials and relative abundance of resources make the country popular as a tourism destination compared to 'too hot' California or 'no snow' Europe.

- New Zealand's tourism tax for international visitors balances the needs of the environment with economics. This sustainable approach to tourism taxation is off set if tourists undertake a number of community based projects.

- A strong domestic economy is the main driver of tourism growth to 2050.

# Shanzhong Zhu

## Vice Chairman of China National Tourism Administration

## Making better use of the multiple functions of tourism

Shanzhong Zhu is Vice Chairman of China National Tourism Administration, the agency in charge of tourism directly affiliated to the State Council of China. He is responsible for external affairs, market development, and informatization, and in charge of the Division of Tourism Promotion and International Cooperation, the Division of Integrated Coordination, Information Centre, and Offices.

There is no doubt that tourism has a powerful role to play in promoting sustainable economic growth and job creation. Looking around, the impact of the international financial crisis is still deep, economic growth in major tourist source markets is slowing down, and protectionism is resurfacing on the world stage. All these have made tourism trade even more difficult.

Being open to the outside world, China's tourism sector is facing the same situation. Yet with a firm conviction and practical steps, we have succeeded in keeping the tourism sector steadily moving forward. Between January and November 2011, China received 124 million inbound tourists, which was 1.2% higher compared to the previous year; and Chinese outbound tourists reached to 63.9 million, up by 22.4%. For the first nine months of 2011, 1.98 billion domestic trips were recorded in China, representing a 12.6% increase over the previous year. These figures show that tourism is playing a positive role in facilitating comprehensive economic and social development, promoting economic restructuring and boosting domestic demand.

First, tourism is playing a more prominent role in driving China's economic growth. Tourism revenue in China is expected to reach 35 million US$ in 2011, up by 18% year on year. The added value of the tourism sector now already accounts for over 4% of China's GDP, and contributes over 90% of the added value in the hotel industry and over 80% in civil aviation and railway transportation. Tourism also boosts consumption. In 2010, the Chinese people spent 200 billion US$ in domestic travels, which accounted for 9.4% of total household consumption in the country.

Second, tourism is playing a more important role in addressing China's employment challenge. From 2006 to 2010, tourism generated about 3 million direct jobs and 17 million indirect jobs in China. Now, more than 13.5 million Chinese people work in the tourism sector and about 80 million people work in tourism-related jobs. The tourism sector has already become the largest contributor of jobs in China. In the meantime, tourism is also playing an important role in providing jobs for people living in ethnic minority regions as well as women, migrant workers, laid-off workers, newly-graduated job seekers and other special groups.

Third, tourism is playing a more notable role in promoting China's rural development. Issues concerning rural areas and farmers are China's top priorities. According to incomplete statistics, 53,000 villages and over 1.5 million rural households are now offering tourist programs in China, benefiting 15 million farmers. In 2010, more than 400 million tourists visited China's countryside and generated a total of US$ 19 million in tourism revenue.

That is why tourism development is being incorporated into the framework of national strategies. Recently, Chinese leaders have stressed on many occasions the importance of promoting tourism consumption. In December 2009, the State Council issued the *Opinions on Accelerating the Development of Tourism Sector*. In March 2011, the outline of China's *Twelfth Five-year Plan* confirmed the role of tourism in supporting the development of China's countryside, maritime space and western regions. In May, the State Council approved 19 May as China's National Tourism Day to boost the tourism awareness of the Chinese people. In September, Vice Premier Wang Qishan expressed his confidence in the future of China's tourism development in his meeting with UNWTO

Secretary-General Taleb Rifai. The National People's Congress is now coordinating the legislation of China's national *Tourism Law*, and the *National Outline of Tourism and Leisure* is also being drafted.

Local governments and relevant government authorities are now paying greater attention to tourism. Tourism development has already been incorporated into the *Plan for the Rejuvenation of Cultural Industries*, the *Outline of the Medium- and Long-Term Development Plan for Service Trade* and other medium- and long-term development strategies. Now, 27 Chinese provinces, autonomous regions and municipalities have made tourism one of their pillar industries or flagship service industries.

In the future, China will step up support for tourism development in terms of infrastructure building, financial resources and land policies. The State Council has already decided to keep its tourism development fund in place till 2015 and provide more funding for promoting China's national tourism image, making tourism plans, organizing professional training and developing tourism-related public service system.

We will continue to follow the principles of long-term, comprehensive and mutually-beneficial tourism development, and open our tourism sector wider to the world. We are confident that with increased policy support and policy innovation, we will have the conditions and ability to maintain stable and fast tourism development, better utilize the multiple functions of tourism, and make new contribution to sustained and balanced world tourism growth.

# Ghassan Aidi

**President of the International Hotels & Restaurants Association**

## The hospitality sector – advancing the green growth agenda

Dr. Ghassan Aidi is President of the International Hotels & Restaurants Association (IH&RA). He is also President of Cham Palaces and Hotels, Chairman of Royal Regency International Hotels and a member of the Leadership Council of George Washington University. Ghassan has 35 years' experience in the hospitality industry worldwide, presiding over several hotels chains and lobbying to defend the interest of the private sector. He has lectured widely and advised governments on issues ranging from destination management, disaster response, hospitality legislation and labour matters.

It is no secret that hospitality businesses prosper when they offer great quality experiences to customers. Integral to those experiences are the quality of the local environment and the vibrancy of local communities. Just imagine for a moment taking a trip to a ski resort without having the opportunity to enjoy the mountains and ski on natural snow, a stay at the coast without experiencing the salty perfume of oceans, a visit to a cultural site divorced from living heritage, a diving trip to a coral reef that is devoid of fish or a trip to the Mediterranean that lacks the whirring of cicadas. These are all a part of the cultural and environmental resources on which our hospitality industry depends. And it is these resources that are under threat from a range of pressures from increasing population to climate change to the growth in the tourism and hospitality industry itself.

The tourism and hospitality industry has been aware of the nature of this threat for more than two decades. When the Rio Earth Summit first convened in 1992, many of the leading hospitality brands had already started to embrace their environmental responsibilities and developed impressive environmental management programmes. In the intervening years, many more large and small hospitality businesses have joined their ranks. The collective efforts of the industry have produced some impressive results:

- Many hospitality businesses have been particularly effective at reducing energy consumption and associated carbon emissions. The Marriott Hotel group, for example, reduced energy consumption by circa 13% between 2007 and 2009, Hilton Worldwide used the LightStay system to conserve enough energy to power 5,700 homes for a year and IHG have used their Green Engage initiative to deliver a 15% reduction in energy consumption per available room night between 2009 and 2011 in their owned and managed properties.

- Water is a particular concern for many in our sector. Hospitality businesses depend on good supplies of clean water and the Water Scarcity Index makes it clear that this is a resource that will be in increasingly short supply over the coming decades. Many hospitality businesses have already responded. We have seen most major companies, including among others Accor, Scandic, Ramada Jarvis, Rezidor and Taj, introduce a range of highly effective water saving techniques and technologies and these can reduce consumption by 20% or more.

- Waste has also been a focus of much attention by hospitality businesses. On this issue, innovative approaches have been required and we have seen businesses using waste as a resource from which to generate energy, businesses finding partners that view their waste as a resource and businesses that have worked within communities to make sure that products like unused food or toiletries serve a social purpose rather than being destined for a hole in the ground.

- Hundreds of communities have continued to benefit from the hospitality businesses in their midst. The most obvious benefits come from employment opportunities, but so many hospitality businesses have extended their influence further. Hospitality businesses across the globe have actively invested in developing local supply chains to ensure their economic influence supports local communities, helped develop education infrastructure at all levels, supported hotel schools to ensure people from the locale are equipped to become the leaders of tomorrow, cleaned up locations that have become degraded and supported cultural and other events to ensure communities remain vibrant.

Underpinning these programmes is evidence of a significant structural change within the industry to play a role in the green economy. Perhaps most powerful among the initiatives is the way that hospitality business have actively invested in educating their staff to engage in 'green initiatives' at home as well as at work. We should also not overlook the scale of investment that the sector has made in green technologies. From the humble energy saving lamp to complex building management systems, heat recovery processes and increasingly solar, geothermal or wind power. All of these will make a contribution towards a lower carbon future.

Our work in building that low carbon future is, however, far from complete and many challenges remain. Some of these can be tackled by hospitality businesses themselves. These include:

- A need to engage more hospitality businesses in the green agenda. Those that have implemented programmes to tackle their environmental and social impacts report impressive results. The challenge is to pass knowledge and experience on to those hospitality businesses that have yet to engage in the green agenda. These include the millions of small businesses and especially those in newly emerging economies.

- There could also be benefits from expanding our horizons beyond learning from other hospitality businesses to learning from other sectors. Food retail companies, for example, have a wealth of experience in preventing food waste from which many in our sector could learn. Building linkages and leaving our sector silos has the potential to enrich our knowledge and help us make progress towards green economies.

- Finding ways to engage those who invest in and develop hotel infrastructure in the green economy. So many hospitality businesses cannot deliver the carbon and water efficiencies that are essential for the future of the sector because they inherit properties that are built using old and inefficient technologies.

- Changing the attitude of the sector towards waste so it is viewed as a resource (something that already happens in many developing countries of course). Methane emissions from waste are more potent than carbon and food waste, and so a particular issue for our sector. The UN recently reported that around one-third of all food produced is wasted before it reaches the final consumer and there is much that hospitality businesses can do to address this issue.

■ The delicate issue of finding effective ways to communicate about green issues with customers. The market research data may indicate that many would prefer to stay in a hotel that does not damage the environment. The reality is somewhat different. As a sector, we need to find ways to engage our customers as partners in helping us to care for the places they love. This is particularly an issue as globalization makes travel to exotic and delicate regions ever more accessible.

■ Finding new and innovative ways to build broader partnerships with external agencies. Many in our sector have already joined initiatives with non-government agencies to ensure our forest resources are protected both as an amenity for tourism, and as a means of protecting biodiversity and capturing carbon. Our forests, however, remain under huge pressure from the agricultural and timber trade as well urban encroachment. More needs to be done to ensure that these precious resources remain and play their role in stabilizing our climate into the future. What is true of forests extends to coral reefs and other environments that have the potential to help our planet deal with warmer climatic conditions and support biodiversity.

There are other challenges, many of which require immediate redress if our industry is not to become a victim of changing climate. Many of these would logically fall to governments, but a decade of protocols, summits, declarations, meetings, and promises have this far failed to deliver the concrete measures that will safeguarded the future of our industry or the resources on which it is based. Crucial among these challenges is a need to help destinations adapt to the implications of climate change. In particular, there is an urgent need to reinforce costal infrastructure. In some parts of the world the majority of hospitality infrastructure lies in the coastal zone. A failure to reinforce these coastal zones leaves them vulnerable to increased storm activity in the short term and the implications of rising sea levels in the long term. Much more than the destruction of a few hotel properties lies at stake if governments do not recognize the need to act. Not least, the tourism income that sustains the coastal communities and so much more besides. Perhaps as important is the need for government to invest in renewable energy infrastructure. Our industry has demonstrated that, where it is feasible, it is willing to invest in small scale solar and other technologies. For thousands of small businesses, however, such technologies are not easily accessible nor feasible. We can only go so far with energy efficiency and our ability to adapt to a changing climate is restricted as long as hospitality businesses are unable to access cost effective renewable energy solutions.

More is needed to support mitigation efforts too. Governments need to provide clear and coherent signals to industry to encourage them to mitigate against their own carbon emissions. Rumours about carbon trading systems abound, but the industry needs to understand how and when carbon trading will become a reality and what the long terms costs will be. Hospitality businesses around the world have already demonstrated huge willingness to implement programmes to reduce cost and carbon emissions. Like any other businesses, however, capital investments need to be planned for and uncertainty about the scale or longevity of carbon trading systems undermine business confidence. If carbon trading is to become a reality a level playing field is required and penalties need to be matched with consistent rewards and capital needs to be made available to allow businesses – and especially SMEs – to adapt.

The pressure to address these challenges is growing as new travellers emerge from countries such as China and India. This year 50 million Chinese will have an international passport issued for travelling abroad. In 2015 this number will double. This is the new trend of travellers and for countries to benefit from tourism income, they need accommodation.

I do believe strongly our hospitality industry will play a leadership role and address the emerging green economy issues. Hospitality is one of the growth sectors with 10 new hotels opening every day somewhere in the world. That's approximately 3000 every year. These new hotels keep hiring and reducing poverty in the world. This is why we are the leaders in investing, leaders in taking risk, leaders in creating jobs, leaders in employing more than 65 million people in the world and contributing about 1000 billion USD annually to the global economy and leaders in seeking a sustainable future as a part of the green economy.

**A**

# Akbar Al Baker

## CEO, Qatar Airways

## Qatar Airways roadmap for alternative fuels – for sustainable green growth

Mr. Akbar Al Baker, Qatar Airways' Chief Executive Officer, has been instrumental in shaping the development of Qatar Airways into one of the fastest growing and most highly acclaimed airlines in the world today – named 'Airline of the Year 2011' by global industry audit Skytrax. A highly motivated individual, Mr. Al Baker has been a successful businessman in Doha for more than 25 years, holds a private pilot licence, and is also CEO of several divisions of Qatar's national airline – these being Qatar Airways Holidays, Qatar Aviation Services, Qatar Duty Free Company, Doha International Airport, Qatar Distribution Company, Qatar Executive, Oryx Rotana Hotel and Qatar Aircraft Catering Company. Born in Doha, he is a graduate in economics and commerce and worked at various levels in the Civil Aviation Directorate before becoming Qatar Airways' CEO in 1997.

Qatar Airways is the national airline of the State of Qatar and one of the aviation industry's big success stories. Operations began in 1994 when the airline was a small regional carrier and was re-launched in 1997 under the mandate of the country's leader The Emir, His Highness Sheikh Hamad bin Khalifa Al Thani, who outlined a vision to turn Qatar Airways into a leading international airline with the highest standards of service and excellence.

Qatar Airways has since become one of the fastest growing carriers in the world. In April 2011, Qatar Airways reached a milestone with 100 destinations in its global route map and expansion averaging double digit growth year on year. Today, the award-winning airline has pending orders for over 250 aircraft worth more than US$50 billion. And Qatar Airways is set to move to a brand new international airport in Doha, a state-of-the-art facility that is due to open at the end of 2012.

Expansion comes with huge responsibility to ensure continued and maintained success at a time when growth is taking place at a rapid pace. In line with this, the industry is faced with challenges of reducing the environmental impact and improving the local air quality for the communities we serve. We at Qatar Airways take these challenges and realities very seriously and have actively engaged in moving forward towards a future that is focused on a cleaner environment.

Long-term energy security is also vital to ensure the sustainable development and growth of the airline, forming an integral part of the strategic Corporate Social Responsibility approach of Qatar Airways.

## Corporate vision

As an industry leader and pioneer, Qatar Airways and our group of companies strive to be the best in everything we do; and an integral part of being an industry leader is to help lead the charge towards environmental sustainability and corporate social responsibility. We are leaders in new-generation fuel research, and are giving back to the communities in which we serve.

Qatar Airways has realised that it is important to go beyond current industry best practices for fuel and environmental management in order to ensure a sustainable future for the airline, its staff and its neighbourhoods – not just in our home base of Qatar, but in the cities and countries we serve around the world.

We have the responsibility to deal with aviation's impacts on global climate change, noise, local air quality, resource depletion and waste.

Therefore, Qatar Airways created the innovative *'Five Pillar Corporate Social Responsibility Strategy – The Oryx Flies Green'* which embraces Change Management, Environment, Integrated Fuel Management, Communication and ultimately Sustainable Development. The central issue is that our children's future depends on the responsible actions of Qatar Airways, its peers, other industries, and everyone on the planet – we must all strive to make a difference so that future generations can enjoy a world of environmental sustainability.

## One of the most efficient aircraft fleets in the industry

Averaging planes that are four years old, our state-of-the-art fleet of over 100 aircraft is among the youngest flying today, naturally helping to reduce our carbon and noise emissions footprint compared to our competitors. Our newest aircraft-type, the Boeing 777-200LR, is at the pinnacle of our efforts to reduce emissions.

Qatar Airways firmly believes investing in brand new aircraft, and on top of that, new generation aircraft. We are heavily involved with aircraft manufacturers to ensure our requirements are met in all areas – safety, comfort, environment, et cetera.

Our fleet acquisition programme is focused on introducing new planes into the fleet while retiring older aircraft. A fleet renewal programme designed to reduce the average age of our aircraft. After all, passengers want to fly on new planes to give them a great travel experience and value for money – which is why we are continually introducing new generation, highly efficient aircraft into our fleet, from the A380s to A350s and Boeing 787s, offering improved fuel efficiency per passenger. Today, our fleet meets the most stringent ICAO noise levels ever set, and the carbon footprint is declining in relative terms.

In 2007, Qatar Airways was the first airline in the region that had an IATA - International Air Transport Association – 'Green Team' visit which conducted a FEGA – Fuel Efficiency Analysis and implemented its findings. Qatar Airways implemented a state-of-the-art fuel management system and, coupled with its modern fleet, achieved one of the lowest carbon footprints of a legacy carrier with just 94.5 grams/RPK compared with 109 and 111 grams/RPK for established legacy carriers.

## Alternative fuels

Qatar Airways is a travel industry innovator in the study of the potential commercial use of jet fuel derived from natural gas as a means of reducing the impact of aviation on local and global air quality.

We have partnered with companies such as Qatar Petroleum, Shell, Airbus, Rolls Royce, Qatar Science & Technology Park and Woqod with a view to test the use of cleaner burning alternative fuels on commercial flights. Qatar Airways and its partners are striving to make a jet fuel blend, including Gas to Liquids (GTL) kerosene a cleaner-burning fuel of choice for the air transport industry of the future. A Letter of Intent for this project was signed at the Dubai Air Show on 17th November 2007.

In October 2009, Qatar Airways became the first airline in the world to fly a mixed blend of GTL and natural aviation kerosene fuel on a commercial flight from London Gatwick to Doha. Not a test flight, but a proper commercial flight. The flight was operated with an Airbus A340-600 aircraft using Rolls-Royce Trent 556 engines. Shell developed and produced the 50-50 blend of synthetic GTL kerosene and conventional oil-based kerosene fuel, the latest step in over two years of scientific work carried out by a consortium of partners.

Going forward, Qatar Airways aims to be the world's first carrier to operate a commercial flight using 100 per cent GTL kerosene fuel – an environmental breakthrough for the aviation industry. The State of Qatar is already home to the world's largest GTL production plant, opened by Shell in 2011.

GTL jet fuel will likely be used in a semi-synthetic 50/50 blend with conventional jet fuel and can be used without any modifications to existing aircraft and engines. GTL jet fuel is virtually free of sulphur and aromatics. As a result, the aircraft engine will emit less sulphur oxide and fewer particulates during operation. The environmental benefits of this are being quantified and are likely to conclude improved air quality around airports, particularly having a noticeable positive impact at airports that are closely surrounded by towns and cities – an example being London Heathrow.

GTL jet fuel has higher energy content by weight compared with conventional jet fuel, i.e. it has a lower density. It also offers improved thermal stability. Both of these characteristics may lead to potential fuel economy and improved payload / range performance which could result in a limited $CO_2$ benefit for specific aircraft / route combinations. This is currently being studied.

These cleaner-burning fuels could become a major factor in future air quality improvement initiatives for the entire airline industry, further proving that Qatar Airways' product leadership extends far beyond passenger comfort.

## From GTL to Biomass-to-Liquid biofuels – Qatar Airways continues its alternative fuel roadmap

On 10th January 2010, Qatar Airways together with partners Qatar Science & Technology Park (QSTP) and Qatar Petroleum (QP) announced that they will jointly carry out studies into the development of sustainable bio jet fuel, as well as production and supply, with the support of Airbus. The QABP – Qatar Advanced Biofuel Platform – was launched, later attracting Rolls Royce and Qatar University.

This followed a 2009 pact by Qatar Airways, Qatar Science & Technology Park and US company Verno Systems to embark on a very comprehensive and detailed feasibility study on sustainable Biomass-to-Liquid (BTL) jet fuel and possible by-products such as bio diesel. This study looked at all available bio feed stocks that would not affect the food or fresh water supply chain. It also looked at existing and future production technologies with a viability analysis. Based on the result of this in-depth study, the partners agreed to establish the *Qatar Advanced Biofuel Platform (QABP)* to lead activities in the following areas.

- A detailed engineering and implementation plan for economically viable and sustainable bio fuel production
- A bio fuel investment strategy
- An advanced technology development programme
- Ongoing market and strategic analysis

QABP takes a portfolio approach to the development of advanced bio fuels across feed stocks, technologies and geographies in order to meet short-, medium- and long-term goals.

## Conclusion

Energy security and reduction of the environmental impact are key elements to our strategic CSR approach in order to ensure sustainable growth and development.

Airlines worldwide currently depend 100% on crude oil derived jet fuel, but this is changing and with that, we not only de-couple ourselves from the volatile oil market, but give the opportunity to industry to develop cleaner synthetic jet fuel.

The era of cheap oil is definitely over and according to reports from the International Energy Agency and the World Bank, the world will face the 'Oil peak' within the next few years. This will see prices rocket to unprecedented levels.

At the same time, the industry faces operational challenges such as environmental charges implemented by the EU – European Union Emissions Trading Scheme.

Taking all this into account, Qatar Airways is determined to continue to invest into the development of cleaner alternative fuels. Our aim is to have a 100% synthetic jet fuel available, a blend of GTL and BTL, over the next few years.

**A**

# Mike Ambrose

## Director General, ERA

## A fairer environmental balance – aviation's responsible role

Mike Ambrose, Director General, the European Regions Airline Association (ERA). Under Mike's direction since 1987 the Association has become one of the main airline associations in Europe and is well-respected in aviation and in European regulatory circles for its dynamism and the scope of its activities. Mike's career began in Flight Operations in British European Airways in 1966. In 1974 he transferred to the Regional Division of British Airways where he was responsible for aircraft evaluation and fleet procurement. He was later responsible for BA's network-wide User Charges before accepting an assignment as a consultant to the franchise partner Birmingham Executive Airways. Mike was the Vice Chairman (International) of the Flight Safety Foundation until 2005. He is a member of FSF's Executive Committee and has been an FSF Board Member since 1997. He is a Fellow of the Royal Society, Royal Aeronautical Society and Chartered Institute of Logistics and Transport.

*The views of the author are not those of the European Regions Airline Association.*

Legitimate environmental concerns are being eroded through a combination of factors that are clouding what is a fundamentally important global geopolitical and socio-economic debate.

- The certainty of many environmental activists reduces credibility and can dissuade people from supporting their ideals, even where they are legitimate. In many encounters with environmental lobbyists and activists who have been acting with the best of intentions, I have come away with the strong impression of a predisposition to believe that only they and likeminded people have any real concern for protection of the environment and that the rest of us simply are out of step. A softer, more moderate, listening approach could well gain greater support. It would be seen to be more reasonable and constructive than pure evangelism which results in a 'transmit' rather than 'receive' mind-set. It is also just wrong to think that the great majority of ordinary folk are dismissive of environmental protection measures or that their legitimate views on environmental issues are somehow unconcerned, less valid, and insufficient.

■ The failure of the environmental lobby to agree and define a balanced road map to a sustainable society (despite the recognition of triple bottom line requirements) creates, for many ordinary citizens, uncertainty that their legitimate aspirations and economic and social needs will ever be achievable. In fact, the impression is given that, other than the implementation of heavy costly regulation and punitive measures, the environmental lobby has no clear idea of where we should be heading.

■ Moreover, as net consumers of resources, probably the most important environmental issue is the unconstrained growth of the world's population. What is absent from the discourse among environmentalists, is a clear strategy for achieving a sustainable society that balances the imperatives of development and environmental protection with the imperative of moderating population growth

■ Lastly, many governments worldwide have cynically implemented new so-called environmental taxes as a source of additional state revenue – and this is likely to increase with current budget austerity regimes around the world. These environmental poll taxes actually do nothing for sustainable development.

Against this complex background can be added the uncertainty in forecasting, with reasonable reliability, longer term environmental trends, the dangers of straight-line business as usual assumptions and wide differences of opinion as to what is environmentally 'good' and 'bad'.

Mankind is virtually unique as a species. Unlike various animal and marine species that manage to exist in the natural world in a state of balance and migrate essentially for food, reproduction and survival reasons, mankind has an inherent curiosity that creates an instinctive urge to travel and explore. Furthermore, we are net consumers of the world's resources.

It is part of human nature to want the next generation to fare better than the current generation and this desire certainly includes the ability of future generations to enjoy an environment that is increasingly protected by the application of new technology. In this regard, air transport can demonstrate an enviable record. Engine technology improvements, funded by the industry itself, have brought into use progressively cleaner and more fuel efficient technology throughout the last half-century.

However, the development of air transport has also brought other environmental benefits. To many European citizens, especially during these economically straitened times, key challenges are war and unemployment. Far too seldom is air transport given the recognition that it deserves in ameliorating these conditions. Air travel has brought societies together, increasing understanding and creating new bonds at personal and national levels. Likewise, air travel has brought employment and new market opportunities to societies and nations, especially in the developing world, that otherwise would have been unable to exploit their natural assets in a global market.

In spite of the current economic difficulties, it is accepted that European states are industrialised nations. It is also generally true that economically successful states can more easily afford a broad range of environmental protection measures whereas poor states face tough decisions when they have to choose between spending public resources on the basic welfare of their citizens versus environmental protection. It is equally true that in Europe, when times are hard, it is understandable that the populace places more importance on the need to protect and create jobs in preference to further, and perhaps costly, environmental initiatives. In this context, air transport should be seen as a tool for environmental protection rather than as a transgressor. Airlines create jobs, they bring wealth and they stimulate industry. Such qualities should therefore be seen as environmentally supportive rather than a cause for punishment.

Nevertheless, it would be unfair and unjustified to allow aviation a soft ride with respect to environmental protection. It would also negate most of the massive investment in many research projects now underway to develop improved environmental performance technology, but it would be unfair and unreasonable to believe that new technology can be implemented in the short-term. Yes, new engines will become available and will reduce fuel consumption and gaseous emissions, but aviation is generally reliant on a single fuel source and single engine technology. There is no 'golden engine' available.

The greater use of biofuels will help to reduce gaseous emissions, but the resources needed to produce them have their own environmental impact. This will need to be carefully assessed and controlled if significant net environmental gains are to be achieved. The positive environmental contribution that can be made by states should also be given more impetus. States can facilitate the early implementation of direct routings for flights (overseen and controlled with better air and ground technology) through projects such as the Single European Sky. Real reductions in environmental impact of air transport can be achieved relatively quickly but collective action is being forestalled by institutional inertia and the protection of sovereign interests by governments that frequently claim strong green credentials.

Furthermore, the action of some states has been at best insincere and at worst cynically exploitative with regard to the so-called environmental taxes and market-based measures. Take, for example, the Emissions Trading Scheme (ETS) now implemented by the EU. In recent months, it has attracted a great deal of adverse publicity and there is a very serious risk of it creating a trade war with other major states. The final scheme differs enormously from the original scheme proposed by the European Commission. Today it fails to include any binding obligations on states as to how they should spend the money that they will derive from auctioning of ETS permits.

If ETS is to be a sincere measure to improve aviation's environmental performance, then it follows that the monies derived from permit auctioning should be ploughed back into the industry through the funding of appropriate research and development of new technology. However, this is not the case. States can use these funds for whatever purposes they choose.

Likewise, the proposed aviation levy to fund environmental protection projects in the developing world rings loud alarm bells. Little attention was given in the original proposal as to how these funds would be managed, what criteria would be used for project selection, how project progress would be monitored, what accountability mechanisms will be put in place, and generally, which principles will apply to governance and disbursement. States and international institutions are notoriously bad at managing large amounts of money, which is often accompanies by waste, duplication, inflated administration charges and even corruption. Aviation cannot afford such uncontrolled generosity.

The United Kingdom's Air Passenger Duty (APD) is yet another example. It currently generates in excess of £2bn per annum for the UK Exchequer. It was introduced as a tax and it is a tax. Yet, past governments have, on occasions when environmental protection has been a politically correct card to play, labelled it as an 'environmental tax'.

Finally, it is unquestionable that all transport modes have environmental effects – too often the analysis of aviation impacts has not properly examined the full impacts of competing modes. Take for example air and rail in Europe. Traditionally, the debate has been clouded by unsubstantiated claims of the 'greenness' of rail and this has led to a serious bias amongst policy makers when considering future transport policy in Europe.

Any objective comparison between modes of transport must look at the full life-cycle impact of each mode. A typical life-cycle environmental analysis of High Speed Rail (HSR) captures not just the energy used to move the train but also the emissions from power plants, vehicle manufacturing and maintenance, the energy inputs and emission outputs for vehicles, raw material extraction, infrastructure construction, fuel production components as well as end of life treatment of vehicles. An often overlooked aspect of the impact of HSR is its effect to move passengers away from conventional express passenger trains, thus causing them to incur a much higher carbon footprint.

For example, HSR $CO_2$ emissions on the UK London-Manchester corridor are expected to be 35-40% higher than emissions from conventional rail lines for the same quantity of passenger-kilometres. Given the kinetic energy required to accelerate the train and energy required to overcome aerodynamic resistance in order to maintain speeds, reductions in journey times of 25% would lead to an increase in energy consumption of 90%.

Looking deeper into these studies shows some even more startling results for specific HSR projects. If the modal split on the proposed UK London-Manchester HSR route moved from a 50%-50% air-rail split (which is approximately the current split) to 100% HSR and 0% air, then greenhouse gas emissions emitted by building and operating the new HSR route would be larger than the entire quantity of carbon emitted by the air services over a period of 60 years were the current 50-50 split to be maintained.

What is clear is that when a full life-cycle emissions approach is undertaken and when noise, and land take are considered, it is difficult to conclude whether, and under what circumstances, air or rail has an environmental advantage: this alone is further proof of the need for a more balanced debate amongst policy-makers on the future of rail and air in Europe.

In summary, the protection of the environment is important to all of us, not just the environmental lobby. However, for all its relevance, little attention, if any, is being given to population pressure, with some indicators showing the world population will rise from the current 7 billion to around 10.3 billion by 2050. Air transport has a vital role to play in helping to stimulate greater international understanding and economic development which becomes more important as the world's population increases. Aviation does have an environmental impact, but the environmental goals that it is set should be on the basis of rational analysis, objective criteria and an understanding of what is technically feasible by when. Self-righteousness and predisposition towards punitive measures are not good enough and do little to further fair and balanced solutions through rational debate.

A

# Rick Antonson

## President and CEO, Tourism Vancouver

## Vancouver – on a green growth path for residents and visitors

Rick Antonson is President and CEO of Tourism Vancouver which represents over 1,000 member businesses and is responsible for the market development of Metro Vancouver as a convention, incentive, and leisure travel destination. As a tourism industry leader, Rick is a member of the Executive Board for the Pacific Asia Travel Association based in Bangkok, Thailand and a former chair of the board for the Destination Marketing Association International based in Washington, DC. He is also president for Pacific Coast Public Television. Rick is the author of *To Timbuktu for a Haircut; A Journey Through West Africa*. And, in September 2012, Dundurn Publishing of Toronto will release his new book, *Route 66 Still Kicks; Driving America's Mains Street*. Rick was awarded an Honorary Doctorate of Laws from Vancouver's Capilano University in 2011. He travels extensively around the world for business, speaking and on personal journeys and is a firm believer that tourism is a vital force for peace.

S urrounded by a panorama of mountains and ocean, Vancouver ranks among the greenest and most liveable cities in the world. But though the city is already known internationally as an environmental leader, the City of Vancouver and Mayor Gregor Robertson have pledged that by 2020 Vancouver will be the world's greenest city. Residents and civic leaders are making a strong start: Vancouver is already Canada's greenest city, has the smallest per capita carbon footprint of any city in North America and is an industry recognized frontrunner in green building, planning and technology. Drawing 90 percent of its power from renewable sources, Vancouver is a leader in hydroelectric power and is charting a course to use wind, solar, wave and tidal energy to significantly reduce fossil-fuel use. Most importantly, residents and visitors can freely enjoy the city's sprawling green space with 200 parks and more than 18 miles of waterfront. Determined to address and rectify environmental challenges while creating green jobs and strengthening the community, the City of Vancouver has reached significant milestones and created environmentally friendly alternatives for nearly every facet of residents' and visitors' day-to-day living. Perhaps the best way to appreciate Vancouver's leading role in creating globe-wide environmental growth for the future is a snapshot of some of the city's countless green initiatives:

## Greenest city 2020: a citywide pledge

Mayor Gregor Robertson's promise in 2009 that Vancouver will emerge as the world's greenest city led to a comprehensive action plan that aims to rethink and re-evaluate the way residents and visitors interact with(in) the region. A collaborative effort of thousands of community members, organizations, stakeholders and city staff, the Greenest City 2020 Action Plan incorporates improvements to building design, increased access to nature, cleaner air and water, an emphasis on locally grown ingredients and other lifestyle changes. In addition to the detailed examples in subsections below, the plan includes initiatives such as One Day (providing residents with resources and information to reduce energy use in their everyday lives); Green Streets (highlighting opportunities for residents to volunteer as neighbourhood street gardeners); and the EcoDensity Charter and Initial Actions (committing the City of Vancouver to making environmental sustainability a primary goal in all planning decisions).

## Greeted with green: sustainability at Vancouver International Airport (YVR)

Visitors to Vancouver experience the city's eco-initiatives right on arrival. Vancouver International Airport (YVR) features a number of green building techniques, such as solar-powered hot water heating systems that have resulted in energy savings of $110,000 per year. The airport's Energy Reduction Committee implements further energy reducing initiatives, including econo-mode settings on baggage conveyor belts and carbon dioxide sensors to control heating, ventilation and air conditioning (since it was created in 1999, the committee has saved more than 24 gigawatt hours of electricity). YVR was also Canada's first airport to install a living wall, standing 18 metres high and home to more than 28,000 plants. Finally, in 2004 the airport introduced a Taxi Incentive Program that licensed 100 hybrid and natural gas operated taxis to pick up arriving passengers; since its inception, the program has reduced carbon dioxide emissions by 8,422 tonnes every year.

## Build green: Vancouver architecture

Vancouver boasts an abundance of Leadership in Energy and Environmental Design (LEED)certified buildings – among the highest number per capita in North America. The city is also a world leader in the area of policies aimed at promoting energy efficiency in buildings, and planners are tasked with making all new construction carbon neutral by 2030. As part of this goal, the Green Homes program requires that all new building permit applications for single family homes meet specific criteria to collectively reduce energy consumption by 33 percent. The program will also improve air quality in new homes through methods such as installation of heat recovery ventilators and service shafts to allow future roof mounted solar panels. And as of 2010, all newly rezoned buildings are required to meet LEED gold standard, the highest green building standard for rezoned buildings in North America.

Many notable examples of green architecture grace the city, but a few standout structures are particularly well known. The multiple award winning Vancouver Convention Centre is renowned for being the first convention centre in the world to achieve LEED platinum certification. The building features a six acre living roof that houses some 400,000 indigenous plants, a design that reduces potable water consumption by 73 per cent and more than 130,000 square feet of walkways and public space. Also noteworthy is the LEED platinum certified Olympic and Paralympic Village, a product of the Vancouver 2010 Olympic and Paralympic Winter Games and often cited as the world's greenest neighbourhood. Housing 2,800 athletes during the Games, the former industrial brownfield site has been transformed into a mixed use neighbourhood that incorporates strategic energy use reduction, high performance green buildings and easy transit access. In addition, the development has re-established local wildlife habits, native vegetation and also provides for urban agriculture.

## Go green: transportation

Vancouver's commitment to green transportation is exemplified by its growing mass transit system. The original Sky-Train rail line opened in 1985 and, in 2009, just in time for the 2010 Olympic Games, the Canada Line was added, linking the airport to downtown in a 25minute trip. The next stage of this eco-minded transit network is the Evergreen Line, scheduled to open in 2016. Alternative modes of eco-transport include one of the world's largest hybrid taxi fleets, newly expanded bike lanes and an easily walkable downtown core. Car drivers aren't exempt: the city now requires electric vehicle (EV) charging stations for 20 percent of all parking stalls in new condo buildings.

Also prominent in Vancouver are public corridors called Greenways, which provide pedestrians and cyclists with eco-minded pathways from which to enjoy parks, historic sites, neighbourhoods and nature reserves. To date, Vancouver features 65 kilometres of Greenways and approximately 2,100 kilometres of sidewalk by which pedestrians can navigate the city.

## Stay, shop and eat green

A host of Vancouver hotels have been recognized by the global Green Key Eco-Rating Program as exemplifying environmental stewardship. Only a few dozen hotels around the world have achieved the top level Five Green Keys rating, and four Vancouver hotels are counted among these elite. An additional 22 local hotels have been awarded Four Green Keys, and a number of others are stepping up green initiatives within their individual properties.

Vancouver is also home to a number of boutiques, grocers and other retailers and designers that produce and sell environmentally friendly wares. A sampling of labels known locally as well as internationally include Ethical Bean (sourcing only fair trade and organic coffee beans); Happy Planet (a juice empire connecting urban residents with organic farming techniques); and Mountain Equipment Co-op (active-wear made from organically grown and recycled materials).

Seafood is a local dining specialty, but not all dishes are created equally. Pioneered by the Vancouver Aquarium and chefs across the region, the Ocean Wise initiative supports sustainable fishing practices, ensuring that restaurant seafood has been raised, sourced and supplied in an environmentally sound manner. Ocean Wise works directly with local restaurants, markets and suppliers to ensure they have the most current scientific information and helps them make ocean-friendly buying decisions. Consumers are also apprised of eco-friendly options, with the Ocean Wise symbol appearing on menus in restaurants across the city. The City of Vancouver aims to further increase access to local ingredients by ensuring for 2020 that the majority of residents are within a five-minute walk of fresh produce.

## Learn green: eco-events

Vancouver's green initiatives extend to community participation, with several events aiming to inspire green discussion and encourage change. Two of the most well-known include the Projecting Change Film Festival (featuring films that promote discussion about social and environmental issues) and Eco Fashion Week (dedicated to promoting the growth of sustainable fashion brands and practices, and establishing Vancouver as an international hub for sustainable style).

The City of Vancouver also promotes an annual cleanup campaign called Keep Vancouver Spectacular, during which thousands of volunteer residents pick up litter in neighbourhoods across the city. In 2011, more than 18,000 volunteers took part to clear Vancouver's streets and shorelines of detritus.

## Greenpeace and the David Suzuki Foundation: made in Vancouver

Vancouver's environmental reputation has been strengthened by a number of globe affecting campaigns. Greenpeace, for example, is known worldwide for exposing environmental problems and brainstorming solutions to ensure a green future – and it was founded in Vancouver. Forty-one years after it began, Greenpeace now operates in more than 40 countries worldwide and has 2.9 million members. Among its many initiatives, the organization has continued its initial aims to protect biodiversity, prevent pollution, end nuclear threats and promote peace, and has also been nominated for a Nobel Peace Prize.

Another local environmental leader is David Suzuki, award winning scientist and broadcaster who co-founded the David Suzuki Foundation.

Suzuki's lifelong activism to reverse global climate change extends to his internationally known foundation, which works with government, businesses and individuals to conserve the environment through science based education and policy work. The organization particularly focuses on youth, ensuring that future generations understand the importance of protecting the environment and ecosystems.

## Greenest City Fund: reaching our goal

In order to ensure Vancouver reaches its goal of becoming the Greenest City in the World by 2020, the City of Vancouver and Vancouver Foundation teamed up in April 2012 to introduce the Greenest City Fund with an initial contribution of $2 million. Between 2012 and 2015, the Greenest City Fund's three granting programs will fund projects led by residents and community based charitable organizations – resulting in increases to local food supply, reduction of energy use and promotion of green transportation.

With all these initiatives and more in place, and further green projects in the works for the coming years and decades, Vancouver is deeply committed to Green Growth – and well on the way to contributing to a worldwide shift in environmentally forward travel, tourism and living.

*While these thoughts reflect not only my views, but those of the very committed people at Tourism Vancouver, I want to single out Sonu Purhar who worked with me on putting it together and who typifies my young bright environmentally aware colleagues that give such hope for the future.*

A

# Raymond Benjamin

Secretary General, the International Civil Aviation Organization

## Aviation's and ICAO's climate change response

Raymond Benjamin is Secretary General of the International Civil Aviation Organization since August 2009. His extensive career in civil aviation includes 13 years as Executive Secretary of the European Civil Aviation Conference (ECAC) where he was responsible for the development of policy advice and strategic options. Prior to joining ECAC, Mr. Benjamin was Chief of the Aviation Security Branch of the Air Transport Bureau of ICAO from 1989 to 1994. Among his responsibilities was the provision of advice to the Secretary General and the President of the Council on security policy matters and the development of a worldwide airport assessment and technical assistance programme. He served as Air Transport Officer and Deputy Secretary of ECAC from 1982 to 1989 and held various positions in the Civil Aviation Administration of France from 1973 to 1982.

## Sustainable development of air transport

Air travel, an integral part of our global society, is the lifeline of economies throughout the world. It provides increased efficiency, affordable access to global markets and contributes to the improvement of living standards by offering an opportunity for all-inclusive growth. It also plays a major role in spreading various social and cultural benefits, as well as to effectively deliver public services such as emergency and humanitarian aid to remote and least developed areas.

The international community recognizes the economic contribution of civil aviation to the development of States, the world economy and trade, as well as to the development of travel and tourism. Each year, 2.6 billion passengers travel by air and more than 35 per cent of goods by value are carried on passenger and cargo aircraft. The aviation industry directly employs about 5.5 million people worldwide and supports millions more. In fact, if aviation were a country, it would rank 21st in the world in terms of gross domestic product (GDP), generating $425 billion of GDP per year (7.5 per cent of global GDP). Worldwide, the amount contributed to the global economy from aviation jobs is roughly four times higher than that contributed by other employment.

Air transport also leads in the progress in eco-efficiency, which has already paid off in terms of reduced fuel consumption, reduced emissions and less noise; if not in absolute, certainly in relative terms. It is estimated that total aviation accounts for 2 per cent of global $CO_2$ emissions, of which 60 per cent is from international flights. Aviation operations today are 70 per cent more fuel efficient and 75 per cent quieter than they were 40 years ago. This success has been made possible through increased use of low-carbon technologies, environmentally friendly materials, new aircraft systems and sustainable energy sources.

ICAO recognizes its essential role in leading air transport to a more sustainable future. The challenge is in how to strike a balance between the social, economic and environmental objectives of sustainable development, which, once applied to international aviation, will allow the sector to grow in an environmentally sustainable manner while at the same time continuing to ensure freedom to travel and economic access to mobility. Sustainable development of air transport seeks to secure the well-being of present and future generations. ICAO and its 191 Member States, in cooperation with other UN bodies and the aviation community, are committed to the development of global solutions for the sustainable future of international aviation.

## ICAO's key activities to respond to climate change

Demand for air traffic is projected to grow by 4.5 per cent per year. What will this mean in terms of the future contribution of aviation operations to climate change? And what can be done to effectively address $CO_2$ emissions from the sector? In this regard, the global policy framework adopted by the 37th Session of the ICAO Assembly in 2010 was an important milestone towards a sustainable future for international aviation, making it the first sector with a shared commitment to increase fuel efficiency and stabilize $CO_2$ emissions at 2020 levels.

The Assembly also requested the further development and global implementation of a basket of mitigation measures to limit or reduce $CO_2$ emissions from international aviation.  These include aircraft-related technologies, improved air traffic management and infrastructure use, more efficient operations, market-based measures (MBMs) and sustainable alternative fuels for aviation.

Sustainable alternative fuels for aviation offer one of the most exciting and promising opportunities for reducing the sector's greenhouse gas (GHG) emissions while improving local air quality, and ICAO has been providing a forum for the exchange of information on the state of worldwide activities. On the use of such fuels, aviation is a real and concrete example of how much can be done within a relatively short timeframe to turn a dream into reality. Today, the drop-in of biofuels in aviation does not require changes to aircraft or fuel delivery infrastructure and airlines have already started using biofuels in commercial flights. Technological aspects are proven to be viable; and the next challenges are to ensure that such fuels are available in a timely and commercially viable manner and in sufficient quantities for use in aviation. ICAO will continue to be at the forefront of international efforts to facilitate the development and deployment of such fuels on a global scale.

With respect to MBMs, it is paramount that a patchwork of uncoordinated measures undertaken by different States and regions be avoided. In this regard, the 37th Assembly of the ICAO agreed on the development of a framework for MBMs, including the further elaboration of the guiding principles adopted by the Assembly, and decided to explore a global scheme for international aviation. ICAO has undertaken intensive work to develop a global solution and the Council will provide a report to the next Assembly in 2013, as requested by Member States.

The agreement by the 37th Assembly on the voluntary submission of Member States' action plans to ICAO by June 2012 led to a dynamic shift in the Organization's policy outlook on climate change, shifting from a 'policy-setting' phase to more action-oriented 'implementation' mode. The action plans allow States to identify their basket of mitigation measures as well as their needs for assistance in the implementation of these measures. In turn, the compilation of information from States' action plans will enable ICAO to assess progress towards reaching the goal of increased fuel efficiency and the stabilization of carbon emissions at 2020 levels. In addition, it will enable ICAO to facilitate support and assistance as required.  Since the 37th Assembly, the Organization has been providing support to States, including the development of guidance material and hands-on training workshops for the preparation and submission of their action plans to ICAO.

## Message for Rio+20

Innovative thinking and co-operation have always been key to overcoming aviation's biggest challenges and it will be no different as we tackle the sustainability challenges before us. ICAO is ready to lead the sector through the sustainable development agenda and to ensure guaranteed access to a sustainable air transport system for generations to come as part of a new green economy.

Global problems require global solutions. ICAO is keenly aware of the leadership role conferred on it by its Member States, and it is totally committed to a sustainable future for international civil aviation — a safe, secure and economically viable global air transport system, with minimal adverse impacts on the environment.

ICAO fully supports the Millennium Development Goals (MDGs), in particular Goals 7 and 8 relating to environmental sustainability and the cultivation of a global partnership for development. ICAO also cooperates with the work of other UN bodies, namely the United Nations Framework Convention on Climate Change (UNFCCC) and its ongoing negotiation process towards a future global climate change agreement.

Rio+20 is expected to set clear objectives and establish a strong framework to address new energy challenges in the context of the transition to a green economy. ICAO hopes for an agreement at Rio+20 that will recognize the positive contribution of air transport to the three pillars of sustainable development and specifically the challenges of ensuring the availability of alternative fuels for use in aviation.

B

# Madan Prasad Bezbaruah

Representative of UNWTO India,
Former Secretary of Tourism, India

## Everybody's action or nobody's action? Rio+20, tourism and India

Madan Prasad Bezbaruah is a retired Indian civil servant who worked in the highest levels of government policy formulation and implementation in many sectors both in the Federal and State Governments. Currently he is the honorary Permanent Representative of UN-WTO and also Director (Hon.), Administrative Staff College of India. He has vast experience and expertise in national and international tourism planning and management, and steered India's tourism development for a long period as Secretary in the Ministry of Tourism. He was a member of the Strategic Group of UNWTO for several years and was unanimously elected the Chairman of Pacific Asia Travel Association (PATA) for 2000-01. Mr. Bezbaruah has written three books and innumerable articles on tourism, and is the Chief Editor of five volume encyclopaedia, *Fairs and Festivals of India*.

Ten years after the Rio Earth Summit, when President Jacques Chirac of France lamented at the World Summit on Sustainable Development in Johannesburg that 'our house is burning down and we are blind to it' he seemed to echo the sentiments of an anguished world. The optimists among the tens of thousands of participants from about a thousand organisations found his use of the possessive pronoun – 'our' – significant. It revived hopes of common action beyond the usual divides of rich-poor, developed-underdeveloped and north-south.

The Summit did underscore the urgency of common global action to meet the pressing challenges before humanity, as did almost all conferences before and after it. But common action has been most elusive. The telling testimony is the world's response to the implementation of the Millennium Development Goals (MDGs), adopted with so much enthusiasm and optimism.

Two years after Johannesburg and four years into the MDG mission, when the Secretary General of the United Nations reviewed the progress of the global partnership, he rued the rapidly diminishing window of opportunity and the almost absent political will. After a decade, the official review still admits that improvements in the lives of the poor have been unacceptably slow and the Secretary General has to remind the world not to fail the billions who look to the international community to fulfil the promise for a better, happier planet.

The world has missed the bio-diversity loss target for 2010 with potentially grave consequences. The Millennium Ecosystem Assessment of 2005 brings out the grim realities of ecosystem degradation but says the self-destruction process can still be checked if, and this is a big *if*, concerted action is taken. Common action denotes everybody's action. Unfortunately, the problem with everybody's action is that it is invariably nobody's action.

Rio Earth Summit Agenda 21 was premised in the hope that humanity would change course. Together we can, it had optimistically proclaimed. Is that hope belied? The primary challenge before Rio+20 will be to achieve commitments on a doable action plan with a time frame for implementation. Otherwise it runs the risk of going down in history as another gala event of diplomatic statements of shared concerns and pious declarations.

Twenty years before Rio, at the Stockholm conference India's Prime Minister Indira Gandhi had made that oft quoted statement: 'Poverty is the greatest polluter'. Back home, NGOs, social activists and others criticised the statement then, and do so even now, as anti-poor. After all, they continue to point out, haven't the rich nations, in their journey towards prosperity, used up resources in such a way that the carrying capacity of the world has been exceeded by 20 per cent. And this despite half the world population still living on less than $2 a day.

Yet the statement reflects what every study, every initiative in the past 50 years has established without ambiguity. Sustainable development will remain a distant dream unless the problem of poverty is addressed and tackled. The report of the Brundtland Commission, appropriately named *Our Common Future*, in fact starts with the assertion that 'a world in which poverty is endemic will always be prone to ecological and other catastrophes'. Hunger and poverty, noted Maurice Strong, Secretary General of the United Nations Conference on Environment and Development in Rio Agenda 21, are both a cause and an effect of environmental degradation.

Every succeeding generation has pledged itself to do something to alleviate poverty and every generation has ended up worse than where it began. During the final decade of the 20th century, total world income increased by 2.5 per cent annually. In this same time, points out Nobel laureate Joseph Stiglitz, the number of people living in poverty actually increased by almost 100 million. A World Tourism Organisation (the present UNWTO) report in 2004 minced no words in calling mankind's achievements in alleviating poverty 'shameful'.

That close to two of every four people on our planet live on less than $2 a day, that the number of malnourished and hungry has increased to a billion is indeed a disgrace to humankind. But the more worrisome danger is the increasing inequality around the world. Even in an emerging economy like India, which has achieved 8-9% GDP growth in recent years, there has been a stark increase in inequality. The share of the bottom 60 per cent has declined from 39 to 28 per cent of GDP while the share of the top 20 per cent has gone up to 50 per cent in the 15 years ending in 2010.

The brewing discontent has very dangerous portents capable of threatening stability and security around the world. Occupy Wall Street (OWS) was a symbolic outburst of that anger. Rio+ 20 will have to address the depth of that anger even if OWS has petered out.

The United Nations World Tourism Organisation has been arguing that tourism is better placed than many other sectors in relating to the needs of the poor. That tourism can help alleviate poverty is by now well known. It provides the main source of income of many developing countries, it provides almost one tenth of the total employment, benefits backward areas, provides employment and income to women and creates demand that has strong ripple effects on many other sectors of the economy. Ninety to ninety five per cent of income of the craftsmen and artisans in Rajasthan and Kerala provinces in India comes from tourism. An oft repeated sample survey in India shows that 100 million rupees invested in tourism gives four times more employment than in manufacture. The list can go on.

Though the contribution of tourism is much talked about, the evidence is not always very apparent. In India, tourism earnings are tucked away as invisible in the national accounting system. Moreover, it is a multi-dimensional activity. The World Travel and Tourism Council (WTTC), for example, has estimated that at least thirty economic activities, as diverse as car rentals and ship building, are at the core of the travel and tourism business. In practice only four or five of them, the tip of the iceberg, like travel, accommodation and transport, are seen as part of tourism. Tourism also often hangs in isolation as an economic activity in national development planning, without links to poverty reduction strategies in health, education and so on.

That may explain why tourism has a very low-key presence in the Rio Agenda 21. It is mentioned cursorily only in three places and always in relation to its impact on the environment. This is surprising because in the forty years preceding Rio, tourism was growing at an average annual rate of 6.5% and earnings were growing at a staggering rate of over 11% a year. As John Naisbitt pointed out in *Global Paradox*, as a contributor to the global economy tourism had no equal. The gap in Agenda 21 was largely filled up by the Travel and Tourism Local Agenda 21, which charted out a definite road map for tourism in combating poverty.

The introduction of the Tourism Satellite Accounting (TSA) system has changed the perception about tourism in many countries and has helped in logically demonstrating the impact of tourism. Rio+20 must recognise the positive contribution and role of sustainable tourism in poverty reduction and should integrate total tourism into its future plan of action. In any case Rio+20 cannot overlook the likely impact of the footprints of 1.6 billion international and 10 billion domestic travellers.

To showcase tourism's contribution to poverty alleviation, UNWTO designed the Sustainable Tourism for Eradication of Poverty (ST-EP). The Indian response came in vigorously pursuing the concept of Rural Tourism. In a country with about two-thirds of the population in rural areas and about one-third below the poverty line, it is the most logical option. The policy is also the closest approximation to a local agenda that Rio envisaged.

Yet there are many gaps. Tourism often fails to travel to the frontiers of 'travelism', which requires that it be integrated with the total poverty reduction initiatives of the government. Rural tourism, implemented without passion and imagination, can be just urban tourism transplanted in rural areas. Often there are leakages on the supply side; benefits not coming to locals because tourism supplies come from outside. This drains out much of the benefit that should go to the local community.

Internationally such leakages have been estimated to be around 55% on the average. Much needs to done, and quickly, to create supply-side value chains involving local communities, building capacity locally, facilitating growth of SMEs, sharing technology and innovations to improve productivity and so on. Rio had asserted that 'human beings are at the centre of concerns for sustainable development'. Meaningful rural tourism can bring people to the core of concerns; it can be a first generation manifestation of the currently popular concept of a Green Economy.

Game changing innovations and technology aligned with nature and people's active participation can work wonders. Barefoot College in Rajasthan, India, was founded with the firm conviction that solutions to rural problems lay with the community. It used local and traditional knowledge to provide safe drinking water, health and education to 100,000 people in 111 villages. This is not a solitary example but the message is clear, empowered people can make the change that they need. ITC, the Indian business conglomerate, has led corporate sustainable strategies with innovative ideas, saving 15 lit of diesel per hour in its operations in one case, by using solar energy. It has also forested 1.5 m hectares in rural areas.

The impact of climate change, described as 'the defining challenge' for humanity by the Secretary General of the UN, adds another dimension to the problem of poverty. Scientific studies of climate change are not new. They go back at least two centuries. But the content and complexion of the concerns have changed tremendously, from a preoccupation with glacial changes to the overwhelming impact of human action on the climate; from lurking suspicion of a return to the ice age to the disastrous effects of global warming; and in a sense from the realm of science fiction to the dreadful reality staring us in the face.

Globally, India subscribes to the principle of 'common but differentiated responsibilities and respective capabilities' that acknowledges, for example, that between 1860 and 1990 some 75 per cent of the total accumulated $CO_2$ emissions was from industrialised countries. Internally India was jolted out of complacency by, ironically, an error on the part of the Intergovernmental Panel on Climate Change (IPCC), headed by an Indian technocrat.

The IPCC's frightening assessment was that the Himalayan glaciers were melting so fast that they would disappear by 2035, if not sooner. This alarming assertion was quickly challenged and subsequently modified. But the controversy does not die down. A study by Jawaharlal Nehru University in Delhi, while admitting that depletion had been greater in recent times, called the fear of disappearance a 'myth'. A Bristol University glaciologist has also come up with the stunning discovery that in the past decade the Asian mountains have lost no ice.

The Himalayas are crucial to the climate and ecology of India and therefore it is good news that the ice is not melting. But India recognises that the threat of climate change is real. Though on a per capita basis India's emissions are 70% below the world average and 93% below the United States, India has committed itself to a low-carbon economy and unilaterally decided to reduce the emission intensity of GDP by 20-25% by 2020, based on the 2005 level. Its National Action Plan on Climate Change has eight Missions, two of which relate to the Himalayan Ecosystem and to the 'Greening of India', by increasing the forest cover by 33 per cent.

However, national policy making is often a tightrope-walking exercise, and balances conflicting options and unavoidable compulsions. Addressing India's parliamentarians, the noted economist Jagdish Bhagwati articulated why high growth was an essential even if not sufficient condition for a pull up strategy to reduce poverty. It is estimated that to maintain an 8% or higher pace of growth requires 20% more primary resources than are produced sustainably and by 2030 will require 4/5 times as many resources.

Some of the resources can come from innovations, productive efficiency, and resource efficiency. But the figures of deprived people in India who need more resources to improve their lives is staggering;

more than 300 million below the poverty line, more than 250 million without access to safe drinking water, more than 700 million without proper sanitation, more than 150 million without proper shelter and more than 500 million without electricity.

On the other hand, fuel wood trade is estimated to have an annual turnover of $1.7bn and main source of livelihood of about 11 million people. About 27% of India's population depend on forests for their subsistence in different ways. Forests meet nearly 40 per cent of the energy needs of the country and 80 per cent of those in rural areas. The crucial question is: how do we maintain equitable consumption flows to the present generation while ensuring intergenerational equity? Sustainability is a future concern. Hunger is of the present. So, how do we blend both imperatives? How do we provide economic alternatives to those who are hungry and malnourished but are willing (or are required to) to sacrifice for the future?

Many countries face this dilemma. Rio+20 must seek plausible answers to such questions. At the same time the cost of not taking action to mitigate the impact of climate change can be, as the Stern report warned in the global context, very costly for India. Any major impact on the monsoon, which is India's lifeline, will completely change the socio-economic fundamentals of the country. A World Bank report has indicated the climate change impact may reduce food production by 20 to 40 per cent in India, and affect the economy of a 7,600 km long coastal area, uprooting 20 per cent of the population and 20,000 villages.

The impact on the travel and tourism industry could be even more serious. The aviation industry, domestically and internationally, is passing through prolonged turbulence. It has survived the past forty years on a fragile margin of 0.1 per cent. Ninety-four per cent of India's international tourists arrive by air. The much-reformed and modernised domestic aviation sector is boosting tourism by carrying 52 million passengers (2010 figures), showing a robust growth of 18 per cent.

But almost all airlines are in serious financial difficulties caused in India, as elsewhere, by high fuel cost and growing cost of operations. The International Civil Aviation Organisation (ICAO) has listed Four Pillars of Survival for the industry:

- Air traffic management
- Efficient infrastructure
- Technology-based solutions to meet security
- Addressing environmental challenges

Progress is far from satisfactory on these counts. The Annual Report of India's Civil Aviation Ministry, submitted to Parliament, makes no mention of initiatives on the challenges of climate change. And the aviation industry continues to complain of government apathy on issues like fuel taxes, structural changes and more commercial freedom. Again the world is poorer in taking action because of a lack of a common approach.

ICAO has announced a self-regulated target to reduce $CO_2$ emission to half of 2005 level by 2050. But the European Union's carbon tax has split the industry, reeling under the burden of a four billion euro impact of departure taxes in the United Kingdom, Germany and Austria. ICAO strongly advocates global problems should be globally managed and not clouded by regional initiatives. A conclave of thirty-three countries has decided to take retaliatory measures including law suits. Forty-three countries have publicly opposed the EU stand. An industry that causes two per cent of all carbon emission at the least is a divided house in taking action to mitigate it.

'Together we can' Rio Agenda 21 had stated. After 20 years Rio+20 would do well to remember the words of the ancient poet Virgil:

*They can,*

*Because,*

*They think,*

*They can*

We can. When will we?

B

# Giovanni Bisignani

**Chairman WEF Global Agenda Council (Aviation, Travel & Tourism), Visiting Professor Cranfield University**

## The mystery of governments' aviation policy

Giovanni Bisignani is a member of the Board of NATS Holdings Limited, the UK's air traffic services provider. He is also a member of the Board and Strategic, Remunerations and Nominating committees of SAFRAN Group and a member of the Board of AirCastle (US). He chairs the World Economic Forum Global Agenda Council on Aviation, Travel & Tourism (Switzerland) and is a Visiting Professor, at Cranfield University - School of Engineering (UK). Mr. Bisignani was Director General of the International Air Transport Association from June 2002 to July 2011. He became Director General Emeritus from June 2011 until his retirement in October 2011.  During his nearly 10 years with the organization, Mr. Bisignani drove major industry changes. The most important was making the IATA Operational Safety Audit (IOSA) a condition of IATA membership. This contributed to a 42% improvement in safety over the period 2000-2010.  He also played a leading role in aviation's response to climate change and the adoption of paperless ticketing.

The evidence is clear and comes direct from the Intergovernmental Panel on Climate Change (IPCC); aviation contributes just 2% of man-made emissions. This small figure should be no surprise. The industry has the strongest possible motive for reducing emissions. They are a by-product of fuel burn and fuel is the largest cost centre airlines have. The 2012 IATA forecast suggests fuel will cost the airlines $198 billion, which is around 30% of costs. Over the years, the industry has developed new technology to reduce the fuel bill. Modern planes are more fuel efficient than a compact car and each new generation of aircraft is approximately 20% more efficient than the model it replaces.

Airlines are winning the battle. Emissions are now decoupled from traffic growth. On average, emissions will increase by 3% annually (about 20 million metric tons) while air traffic will grow 5%. And approximately 80% of these emissions will come from journeys of over 1,500km for which there is no realistic alternative.

If you are still unsure about aviation's commitment to the environment, look at its track record in confronting the big issues. Noise used to be the major problem. It emerged as a concern in the 1970s and some tough regulations came into force. As ever, governments argued among themselves—there was the infamous hush-kit battle, for example—while airlines and airports worked together to solve the problem. Airports insulated the homes of affected communities and improved planning processes on their borders while airlines worked with manufacturers to make aircraft quieter without losing performance. Today, the latest generations of high bypass ratio engines are 50% quieter than they were just 10 years ago.

And still the bar is being raised. The International Civil Aviation Organization (ICAO) is now considering a 'Chapter 5' regulation, making aircraft even quieter from 2017 onwards. In my Vision 2050 project, prominent business leaders extrapolated the current progress to suggest that by 2050, noise will not be an issue outside the airport perimeter.

The advances being made in emissions reduction suggests that by 2050, emissions could join noise in the history books.

## The industry story

Despite all of this, aviation's 2% contribution to man-made emissions is not a figure to hide behind. Unless further improvements are made, emissions will grow as air traffic increases.

When I joined IATA I knew I had to address this concern and make air transport the most pro-active industry in the world when it comes to environmental mitigation. For a while, 9/11 forced other priorities on the industry but at the end of 2005 the IATA Board endorsed a four-pillar strategy; new technology, more effective operations, more efficient infrastructure, and positive economic measures. This had the advantage of engaging all stakeholders so no one sector of the industry felt isolated. Air transport would be united in its environmental efforts.

A robust framework was a good start but as I always say, 'no targets, no business.' It was important to show the strategy was more than public relations. At the 2007 IATA AGM in Vancouver, I took a calculated risk and announced that aviation was on track for a carbon-free future. It stunned the audience and generated a huge amount of press around the world. By the time of a preparatory meeting for the United Nations Framework for Climate Change Convention (UNFCCC) in May 2009, the perception of aviation's role in the environment was beginning to change. I was invited to speak at the meeting, not to defend air transport but to explain to other industries how to create a viable environmental strategy.

A month later, at the IATA AGM in Kuala Lumpur, the industry took the next step. We had a hard-won consensus on targets. I announced aviation's three sequential goals:

1. a 1.5% average annual improvement in fuel efficiency from 2009 to 2020;

2. a cap on carbon emissions with carbon-neutral growth from 2020 and

3. a 50% absolute reduction in carbon emissions by 2050 compared to 2005 levels.

No other industry has come close to such an ambitious undertaking.

## Time for governments to step up

Aviation has clearly shown its commitment to climate change. Even United Nations Secretary General Ban Ki-moon has congratulated aviation and said it was a role model for other industries to follow.

Unfortunately, there are no role models at the government level. The prime offender is the European Union and specifically the Emissions Trading Scheme (EU ETS). There is no problem with positive economic measures—it is one of aviation's environmental pillars and the industry will not achieve its targets without them. But the EU ETS in its current form is ill-conceived. When it was proposed at the intra-European level, IATA supported the idea. But now the scheme has gone global. If Cathay Pacific is flying to Europe, for example, it needs to pay the EU for emissions over Hong Kong. That can't be right and the United States, China, India, and some 40 other countries agree.

A letter by Secretary of State Hillary Clinton and Transportation Secretary Ray LaHood on 16 December 2011 to the European Commission stated:

'We urge the EU and its member states ... to return to working with, rather than against, the international community in the appropriate multilateral forum—the ICAO—to address the important challenge of reducing aviation emissions. Failure to resolve this issue will hamper our efforts to make progress in reducing emissions from international aviation.'

The letter is right. ICAO is the place to agree a global solution. In fact, I have met with representatives of the European Commission and most of the other governments concerned to work out the specifics.

My proposal has three steps:

1.  Governments fighting against the EU ETS should recognize the positive role played by Europe for a stronger environmental commitment

2.  The EU should modify its approach and restrict itself to a intra-European ETS by 2013

3.  All countries should commit to a global ETS by 2014 under the leadership of ICAO.

I believe this is a fair and balanced solution to the current deadlock. The European Commission and other governments should consider this proposal, which provides a way for all parties to be winners; the environment, governments, and the aviation industry. I am confident we will see progress by the end of 2012.

It is also worth noting that ICAO is studying an aircraft global standard for $CO_2$ emissions and through its Committee on Aviation Environmental Protection will implement a stringent nitrogen oxide standard for engines issued after 2013.

**Tax heaped upon tax**

Aside from its attack on other nations' sovereignty, the EU ETS has one other big failing. It has not stopped other so-called green taxes in Europe. Germany, Austria, and the United Kingdom all have aviation taxes that were introduced under an environmental disguise. And like the EU ETS not a single cent or penny is obligated for environmental mitigation. This is a shame, because at early 2012 market prices for UN-issued Certified Emissions Reductions the $5.3 billion these three taxes collect annually would pay for aviation's total global emissions (approximately 650 million metric tons) 1.5 times. And remember, this is before airlines even start to pay for emissions through the EU ETS.

This is not all that Europe has to be embarrassed about. The Single European Sky (SES) has been talked about for at least 20 years. If implemented it would save some 16 million metric tons of $CO_2$ annually. But the targets for implementation are weak and the countries' commitment weaker still. The last SES progress report suggested only five out of 27 countries are on track and only one out of the nine Functional Airspace Blocks is expected to be ready by end 2012. The situation is now critical because the EU is falling short. The SES project needs leadership and a show of political will. European rhetoric about the EU ETS is empty while the SES remains a 20-year-old dream.

NextGen in the United States and a Seamless Asian Sky could deliver similar $CO_2$ reductions to SES. The US FAA Reauthorization and Reform Act should finally provide the funding for the former while the latter has a great chance of success in what is now aviation's largest market, Asia-Pacific. Governments there show a better understanding of aviation's role in the wider economy. They appreciate that aviation supports 33 million jobs worldwide and $3.5 trillion in economic activity.

It is also time for governments to make the necessary investment in air traffic control so that airlines can take full advantage of the advanced avionics on board aircraft. We've managed to get Reduced Vertical Separation Mimima implemented globally but there is still much that can be done on shortening air routes, green departures, and continuous descent approaches.

## Commercial biofuel

A major part of aviation's environmental work is alternative fuels. Biojet fuel could reduce the industry's carbon footprint by 80% over the lifecycle of the fuel. Again, airlines have pushed the boundaries as far as they are able to. Test flights have taken place around the world. Lufthansa did a successful six-month trial on a Hamburg-Frankfurt service. A biokerosene mix in one engine on an Airbus A321 reduced $CO_2$ emissions by 1,471 metric tons. We know biojet fuel works. The challenge is to make it commercially available in sufficient quantity and for that we need governments and big oil companies to step up to the mark.

Under current EU legislation there is little incentive to produce aviation biofuel. It is thought to be worth about $33 per metric ton for airlines to switch over to biojet fuel, the small saving coming from a reduced need for carbon allowances. That $33 would barely cover the cost of filling out the extra forms. Governments must legislate to take the risk out of scaling-up biojet fuel production. At the moment, big oil companies worry they could find themselves on the wrong side of bad regulations in the future and never recover any money they invest. But oil giants won't lobby on aviation's behalf. Airlines pay them the best part of $200 billion for normal jet fuel every year and they make healthy margins. Oil companies lack the motivation to be involved in this struggle.

There are other issues to resolve. Some argue that biofuel production eats up land needed for food production. They are wrong. Second generation biofuels use crops and land that would otherwise stay idle. In fact, biojet fuel production is a force for good. It will reduce dependence on oil and create a vibrant new industry, employing many where previously there were no jobs.

The industry environment strategy targets 4% biofuels by 2020, but this will be a tough target unless governments and oil suppliers support this fledgling market. President Obama's Administration has pledged support through its energy policy and Europe included biofuels in its Transport 2050 assessment. But lack of money and half-hearted policies mean specific mechanisms to encourage the production of biojet fuel are still lacking.

**B**

## A green future

Airlines do understand the power of the climate change debate and they do understand the air transport business model, which focuses on keeping the fuel bill down. The incentive for reduced emissions is strong. Working with their partners they have squeezed out fuel efficiencies wherever possible. IATA launched a 'save a minute' campaign. Just 60 seconds shaved off a flight though better airspace design and management saves about 62 litres of jet fuel, about 160kg of $CO_2$.

The industry has many such success stories, from global strategies to local improvements. The evidence and the available figures back up the work that has been done. Over the past half century, the industry has reduced noise by 90% and $CO_2$ by 70% through a comparable increase in fuel efficiency.

But the industry working alone cannot deliver the results that climate change needs. Governments must see the bigger picture and recognize that the environment is a global concern that can't be addressed with location-specific taxes and regulations. Too often, governments are fighting against aviation and not fighting for it. Considering that airlines are vital to the global village, their attitude is a mystery.

# Richard Branson

## Founder and Chairman, Virgin Group

## Why aviation can respond positively to climate change

Sir Richard Branson is Founder and Chairman of the Virgin Group. Virgin is one of the world's most recognised and respected brands and has expanded into everything from air and ground travel to telecommunications, tourism, banking, health, space travel and renewable energy, employing approximately 50,000 people in more than 30 countries. Richard works with partners to tackle tough social and environmental challenges with talented people and innovative approaches. In addition to launching the Virgin Earth Challenge, a $25 million prize to encourage a viable technology which will result in the net removal of anthropogenic, atmospheric greenhouse gases, he has created Virgin Unite, the not-for-profit foundation of the Virgin Group. Virgin Unite has helped to form The Carbon War Room, The Elders, and has supported the Global Drugs Commission. Richard and Unite are also fostering young entrepreneurs through the Branson School of Entrepreneurship in South Africa and the Caribbean.

There's no getting away from the fact that aviation has an impact on the environment, but flying is also crucial to the global economy and central to many people's lifestyles. It connects countries, fosters businesses and links families and communities around the world.

Looking ahead, the aviation industry must respond positively to the challenge of climate change if it wants to maintain its key role in the world's future. As the founder of a number of airlines I am determined that we grow responsibly, and keep working hard to find new solutions that will make low carbon aviation possible in the foreseeable future.

Today, we are very focused on fuel efficiency; reducing both the demand for fuel and carbon emissions. Virgin Atlantic has invested in new efficient aircraft, as well as making changes to operational and maintenance procedures. Last year it took delivery of the first of these new, more fuel-efficient aircraft – the Airbus A330s – which will shave up to 15% per seat off their fuel and carbon emissions compared to the aircraft they are replacing. In 2014, Atlantic expects to receive the first if its new Boeing 787-9 'Dreamliner' aircraft, which are 25% more fuel efficient on a per seat basis.

Virgin Australia will also be investing $2.5billion (AUD) into its fleet over the next six years to keep it modern and fuel efficient. For example, it has introduced the ATR turboprop aircraft, which are up to 40% more fuel efficient than existing aircraft on short- to medium-haul routes.

Already Virgin America's existing A320 family fleet is up to 25% more fuel efficient than other domestic fleets and one of the most carbon-efficient in the United States. Despite this, Virgin America is still investing and has selected the CFM International advanced LEAP™ engine to power its new Airbus a320neo aircraft, scheduled to come online in 2016. Together, these two investments promise to deliver one of the world's most fuel-efficient commercial aircraft, with a further 15% improved fuel efficiency, reduced engine noise and double digit reductions in NOx emissions.

Although increasing efficiency has been the main focus for all our airlines, it can only take us so far. We are also looking at alternative fuels that have a lower carbon footprint. In 2008, Virgin Atlantic was the first airline in the world to operate a commercial aircraft on a biofuel blend (ground-breaking stuff at the time!). We understand the negative unintended consequences biofuels can have, if not carefully chosen.

That is why Virgin America, Virgin Atlantic and Virgin Australia have all pledged their commitment to sustainability through the Sustainable Aviation Fuel Users Group (SAFUG), which supports the Roundtable on Sustainable Biofuels (RSB) – a leading, international, independent multi-stakeholder organisation responsible for rigorous sustainability standards for biofuels. The RSB process ensures that we avoid the problems associated with earlier generations of fuels (like competition with food or deforestation issues) and establishes that the true life cycle carbon emissions of new fuels are lower than those for fossil fuel alternatives.

The other problem facing the nascent fuel industry is that the supplier companies are not yet large enough to make sufficient volumes at commercially viable prices. Many need money to scale-up, but the banks won't provide loans without orders from airlines, who in turn won't place big orders without the certainty on future costs – which are often unclear until they get to scale.

This is the information barrier which the Carbon War Room (CWR) is keen to address. In 2009, I and some partners set up the CWR, a not-for-profit organisation, aimed at eliminating market failures around climate change. It has been very effective in getting capital moving to entrepreneurs in clean technology and breaking down barriers, and to help them scale-up in a range of industries.

We now hope they can do the same for the aviation sector through their 'Renewable Jet Fuels Operation'.

Virgin Atlantic is a partner of the 'battle', but Airlines have a lot of different considerations to compare – such as supply chain risks, technology performance, differentiation, scalability and sustainability.

They need to be able to get their heads around all of these areas before they can confidently form partnerships, sign contracts, and provide what the finance companies need to scale up. That is why Carbon War Room and Elsevier created an online tool do exactly that. It is called renewablejetfuels.org and it collates and analyses a large amount of information about the entire renewable fuel supply chain: from feedstock and capacity to price and environmental compliance.

Providing this level of information transparency will hopefully assist Virgin and other airlines to have the confidence to place bigger orders with biofuel companies, enabling suppliers to raise money, scale up production and bring down the prices.

Personally, I believe the airline industry can move from being a polluting industry to one of the cleanest industries in the world within 10 years. Unlike other industries, it only has 1 800 fuel pumps to fuel the world's aircraft and therefore once clean fuels are ready for delivery, it is easy to transform the whole industry.

Virgin airlines are already starting to show their confidence in the biofuel industry. Recently, I made a very exciting announcement around

Virgin Atlantic's partnership with fuel company, LanzaTech, to develop a next generation low-carbon fuel. LanzaTech has a unique patented fermentation technology that uses a microbe to convert waste carbon monoxide (CO) gas from industrial steel mills into ethanol. Then using technology from Swedish Biofuels, the ethanol is converted into jet fuel through a second stage process. Currently these waste gases are flared off directly to the atmosphere, however with this incredible breakthrough technology these gases could instead, soon be recycled into jet fuel. The great thing about LanzaTech's biofuel is that not only does it have less than half the total life cycle carbon content compared to kerosene, its prices are on a par with current commercial aviation fuel and it scores the maximum three stars in each category of Renewablejetfuels.org.

Virgin Australia has also announced its support for two highly promising projects that use sustainable means and methods to achieve high-quality bio-crude oil. The first involves working with Renewable Oil Corporation, GE and Future Farm Industries Co-Operative Research Centre, to develop a sustainable aviation biofuel through the use of an innovative fast pyrolysis technology, which processes mallees, a eucalypt tree that can be grown sustainably in many parts of Australia.

The second involves Australian-based biofuel company, Licella, to support the commercialization of a Catalytic Hydrothermal Reactor which uses water technology to process high-quality bio-crude oil from a range of different biomass including agricultural and farm waste.

With a highly regulated industry like aviation, policy has a large impact on how efficiently businesses operate, and whether innovation is promoted or penalised. As founding members of Aviation Global Deal, Virgin Atlantic and Virgin Australia have been campaigning for an effective carbon cap-and-trade scheme for the whole industry, worldwide. Cap-and-trade is much more environmentally-effective and cost-efficient than taxation for reducing carbon emissions. It incentivises fuel efficiencies and the funds can be used for both climate change mitigation and adaptation schemes.

The airlines also have large social impacts - by building businesses which create jobs and wealth, not only within the Virgin group, but in local communities globally. There are also knock-on effects through tourism which brings millions of dollars every year to the Caribbean and aviation has played a large part in that. But as with everything, tourism can have a downside too – from over-reliance on tourism for economic growth to depletion of destinations' natural resources. I believe that locals should benefit as much as visitors from tourism and we should ensure that the resorts we enjoy today are preserved for others to enjoy in the future.

Virgin Holidays has established its Human Nature Promise, which promises to get its business in order, encourage suppliers to be more sustainable and give something back to the people and places in the destinations we visit. This is why we established The Branson Centre for Entrepreneurship Caribbean, which acts as a hub for aspiring young entrepreneurs. The Centre, a joint project between Virgin Holidays and Virgin Unite, offers practical business skills and access to expert mentors and financing opportunities, enabling Caribbean businesses to grow, and creating jobs for disadvantaged communities across the region.

I know we at Virgin still have a long way to go, but we are committed to the path we have chosen. I believe we can make it happen. Addressing the challenges of climate change should not be about sacrifice but about opportunity. There will be a healthy aviation industry, even when we have achieved the low carbon world of the future. But to make that a reality, we need to support new technologies, work with those developing new fuels and push for better policy - that is what I make sure my airlines are doing.

It's important for us to stay positive in the fight against carbon and in attempting to overcome all problems. As I've said before – Martin Luther King did not get his message across by saying 'I have a nightmare'!

B

# Geoff Buckley

**Managing Director, New Earth Tourism, Former MD Tourism Australia**

## Establishing a destination brand framework for a green growth strategy

Geoff Buckley, Managing Director of New Earth Tourism Pty Ltd, a specialist destination management and marketing company. The firm undertakes a range of strategic planning and marketing consulting/contracting projects mainly in the tourism sector. He is also a Principal with KPMG Australia, leading their tourism and travel advisory projects within the Asia Pacific region. Before establishing his own business, Geoff was Managing Director of Tourism Australia, the country's national tourism body, and one of the most successful and innovative National Tourism Organizations in the world. He has a strong interest and a wide range of practical experience in destination management, marketing and branding. Recognizing that tourism is an important industry growth sector for the world and has a key part to play in helping achieve economic and social well being in many developing countries across the globe, his belief is that effective destination management is the way to sustainable growth.

Under any green growth strategy one key element in shifting a destination to a stronger environmentally sustainable position will be through the repositioning of the destination's brand.

It's commonly accepted that strong brands accelerate business performance, with the power to lift destinations, their products and services from a low level of awareness and status to positions of pre-eminence in the marketplace.

We define brand as the recognition and personal connection that forms in the hearts and minds of customers through their accumulated experience with the brand, at *every* point of contact. Ideally the brand that emerges is a positive one, leading to trust, loyalty and advocacy for the offerings, increasing demand and establishing a long-term advantage in the marketplace.

With the rise of a new, ethical, green consumer, destinations that put themselves on a green growth path have an opportunity to take advantage of this growing global visitor demand but will need to do this via a changed brand emphasis.

## How to create a green growth based destination brand?

It should be understood that to be effective, branding is much more than just a marketing responsibility; it is an integrated business practice, particularly for a destination. It needs to underpin all the decisions and actions regarding the green growth development and marketing of a destination; from investment and product development, through to culture, communications and the delivery of experiences and services. It should reflect and inform all the business decisions and should guide all of the customer contact points.

The best response to this challenge is the development of a Destination Brand Framework for the green growth destination. This framework helps work through all the processes needed to design, create and manage a broadly integrated destination branding program.

The Branding Framework is built around four core processes, each of which plays a vital role in creating a viable 'green growth' destination brand. They are:

## 1 Developing a destination brand strategy

The brand strategy is critical because it sets the foundation for all other marketing activities and also it establishes a focused understanding and direction that's agreed upon at the highest levels of destination management, preferably before creative development work begins. It also helps prevent the brand chaos that sometimes arises from conflicting goals and personal beliefs, plus provides vital input to align the creative and management processes.

Based on a detailed understanding of the destination, its offerings, audiences and competitive marketplace, the strategy defines the overall brand architecture, a differentiated position in the marketplace, a hierarchy of messages crafted to resonate with customers, a distinctive but authentic brand promise and a projection of the customer's ideal overall brand experience.

The brand strategy will, importantly, also establish the brand attributes.

## Brand attributes

The main objective is to firstly decide what are the key attributes of the destination (and how do they relate to the green growth philosophy). Often not easy decisions, those attributes should be:

- *Relevant:* important to the potential visitor.
- *Distinctive:* that are unique to the destination and that will help separate it from the more than 160 other global tourism destinations now competing for the international traveller.
- *Superior:* that the destination delivers better than the competitors.
- *Tangible:* that can be quantified in some way, e.g. value for money or customer satisfaction.

In addition the brand positioning attributes that are developed must be:

- *Affordable:* The potential visitors believe they can afford the experience being promised.
- *Return on Investment:* The cost to maintain the differentiating attribute(s) does not exceed the visitor benefit to the destination.
- *Believable:* The attribute is aligned with the authenticity of the experience, that is, credible and achievable for the visitor.

The key output from this process is a recommended destination brand strategy that would be a subset of any integrated green growth strategy.

Once the brand strategy has been developed and endorsed the next phase would be toward implementation.

## 2 Creating a brand identity

With a strategy in place, a brand identity then needs to be created. This brand identity is the highly distinctive outward expressions of the destination's values, personality and promise. It will consist of elements such as the name and logo that are going to be used repeatedly to provide instant recognition in a crowded marketplace.

It is here that the difficult task of expressing the 'green growth' vision and key initiatives being undertaken by the destination to deliver that green growth get put into some simple communication messages. Beyond name and logo, the brand identity expresses the destination's purpose and personality usually through a well-defined colour palette, a characteristic design system and additional verbal branding such as a tagline.

In addition to the destination identity, identity systems may also be developed for specific sub-destinations (precincts), products, services and programs, e.g. business events, education, etc. These systems may be designed to work closely within the main destination identity or stand on their own, depending on the architecture defined in the brand strategy. All of these identity elements, along with assets such as the graphics and photography are then available to key stakeholders for repeated application to give the brand its consistency, distinctiveness and recognisability as a 'green growth' based destination.

## 3 Success depends on brand management

With the identity system in place, the next step is the application of its elements into the full range of branded communications and interactions. However, experience has shown that the establishment of some brand management discipline at this point in the process is critical for success. It requires three key actions:

- Planning a coordinated launch and delivery of brand messages, both internally and externally. This should be integrated with business and marketing plans to optimise impact and cost-effectiveness.
- Actively cultivating brand understanding, adoption and ability among industry and others who will be creating the customer's brand experience. This means providing them with brand training, assets and tools so they can consistently deliver 'on-brand' communications, personal interactions and products.
- Setting up a system and tools for monitoring and assessing the brand's health (the brand metrics), so that resulting insights can be used not only to maintain brand alignment, but also to evolve the brand strategy, identity, experience and management over time.

## 4 Delivering the brand experience

Finally, a customer's experience with a destination brand is too often the accidental result of uncoordinated communications and random customer contacts. The goal of using this approach to destination branding is to enable a destination (and encourage its industry operators) to establish and deliver a range of experiences that the visitor will find meaningful, memorable, and associate explicitly with the green growth destination brand. Doing this is the surest path to building brand trust, loyalty and advocacy.

And again it is important to emphasise, that this brand development process must extend well beyond traditional communications to include all the points where the visitor interacts with the destination. The green growth brand message should be reinforced in the personal interactions between the visitor and the local community, local events, the whole experience with the environment and also the quality and style of products and services that the customer will experience.

The goal should be to make every point of contact with the customer as remarkable, engaging and compelling as possible, clearly tying these positive experiences to the green growth destination brand.

## Conclusion

For destinations which wish to take advantage of the emerging green economy, there are significant opportunities to attract new consumers attuned to this changing paradigm.

However, to capture this opportunity requires two important steps.

Firstly, destinations must make the structural changes needed to put themselves onto a green growth path - by reducing GHG emissions, solid and liquid waste, conserving water and natural resources, all of which also delivers enhanced benefits to local communities. With this pathway in place destinations can then review their brand to attract these new consumers.

Secondly, to help build and strengthen the brand connection between a destination on a green growth path and their customers, establish a Destination Branding Framework. This will serve a number of needs. It brings together what are often disparate business and marketing efforts and applies specific branding disciplines to them. It defines the critical facets of the brand, relates key processes and elements to each other, and provides a common terminology and approach.

Ultimately, the framework serves over time to build a brand's strength, connect the brand inextricably to a paradigm of green growth and with it a destination's long term success.

# Lucian Cernat

## Chief Trade Economist of the European Commission

## Tourism performance benchmarking for sustainability development policy

Lucian Cernat is the Chief Trade Economist of the European Commission. Until 2008, he held various positions at the United Nations in Geneva dealing with trade and development issues. He has authored more than 20 publications on the development impact of trade policies, WTO negotiations, EU preferential market access, regional trade agreements, competition policy, corporate governance. Prior to his UN experience, he has been a trade diplomat with the Romanian Ministry of Foreign Affairs, and part of the negotiating team of bilateral FTAs with the EuroMed area and Baltic countries, preceding Romania's accession to the EU. Lucian Cernat obtained a PhD from the University of Manchester and a postgraduate diploma from Oxford University. He is also the author of *Europeanization, Varieties of Capitalism and Economic Performance in Central and Eastern Europe* (Palgrave Macmillan, 2006).

## Transforming tourism into a driver of sustainable development: between reality and potential

Tourism has already emerged as one of the world's most important socio-economic sectors, and has been steadily expanding at an average rate of about 4-5 per cent annually during the latter half of the 20th century. In spite of occasional shocks, like the 2009 financial crisis international tourist arrivals have shown virtually uninterrupted growth, being projected to cross the symbolic 1 billion tourist arrivals in 2012. The combination of domestic and international tourism is now acknowledged as comprising the world's 'largest industry'.

Tourism has a particularly promising development potential. Unlike many primary products whose share in world consumption might decrease, in the case of tourism, there is a favourable income elasticity of demand. With increasing incomes, tourist expenditures increase at a faster rate than income. Moreover, even though the tourism sector has been severely hit by a number of crises (e.g. international terrorism, SARS, natural disasters, the global financial crisis), the standard deviation of growth rates of 'export value' for several primary commodities and tourism shows that tourism revenue is less volatile than commodity revenues. Finally, tourism activities bring much needed foreign exchange which allows developing countries to finance the import of capital goods and raw materials required for the economic development and diversification of their economies.

If tourism activity is bustling in many regions in the developing world, this is still not the case for all. And certainly not for all those that need the most to unleash this potential. What's more is that, the reasons behind one country's success are hard to replicate and policy failures can't be prevented elsewhere.

Significant sustainability problems have emerged in some countries. Increasing tourist flows may create shortages that have negative effects on the local population (e.g. increases in food prices, lodging problems, water supply, etc.). Moreover, the local population in particular the poorer social segments of host countries do not always benefit from tourism revenues. Sometimes a large share of the price that tourists pay for their holidays goes to different parts of the global supply chains in the travel and tourism sector.

## Sustainable tourism performance and evidence-based policy benchmarking

This brings us to the issue of policy effectiveness and sustainable development, the latter being a key theme at the Rio+20 Summit. The international community and key stakeholders (domestic constituencies as well as international organization such as the World Tourism Organization, World Bank, various other UN agencies, the business sector, etc) have long recognized the need for evidence-based policy making in the area of travel and tourism.

History has shown that for those countries that managed to engage on a successful development pathway it was not always as a result of textbook policies. It was often a mishmash of common-sense policies, experienced policy makers, a bit of guesswork, and sometimes even blind luck. But there is little reason to rely predominantly on guesswork or blind luck rather than rigorous analysis and evidence-based policy making. For such a rigorous approach on how to promote successful tourism development, one needs a comprehensive approach and the right tools.

In spite of all the initiatives that have been put into effect in the past decade, the main challenge to overcome in achieving sustainable tourism is to fill the current gap between policy design and the implementation of those blueprints. Part of the problem is that often policymakers need to advance 'in the dark', without proper indicators, benchmarks and international best-practices to follow. Although there have been notable advances in the design of indicators in the past decade, the results are still only partial. There is still no agreement on a universal list of indicators enabling the comparison of sustainability levels in different tourism destinations. This is due in part to the multivariate character of sustainability, together with the difficulty in aggregating the considerable amounts of information required.

## The Sustainable Tourism Benchmarking Tool: the '7-faceted diamond of success'

There is general agreement in the literature that one of the main obstacles to attaining sustainable tourism is the difficulty in measuring the sustainability level that has been achieved by any given tourism destination. This has hindered decision making in the corresponding management processes and made it difficult to recognize and meet the specific needs of these territories.

A comprehensive and coherent analytical benchmark would clearly help countries that are dependent on the tourism to improve the sustainability of the sector. Most studies and approaches assessing tourism activities often deal with one or a few aspects of the travel and tourism sector.

The Sustainable Tourism Benchmarking Tool (STBT) uses a comprehensive range of policy-relevant indicators along seven key dimensions (Figure 1) and across 75 countries to produce a coherent benchmarking tool against which the sustainability of the tourism sector in a particular country can be assessed.

These seven key dimensions cover a wide range of tourism-related issues:

(i) *economic sustainability* (tourism assets, tourism activity, linkages and leakage effects),

(ii) the role of *supporting policies* and overall quality of infrastructure,

(iii) *environmental* and

(iv) *social sustainability.*

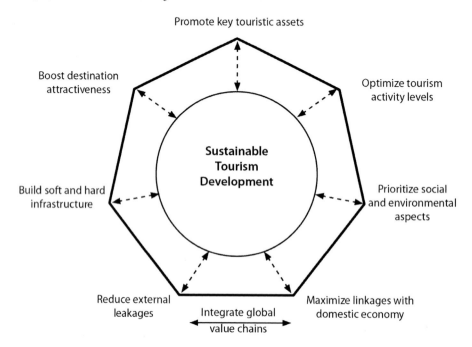

**Figure 1.** The STBT approach for tourism policy-making: the 7-faceted diamond of success

The STBT benchmarking tool uses quantitative indicators that are policy-relevant and, as such, it is hoped that it will become a useful tool for decision-makers, researchers and businesses involved in tourism activities in developing countries. While the STBT methodology used in this paper may need further refinement and elaboration, the results and findings obtained suggest that the STBT can become a valuable tool for researchers and policymakers involved in the assessment and design of sustainable tourism strategies.

## Some examples: linkages, leakages and synergies between different key dimensions

The STBT benchmarking tool can address several critical questions any tourism policymaker in developing Africa, Asia, Latin America or OECD countries has to struggle with at some point. For instance, the STBT can show that an equal level of tourism activity might induce different sorts of domestic and international dynamics and might have different consequences on local development. When comparing Indonesia with other countries in the region, it appears that Indonesia has one of the highest score for tourist assets, whereas Malaysia and Thailand rank far below. However, despite lower tourist endowments, the level of tourism activity is very close for all three countries. Therefore, Malaysia and Thailand appear to be more efficient in the exploitation of their assets than Indonesia.

The STBT benchmarking tools can shed light on missing elements preventing various countries from building linkages with the rest of the domestic economy. Using the same country example of Malaysia, the STBT benchmark suggests that despite having a very good score for building linkages with the rest of the domestic economy, Malaysia has also a low score for external leakages. This apparent paradox may be explained by the fact that a large part of the tourism-related activities generated in other sectors needs to import most of their input to supply the required products by the tourism sector.

In contrast, tourism in Indonesia provides 'relatively' less leakages but this activity is conducive to larger linkages with the local economy, along the value chain. Several policy recommendations to contain leakages could be advanced. To reduce leakages generated by imports of goods and services, developing countries need to encourage invest-ment by local entrepreneurs to improve their existing products and to diversify into new products. Similarly, leakages generated by foreign management personnel could be reduced if such the education system would train highly skilled managers according to international stand-ards. Policies should also aim to provide incentives to reinvest profits that otherwise would be repatriated or invested abroad. The bottom line is that simply looking at leakages as 'liabilities' does not pay off. Today, global value chains are pervasive and the tourism sector cannot be an exception. An optimal level of linkages-leakages, attractiveness based on international standards and local branding is more likely to be successful than an 'import-substitution' strategy.

The STBT can lead to additional policy insights. For example, Malaysia tends to attract a large number of tourists but the expenditure per tourist is quite low. In contrast, Thailand seems to be oriented towards higher-value tourism. At the same time, both Malaysia and Thailand score low on the length of time tourists spend in these countries. While Indonesia does not have a very good score on the number of tourists, it achieves a good score on revenues per tourist, not necessarily due to high value tourism but because tourists tend to stay longer in the country. Based on such STBT benchmarking indicators, Malaysia would needs to raise expenditure per tourist and length of stay. Concrete policy measures that could lead to such improved results would be to develop tourist assets that attract special interest tourists, leading to a higher value-added tourism. On the other hand, Thailand would need to take actions aimed at raising the length of stay of tourists by providing, for instance, new attractions or special events, or promoting longer tourist packages. In contrast, Indonesia would need to improve its score on the number of incoming international tourists, by using more actively new marketing techniques and online presence on social media and networking tools, for example.

## Cluster analysis and the role of global value chains

The STBT benchmarking tool also allows the use of cluster analysis that could identify the relevance of each of the seven 'diamond facets' (tourist asset, activity, infrastructure, sustainability, linkages, leakages and attractiveness) to detect correlations and more complex interactions. For instance, the results for the leakages-linkages clusters show a clear relationship between them and the level of activity. So tourism activity which creates output for the entire economy will also increase imports in the economy. So, like for global value chains in other economic sectors, successful exports of tourism services require an open overall trade regime and an unavoidable need for certain imported interme-diate inputs. The STBT therefore reinforces another more general axiom for a successful integration in the global economy and economic development: imports are key determinants of export competitiveness.

Overall open trade and investment polices become therefore important determinants of excellence in international tourism.

## Way forward

The STBT approach follows and builds on the several decades of sustained efforts to put in place Tourism Satellite Accounts (TSAs) have been pioneering a robust approach to account for the real value-added of the travelism sector in the quest for sustainable development around the world. While tourism satellite accounts initiatives have been ongoing and advancing for several decades it is only recently that a similar logic has been extended to 'value-added' approaches along the global value chains in the rest of the economy. This year is one of major advances on evidence-based policy making and the role of global linkages across countries. The WTO's 'Made in the World' initiative, the OECD various initiatives or the EC-sponsored WIOD project (www.wiod.org) will all lead to a greater realization that globalization has been a major engine of prosperity around the world. Parallel efforts are ongoing on new and innovative indicators on sustainable development indicators blending 'hard data' like geospatial satellite observations and more behavioural-based like 'better life' or ecological footprints and 'Happy Planet' indicators. The STBT benchmark tool offers an 'open source' platform that can further incorporate such indicators and create multidimensional layers of analysis on the true impact of travelism.

The Rio+20 Summit should give a fresh impetus to such evidence-based policy making on tourism and travel, particularly in LDCs and other developing countries where such insights and policy advice is most needed. Since a large number of countries still do not have full TSAs, it is hoped that the STBT benchmarking tool can provide a simpler solution to ensure that successful and sustainable tourism development becomes less of a 'miracle' and more grounded on best practices around the world.

C

# Tony Charters

## Founding Director, Ecotourism Australia

## Ecotourism spearheads the green growth of travelism

Tony Charters, Principal of Tony Charters and Associates, has over 20 years experience in tourism planning, development and management in the public and private sectors. He was a founding director of Ecotourism Australia and has served continuously on its board since 1991. For many years he also served on the board and executive of The International Ecotourism Society. An environmental scientist and urban and regional planner by profession, Tony entered the tourism industry after a successful career in World Heritage Area and multi-tenure protected area management. Tony convenes the annual Tourism and Events Excellence Conference and the Global Eco Asia-Pacific Conference. Since 2005 he has served as a Finalist Judge in the Tourism for Tomorrow Awards hosted by the World Travel and Tourism Council, and as a Destination Stewardship Committee member for the Global Sustainable Tourism Council.

Ecotourism was first described and defined in the late 1980's and in 1990 the International Ecotourism Society was formed in the United States. One year later Ecotourism Australia was established. Ecotourism is about operating sustainably; but it is also about tourism based on natural and cultural heritage with positive interactions and involvement of local communities, and putting something back into conservation of heritage.

Partially as a result of the rapid emergence of ecotourism in the nineties there developed a sense in some quarters that this newly described form of tourism was a 'flash in the pan', a transitory trend, enjoying a period of notoriety but likely to decline just as quickly. Some nations shunned the term ecotourism, believing that it was being used and abused as a term and was too often used by operators seeking to jump on to this popular new tourism sector. There was a concern, particularly in Europe, that ecotourism was largely 'greenwashing', where only superficial efforts were made to adopt sustainability principles. The International Year of Ecotourism in 2002 re-focussed attention on ecotourism and over the next ten years through to today ecotourism has matured to the point where there are now scores of ecotourism industry associations around the globe. Ecotourism is as an important tool to pursue sustainable tourism growth and to achieve better yields from tourism. Critically, ecotourism is seen as a sector of the industry that is scalable from micro-businesses to multi-national and it is highly suited to community based tourism projects.

Ecotourism was for many years regarded as a niche market, a highly specialised component of the tourism industry, dominated by micro, small and medium operators. And yet if you take the Australia as an example, ecotourism is estimated to account for 25% of the total tourism industry. No longer a niche, more likely the largest sector of the industry, operating across tours, attractions and accommodation and dominated by small and medium sized operations.

It is true to say in their infancy, ecotourism bodies around the globe became a little fixated with defining ecotourism. There was quite a purist approach to in the early years, driven in part by a notion that there were dedicated ecotourists looking for travel options that were purely ecotourism focused. It was soon realised that just like any other sector, people participating in ecotourism activities cover a whole spectrum ranging from purists, who only undertake eco activities, to travellers who mix up their holidays with a wide range of activities. These travellers may variously enjoy ecotourism activities, theme parks, casinos and shopping tours or a whole host of other tourism activities.

Ecotourism shuns the commoditisation of tourism products and celebrates variety and diversity. It seeks to draw out the unique natural and cultural values of a destination. Ecotourism provides the opportunity for destinations to wear their natural and cultural credentials with pride. The rare and unique values of a destination become its competitive advantage. No more the need to emulate other destinations and products. The 'differentness' of destinations, both natural and cultural is the very thing that sets them up for a thriving industry based on ecotourism.

Quality experiences, authenticity and good value for money are seen as vital ingredients for the prosperity of the tourism industry. Perhaps there can be no better exemplar of these values than ecotourism. Destination values, made up of the natural landscapes, local food and wine, music, dance, architecture, wildlife, political history and so many other attributes that make a destination unique, provide competitive advantages. These competitive advantages in effect mean that rather than the next door destination being seen as a competitor, it is a partner with a complementary product. Take the ten ASEAN nations. Collectively they have adopted the marketing brand Feel the Warmth. Governments are simplifying travel between the borders and are moving to co-ordinate efforts in infrastructure, product development and marketing. A sensible strategy, and one that enables ASEAN destinations to be presented as a suite of experiences.

In examining the opportunities for ecotourism to further contribute to green growth and to accelerate the transformative capacity of tourism there are several areas in where ecotourism in particular can play a greater role.

## Ecotourism's role in advocating for protected areas

Often ecotourism occurs on or around protected areas. These may be publically managed protected areas such as national parks or privately funded protected areas both of which are a core resource for ecotourism. There is much to be gained from strengthening the linkages between ecotourism and protected area management. This natural alignment provides opportunities for ecotourism to advocate for conservation and present and communicate heritage values to a wider public. There are examples from around the globe where protected area managers have been extremely proactive in developing ecotourism on their lands and waters as they can see the positive conservation and presentation outcomes that can develop. This foray by protected area managers into supporting ecotourism is a natural evolution and one that can be very instructive to destinations who are establishing a fledgling industry. Critically the emergence of credible certification schemes such as Ecotourism Australia's Eco Certification program provides protected area managers with important management tools that aid protected area sustainability, interpretation and monitoring.

## Sustainable resource management

As ecotourism is aligned to nature, culture, community and sustainability it is a natural fit for destinations who wish to develop an economic base yet maintain the integrity of their natural resources.

Ecotourism offers communities an economic base that is respecting of their culture, environment, customs and values. Importantly, ecotourism offers the potential for a sustainable future. Unlike many resource-based industries, ecotourism it is not based on a one-off exploitation of a particular non-renewable commodity. Economic studies repeatedly show for example that the value of a whale shark or manta ray for dive or marine tourism is many times greater than their value for shark fin or gill rakes.

Ecotourism is at its best when it is conducted by local people, who invite guests into their destination to experience an authentic taste of local life and conditions, an understanding of special areas and an approach to management that sustains both the resource and the community. This creates a high value tourism product, a unique product and an ongoing economic base. It just makes good business sense. It also makes good conservation sense.

## Sidestepping technology limitations with labour solutions

The affordability of technology in developing countries can often be a barrier to achieving best practice. However in countries where wage costs are comparatively low it is often possible to sidestep the cost barriers of technology through the application of greater human resources. Practices which may be uneconomic in the developed world can be undertaken in developing countries with excellent sustainability outcomes. Areas such as recycling, use of local and traditional building materials rather than imported materials, use of low energy solutions can sidestep technology and also provide more jobs for local people. Inevitably such an approach also leaves guests with a greater appreciation of the local culture and a sense that the destination is being well stewarded. Ecotourism provides an ideal vehicle for development of green jobs.

## Climate change action or sustainability?

The debate about climate change is at varying stages across the globe. After being a late starter in its response to climate change, Australia has had a tumultuous involvement with the issue over the past 5 years. In what must be one of the most rapid cycles of building and then losing community support, climate change in Australia has gone from an issue in 2007 that engendered extraordinary mainstream community support to a point in 2012 where the community is largely confused about what to think about the issue. Back in 2007 the community strongly embraced the notion that they could do something positive about climate change through its own actions at home and work to reduce its carbon footprint. Unfortunately as the Australian government moved to respond to climate change at a more global level, dealing with the big carbon emitters, proposing carbon trading and carbon taxes, it effectively shunned voluntary efforts and direct actions at a community and individual level. Individuals, 'doing the right thing' for climate change felt disenfranchised and irrelevant to the climate change actions of government. Compounding the problem was the multiple iterations of climate change response proposed by international forums such as at Copenhagen which left the community totally confused.

With the emergence of the climate change debate there was a tendency for sustainability as a topic to be set aside. Climate change effectively became the proxy for sustainability. Maybe the time is right to get back to speaking about sustainability. Inevitably good sustainability practices will address the mitigation issues of climate change. Ecotourism has a proud record in presenting sustainability in a way that has meaning and relevance to travellers. Perhaps the time is right to place climate change response back into its sustainability context. Few would argue that sustainability is unimportant. However the climate change debate has in many ways opened the door to a distracting discussion about the evidence or truth of climate change. In the end the key issue the world must come to terms with is sustainability. Climate change is but one indicator that the world's approaches to development are not sustainable. Ecotourism plays an important role in leading the way for the tourism industry with sustainability. Ecotourism should play a greater role in presenting climate change through the prism of sustainability.

## Conclusion

Ecotourism products still pave the way in setting the standards for best practice in a triple or quadruple bottom line approach to sustainability. Ecotourism has been at the pointy end of innovation across environmental sustainability, community involvement, heritage interpretation and contributing to conservation. Many of the early practices of ecotourism have now been adopted by more traditional areas of the tourism industry, particularly in the areas of energy, waste and water management and in the areas of community engagement and destination stewardship. Increasingly what was once seen as niche is now seen as mainstream. Many practices that were once only adopted by purist eco-operators are now seen as routine. But to be true to its roots ecotourism must remain at the cutting edge, keep pushing the boundaries and maintain its commitment to sustainability, including involving local communities and putting something back into conservation.

The pioneers of ecotourism identified very early the role tourism plays in transforming traveller's attitudes, perspectives and actions. While travelling, people are exposed to new paradigms and have their perspectives broadened. People on travels are more open to learning new approaches then when they are in their normal day to day routines. Therefore a tourism industry that exhibits good green practices will inevitably influence travellers and other industry sectors. As the largest industry in the world the tourism industry has a duty to respond.

If travelism is playing a vital role in spearheading the move to global green growth, then ecotourism is the spear carrier for travelism.

C

# Felix Dodds

## Executive Director of Stakeholder Forum for a Sustainable Future

## Traveling to tomorrow – stakeholders on the same planet

Felix Dodds is the Executive Director of Stakeholder Forum for a Sustainable Future. He has been active at the UN since 1990 attending the World Summits of Rio Earth Summit, Habitat II, Rio+5, Beijing+5, Copenhagen+5, World Summit on Sustainable Development.  He chaired the 64th UN DPI NGO Conference 'Sustainable Societies – Responsive Citizens (2011) the major stakeholder conference for Rio+20. He co-chaired the NGO Coalition at the UN Commission on Sustainable Development from 1997 to 2001. He has written or edited nine books; his most recent is *Only One Earth* with Michael Strauss and Maurice Strong.

In preparation for Rio+20 he has been a member of the advisory boards of the Bonn 2011 Nexus Conference, Planet under Pressure (2012): new knowledge towards solutions and Eye on Earth Summit. He has been advisor to the UK and Danish Governments and to the European Commission.

## Introduction

Forty-five years ago, Kenneth Boulding, President Kennedy's environmental advisor, said 'Anyone who believes in indefinite growth in anything physical, on a physically finite planet, is either mad – or an economist.'

The decision by the United Nations General Assembly in 2009 that the next Earth Summit in 2012 would be on two subjects, the Institutional Framework for Sustainable Development and the Green Economy in the context of Sustainable Development and Poverty Eradication, has opened a critical discussion for how the tourism sector should react.

Both issues will play an increasing role in the future as we try and balance the challenges of an increased population now topping 7 billion and increasing to 9 billion by 2050, with an increased number of people travelling and consuming. For an industry that is forecast to continue to grow over the next decades, it will need to be at the forefront of creating a more sustainable planet.

The generations that took responsibility from 1992 to 2012 is increasingly being seen as the irresponsible generation. It's not as if the problems that needed to be addressed were unknown. In 1992, Rio identified them and outlined the blueprint for a sustainable future in Agenda 21. The tourism sector responded positively two years later with the 'Agenda 21 for the Travel & Tourism Industry.'

It is clear that one of the biggest problems with advancing this agenda has been *implementation*. Instead of bedding sustainable development in economic policy decisions, the 1990s, in particular, became an unregulated free market bonanza with little or no regard for the environment and the impacts that this might have on future generations. And while the 2002 Rio follow-up Summit in Johannesburg sounded further alarms, it did little to make any directional change.

The financial crisis brought home many of the harsh realities of the growth agenda and for a moment some of the governments started focusing their recovery packages on green industries or associated actions through new investments. As the UN Secretary General said in his 2011 Davos Speech:

> 'We mined our way to growth,' he said. 'We burned our way to prosperity. We believed in consumption without consequences. Those days are gone. In the 21st century, supplies are running short and the global thermostat is running high. Climate change is also showing us that the old model is more than obsolete. It has rendered it extremely dangerous. Over time, that model is a recipe for national disaster. It is a global suicide pact.'

### Green economy in the context of sustainable development and poverty eradication

HSBC did an analysis of how green recovery packages were and found that in countries such as South Korea and China they seized the opportunity of increased government spending to re-orientate their economies. As we look forward, making tourism – which is an engine of traditional growth, globally and in key regions – an agent for *green growth* will be the challenge. What is needed is a common vision, principles and breaking down the wall of sector silo-based thinking. For this to change there must be clear leadership and medium to long-term planning that brings together the different sectors.

Globally, tourism is the single largest business sector of the world economy, accounting for a total of10% global GDP, as well as one in every twelve jobs around the world. Small and medium sized businesses play a key role, despite their lack of access to financial capital. What is needed is for Governments and development banks to help facilitate the financial flow particularly where there is a clear link between supporting local economic development and poverty reduction through local sustainable tourism development.

Although Governments are now in deficit reduction mode, it is vital that they return to spending on public goods such as water conservation, waste management, sanitation, public transport and renewable energy infrastructure, which all help to spread the cost of moving towards a greener economic model.

## Some green shoots...

There have been some useful international shifts in recent years – even though they have not gone far enough or fast enough. The Convention on Biodiversity in 2004 has given some clear international guidelines relevant for tourism in biologically sensitive areas – the ecotourism market. Similarly the painfully slow work through UNFCCC to reach new accords on greenhouse gas reduction is establishing national targets that tourism must align to – as a minimum. Perhaps of even greater significance is the idea of a Convention on Corporate Sustainability which has been floated by 40 insurance, banking and investment companies, who manage over $2 trillion in investments

The last twenty years have seen the growth of sustainability reporting and sustainability indexes such as the Global Reporting Initiative, the UN Global Compact, the FTSE for Good Principles for Responsive Investment, and the Carbon Disclosure Project. Yet, according to Bloomberg, only around 80% of listed companies on the stock exchanges are reporting to the standard that they should be.

The foundation of a new convention would be the introduction of mandatory reporting for companies listed on stock exchanges.

For major tourism companies or related companies such as airlines, the introduction of such a requirement by stock exchanges will have a big impact on the supply chain. And small and medium sized companies will need support through instruments like the ISO environment standards and the Global Sustainable Tourism Criteria to integrate this into their policies and practices.

Another relevant idea is the creation of 'Green Economy Councils'. The Rio Conference in 1992 had a huge impact in creating space for addressing local sustainability questions. In Chapter 28 of Agenda 21 it was asked that: 'Each country should have undertaken a consultative process with their populations and achieved a consensus on 'a local Agenda 21' for the community. Some 6,000 local authorities around the world have undertaken Local Agenda 21s and some are still actively using this mechanism to work with their local communities. With the focus on the economy through the 2012 Rio+20 conference, we can expect this process to intensify. Tourism must step up to the plate and actively engage.

Finally there is the idea of 'Stakeholder Democracy'. Perhaps one of the least understood outcomes from Rio in 1992 comes from the under-pinning of Agenda 21 and the enhanced role crafted for stakeholders - those who have an interest in a particular decision, either as individuals or representatives of a group.

Slowly through the 1990s the experiments in 'stakeholder democracy' around sustainable development and Agenda 21 were being tried at various levels. At the local level it was through 'local agenda 21s', at the national level it was done vis-a-vis National Councils on Sustainable Development, and at the global level it was attempted through stakeholder dialogues.

Perhaps the most successful global dialogue was the one in 1999 on Tourism under the able leadership of the then New Zealand Minister of Environment and Chair of the UN Commission on Sustainable Development, Simon Upton. It created a real space for trade unions, NGOs, industry and local authorities to address common concerns. Its outcome resulted in a multi-stakeholder working group that was starved of funds but which did start to address the issue that though tourism is basically a private sector driven activity it does need strong government policies and regulation to ensure that it is supportive of inclusive and sustainable growth and supports sustainable development. This is particularly obvious in the area of financial leakages, which can be as much as 70%, resulting in little support being given to local economies and suppliers of tourism related goods and services.

The Dialogue and working group did help build trust among the key players, which ultimately enhanced stakeholder relations once the UN World Tourism Organization was set up in 2003. There is still much work to be done to integrate stakeholders into the UNWTO, but at least there is a small tentative baseline.

The advancement of stakeholder involvement in decisions on tourism at all levels will be critical as we move towards a more inclusive and sustainable economy. The next twenty years will see an increase in the challenges that we face through the impacts of climate change, energy, food and water security issues. Tourism can and should be seen as part of the solution.

## Travelling to tomorrow

It has taken us forty years to get back to the right discussion, which is 'how do we ensure that the economic system we have is supporting our life on this planet?' The Club of Rome's seminal report in 1972 'Limits to Growth' looked at the available 'natural capital' – the total geophysical and ecological resources of the planet – and the rate of human consumption, and warned of the need to change global consumption patterns and factor in the depreciation of natural capital or to risk the devastating depletion of Earth's resources. Today those concepts seem obvious and the accuracy of the report has become clear.

So the challenge for the tourism industry is to become 'smart', moving to low carbon destinations, lower waste, better water management, conserving biodiversity and ensuring integrated transport systems supporting tourism wherever possible. Perhaps we need to see the development of a Global Building Code Convention that underlines what needs to be done.

There is already the Leadership being shown by Energy and Environmental Design (LEED), an internationally recognized certification system developed by U.S. Green Building Council, a non-profit organization. This is a scheme that measures how well a building conserves energy, water, reduces $CO_2$ emissions, and improves indoor environmental quality. Already, 50 Marriott-branded hotels in design, development or under construction are expected to achieve LEED certification. This could form the basis for all new building construction in the tourism sector.

Over the last twenty years we hoped that voluntary codes will work. They had some impact but what is needed now is a firmer hand of government at all levels working with their stakeholders to help ensure that as much of our future tourism is supporting a 'greener', more sustainable economy that puts people and planet at its centre. After all, time is no longer on our side. In his Davos speech in 2011, the UN Secretary General called for a revolution:

'Here at Davos – this meeting of the mighty and the powerful, represented by some key countries – it may sound strange to speak of revolution,' he said. 'But that is what we need at this time. We need a revolution. Revolutionary thinking. Revolutionary action. A free market revolution for global sustainability.'

After all, tomorrow is now today. We have a journey that brings us all together: how to create a sustainable society in which there are responsive citizens, responsible companies and accountable governments. Tourism will need to play its part in helping that to happen.

D

# Acronyms and abbreviations

| | |
|---|---|
| **ABTA** | Association of British Travel Agents |
| **ACARE** | Advisory Council for Aeronautical Research in Europe |
| **ACI** | Airports Council International |
| **AGD** | Aviation Global Deal |
| **APD** | air passenger duty |
| **APK** | air passenger kilometres |
| **ASA** | air services agreement |
| **ASPIRE** | Asia Pacific Initiative to Reduce Emissions |
| **ATA** | Air Transport Association of America |
| **ATAG** | Air Transport Action Group |
| **ATM** | air traffic management |
| **ATN** | air traffic navigation |
| **BRIC** | Brazil, Russia, India, China |
| **BRICS** | Brazil, Russia, China, India, South Africa |
| **CBD COP** | Convention on Biological Diversity Conference of the Parties |
| **CDP** | Carbon Disclosure Project |
| **CERs** | certified emissions reductions |
| **CCC** | (UK) Committee on Climate Change |
| **CI** | Conservation International |
| **CNG** | compressed natural gas |
| **CNTA** | National Tourism Administration of the People's Republic of China |
| **CO$_2$** | carbon dioxide |
| **CO$_2$e** | carbon dioxide equivalent |
| **COP** | Conference of the Parties |
| **CPR** | Centre for Policy Research |
| **CSD** | Commission on Sustainable Development |
| **CSR** | Corporate Social Responsibility |
| **DANTEI** | Development Assistance Network for Tourism Enhancement and Investment |
| **DTIS** | Diagnostic Trade Integration Studies |
| **EC** | European Commission |
| **ECOSOC** | Economic and Social Council (UN) |
| **EIF** | Enhanced Integration Fund |
| **ERUs** | emissions reduction units |
| **ETS(s)** | emissions trading scheme(s) |
| **EU** | European Union |
| **EUAAs** | European Union aviation allowances |
| **EU ETS** | European Union emissions trading scheme |
| **FAA** | Federal Aviation Administration |
| **FDI** | foreign direct investment |
| **G20** | Group of Twenty |
| **GDP** | gross domestic product |
| **GHG** | greenhouse gas |
| **GNH** | gross national happiness |
| **GPS** | geographical positioning system |
| **GPST** | Global Partnership for Sustainable Tourism |
| **GSTC** | Global Sustainable Tourism Criteria |
| **GWh** | gigawatt hour |
| **HSR** | high speed rail |
| **IATA** | International Air Transport Association |
| **ICAO** | International Civil Aviation Organisation |
| **ICRT** | International Centre for Responsible Tourism |
| **ICTP** | International Council of Tourism Partners |
| **IEA** | International Energy Agency |
| **IHRA** | International Hotel and Restaurant Association |
| **ILO** | International Labour Organisation |
| **INSPIRE** | Infastructure for Spatial Information in the European Community |
| **IMF** | International Monetary Fund |
| **IMO** | International Maritime Organisation |
| **IPA** | Investment Promotion Agency |
| **IPCC** | Intergovernmental Panel on Climate Change |
| **ISO** | International Standards Organization |
| **ITC** | International Trade Centre |
| **ITP** | International Tourism Partnership |
| **ITU** | International Telecommunications Union |
| **IUCN** | International Union for the Conservation of Nature |
| **kWh** | kilowatt hours |

| | | | |
|---|---|---|---|
| **LATTE** | Local; Authentic, Traceable, Trustworthy, and Ethical | **STBT** | Sustainable Tourism Benchmarking Tool |
| **LCG** | low-carbon growth | **STI** | Sustainable Travel International |
| **LDC** | least developed countries | **SWAFEA** | Sustainable Way for Alternative Fuels and Energy for Aviation |
| **LAC** | local air quality | | |
| **LEED** | Leadership in Energy and Environmental Design | **T 20** | Tourism ministers of the G20 |
| **MBM** | market-based mechanism | **T&T** | travel and tourism |
| **MDGs** | Millennium Development Goals | **TBL** | triple bottom line |
| **MtCO₂** | million tons carbon dioxide | **TCCEP** | Trade, Climate Change and Environment Programme |
| **NASA** | North American Space Agency | **TEEB** | The Economics of Ecosystems and Biodiversity |
| **NDT** | National Department of Tourism | | |
| **NGO** | non governmental organisation | **TIES** | The International Ecotourism Society |
| **NOAA** | National Oceanic and Atmospheric Administration (US) | **TFEU** | Treaty of the Function of the European Union |
| **NOx** | mono nitrogen oxides | | |
| **OECD** | Organisation for Economic Cooperation and Development | **TSA** | tourism satellite account |
| | | **UAE** | United Arab Emirates |
| **OWS** | Occupy Wall Street | **UK** | United Kingdom |
| **PATA** | Pacific Asia Travel Association | **UKCCC** | UK Committee on Climate Change |
| **PPP** | public private partnership | **UN** | United Nations |
| **R&D** | research and development | **UNCTAD** | UN Conference on Trade and Development |
| **REDD+** | Reduced Emissions from Deforestation & Degradation in Developing Countries | **UNDP** | UN Development Programme |
| | | **UNED-UK** | UN Environment and Development UK Committee |
| **RBS** | required by science | | |
| **Rio + 20** | UN Conference on Sustainable Development, held in Rio de Janeiro, Brazil, on June 20-22, 2012 | **UNEP** | UN Environment Programme |
| | | **UNESCO** | UN Educational, Scientific and Cultural Organisation |
| **RLKM** | Regionaal Landschap Kempen en Maasland | **UNFCCC** | UN Framework Convention on Climate Change |
| **RPK** | revenue passenger kilometre | **UNWCED** | UN World Conference on the Environment and Development |
| **RSF** | Roundtable on Sustainable Biofuels | | |
| **RTK** | revenue ton kilometre | **UNWTO** | UN World Tourism Organisation |
| **SA** | South Africa | **USA** | United States of America |
| **SAFUG** | Sustainable Aviation Fuel Users Group | **USAID** | US government agency for foreign and humanitarian assistance |
| **SD** | sustainable development | **VOC** | volatile organic compound |
| **SD-PAMs** | sustainable development policies and measures | **VFR** | visiting friends and relatives |
| | | **WEDF** | World Export Development Forum |
| **SES** | Single European Sky | **WEF** | World Economic Forum |
| **SESAR** | Single European Sky ATM Research | **WIOD** | World Input Output Database (EU) |
| **SIDS** | small island developing states | **WMO** | World Meteorological Organisation |
| **SMMEs** | small, medium and micro-sized enterprises | **WSSD** | World Summit on Sustainable Development |
| **STEM** | science, technology, engineering and mathematics | **WTO** | World Trade Organisation |
| | | **WTTC** | World Travel and Tourism Council |
| **ST-EP** | Sustainable Tourism for Eradication of Poverty | | |